How Do You Know?

How Do You Know?

THE ECONOMICS OF
ORDINARY KNOWLEDGE

Russell Hardin

PRINCETON UNIVERSITY PRESS

PRINCETON AND OXFORD

Copyright © 2009 by Princeton University Press
Published by Princeton University Press, 41 William Street, Princeton, New Jersey 08540
In the United Kingdom: Princeton University Press, 6 Oxford Street,
Woodstock, Oxfordshire OX20 1TW

Library of Congress Cataloging-in-Publication Data

Hardin, Russell, 1940–
How do you know? : the economics of ordinary knowledge / Russell Hardin.
    p.   cm.
Includes bibliographical references and index.
ISBN 978-0-691-13755-1 (cloth : alk. paper)
1. Knowledge, Theory of.   2. Knowledge, Sociology of.   3. Decision making.   4. Social
interaction.   I. Title.
BD161.H279 2009
306.4'2—dc22   2008052655

British Library Cataloging-in-Publication Data is available

This book has been composed in Sabon

Printed on acid-free paper. ∞

press.princeton.edu

Printed in the United States of America

10   9   8   7   6   5   4   3   2   1

For Gary S. Becker

Contents

Preface

WE OFTEN SAY of someone's action that it is irrational. I wish to take a charitable view and suppose that people are not generally irrational according to their own assessments of what they are doing. They may seem to be irrational according to some second-party assessment of even a putatively objective account of their interests, and of the means to achieve their ends. There are two general obstacles to bringing a person's subjective rationality into line with any such objective assessment of rationality. First, in contexts of interactive choice, the connection between one's action and the outcome one gets is indeterminate. I analyze this issue in a recent book, *Indeterminacy and Society*. A second general obstacle to achieving objective rationality is that one's knowledge base for making good—meaning objectively rational—decisions is commonly inadequate. The first issue is a problem of the world that we face; the second is a problem of our individual capacities. Here I address this second issue: the knowledge base of the ordinary person making choices.

For explaining human behavior and choice we need an economic theory of knowledge, meaning economic in a very broad and even loose sense. The theory would not be about what the philosophical epistemologist's criteria for truth claims should be, but rather about why we come to know what we know or believe. We can use such a theory to make sense of many behaviors and beliefs, such as religious, moral, and pragmatic beliefs, and of limits on popular knowledge of science. In politics, such a theory makes sense of some aspects of liberalism, cultural commitments, extremism, and voters' lack of knowledge, and it undercuts the median-voter model of party positions in a democracy. Here I present a theory of ordinary knowledge and then apply it to many contexts. Such a theory can explain many seemingly systematic failures of individual choice.

The issue addressed in *Indeterminacy and Society* is the complication that, in contexts of interactive choice as mentioned above, the connection between one's action and the outcome one gets commonly is indeterminate. In strategic interactions, you cannot determine your outcome simply by choosing it from a range of possibilities. You can choose only a strategy, not an outcome. All that you determine with your strategy choice is some constraints on the possible array of outcomes you might get. To narrow this array to a single outcome requires action from you and perhaps many others. You commonly cannot know what is the best strategy choice for you to make, unless you know what strategy choices others will make. But if all of us can know what all others are going to do, then it is not coherent to say that thereafter we can alter our choices in the light of that knowledge, because the altered choices vitiate our supposed knowledge. This is the form of indeterminacy at issue in *Indeterminacy and Society*: indeterminacy that results from strategic interaction. Interactive choice as represented descriptively in game theory is often indeterminate for each individual chooser. For an individual chooser in a moment of choice, this indeterminacy *is not a failure of reason by the chooser;* the indeterminacy is in the world, because it follows from the mismatch of the preferences of all those in the interaction of the moment.

The present book and the earlier *Indeterminacy and Society* are therefore a pair. The implications of problems of knowledge and problems of strategic interaction are quite similar: the individual's capacity for achieving objectively good outcomes is often impaired or even stymied. But problems of knowledge are primarily within the individual, whereas problems of strategic interaction are inherently in the larger world in which individuals find themselves. There should be no doubt or confusion about what the two problems are, although there might be disagreement over how we should deal with them. My focus here is on the broadly conceived economic constraints on knowing what we need to know in order to make good decisions.

There is a vast literature that addresses psychological constraints on our decision making. For those who are not expert in this literature, note that its arguments and conclusions range from the often dazzling and powerful to the ordinary and merely commonsensical. That literature is full of ad hoc labels for countless patterned behaviors. That is not my intellectual world, and I do not canvass psychological limits in this book. Readers might wish to consult Baron [1988] 2000, Kahnemann and Tversky 2000, Margolis 1987, Plous 1993, and Simon 1955 and 1957 for the general problems, and such works as Converse 2000, Delli Carpini and Keeter 1996, Friedman 1998, Popkin [1991] 1994, and Somin 1998 for specific realms of choice in, for example, politics.

R. H.
July 2008

Acknowledgments

THIS BOOK began life in the distant past, as suggested by the dates of some of the papers on which it is based. A version of the first chapter was drafted while I was a Fellow at the Center for Advanced Study in the Behavioral Sciences at Stanford. I am grateful for the financial support provided during that period by the National Science Foundation (Grant # SBR-9022192), the Guggenheim Foundation, and New York University, and for support during the years of the book's writing from New York University, the University of Chicago, the Andrew W. Mellon Foundation, and Stanford University.

I also wish to thank numerous commentators for their reactions to its arguments. Parts of it have been presented to conferences on pragmatism at Washington University, St. Louis, on alternatives to self interest at Potsdam University, to a panel on decentralist thinking and the good society at the meetings of the American Political Science Association, and to a memorial conference in honor of James S. Coleman at the Reimers Foundation in Bad Homburg. Parts have also been presented in the political economy seminar at the Hoover Institution, Stanford University, the Monroe seminar at CalTech, the fellows seminar at the Center for Advanced Study in the Behavioral Sciences, the Department of Political Science at George Washington University, the ANPOCS meetings in Caxambu, Brazil, and the Center for Rationality and Interactive Decision-Making at the Hebrew University of Jerusalem.

During the book's gestation, there were two especially formative occasions. The earlier one was a week of lectures in the philosophy department at the University of Arizona in a series on epistemology funded by the National Endowment for the Humanities; this was at the invitation of Thomas Christiano and his colleagues, who included a collection of several of the best epistemologists anywhere. The second was a similarly intense four days giving the Humphrey Lectures at the University of Waterloo, Ontario, Canada. I am especially grateful to Jan Narveson for inviting me to give these lectures and then gloriously crowning the occasion, in his home, with a live performance of the Bartok quartets 4–6 by the Penderecki Quartet.

A version of chapter 2 (on science) was presented to the Society of Fellows, New York University, 19 March 2002; it benefited from formal comments by Kit Fine and Barbara Kirschenblatt-Gimblett at a further meeting, 18 April 2002. It was also presented at the Fourth Annual

St. Louis Philosophy of Social Science Roundtable at the University of St. Louis, 15 March 2002, and at a session of the weekly Political Science seminar, Stanford University, 9 May 2002. The chapter has benefited from commentary at all these sessions. I thank Natalie Kapetanios for her notes on the Society of Fellows discussions. I especially thank Catherine Stimpson for inviting me to present such a paper at the Society of Fellows meeting, and James Bohman for inviting it for the St. Louis Roundtable.

An earlier version of chapter 3 (on democratic participation) was presented at the meetings of the European Public Choice Society, Lisbon, 7–10 April 1999; at a seminar at Tel Aviv University in June 1999; at a conference at the University of Texas in February 2000; and at the William H. Riker Memorial Conference at the University of Washington, St. Louis, in December 2001. I thank participants at those meetings for their comments.

An earlier version of chapter 7 (on religion) was prepared for presentation at the 14th International Seminar on the New Institutional Economics, on "Religion and Economics," Wallerfangen (Saarland), 11–14 June 1996. The chapter is partly the outgrowth of commentary on several papers (Kuran 1996; Montgomery 1996b; and Stark et al. 1996) at the meeting of the American Economic Association in San Francisco, January 1996. I thank participants in both these meetings for their comments and discussion.

Chapter 8 (on culture) was presented at the World Congress of the International Sociological Association, Brisbane, Australia, 7–11 July 2002.

Chapter 9 was prepared for and presented at the biannual meeting of the Villa Colombella Group at its conference, "Political Extremism," Vichy, France, 24–27 June 1998. I thank the organizers of that meeting and the participants for engaging discussions. Much of the original paper was written while I was a visitor at the Universidad Torcuato di Tella in Buenos Aires, whose people had recently escaped from an era of dreadful, murderous extremism to achieve a remarkable air of decency. I thank Julio Saguir, Geraldo de Paolera, and the Universidad Torcuato di Tella for that visit. The paper was also presented to the UCLA workshop in political economy in March 1999. I thank Kathleen Bawm and Miriam Golden for organizing that session, and I thank them and their colleagues for a spirited and insightful discussion. Finally, I thank New York University for generous general support.

I especially wish to thank Judith Aissen, Sonja Amadae, Nomy Arpaly, Kenneth Arrow, Michael Baurmann, Sebastiano Bavetta, Kathleen Bawm, Andrea Belag, Geoffrey Brennan, Albert Breton, David Brink, Bruce Bueno de Mesquita, Paul Bullen, Thomas Christiano, Ingrid Creppell, Lorraine Daston, Michael Dawson, Alberto Diaz-Cayeros, Keith Dowding, Christoph Engel, William Eskridge, James Fernandez, James Fishkin, Bruno S. Frey, Gerd Giegerenzer, Miriam Golden, Jack Hirshleifer, Geoffrey Keene, Steven Kelts, Jack Knight, Roger Koppl, Timur Kuran, Diana Marian, Robert K. Merton, Leo Montada, James Montgomery, Paul Aarons Ngomo, Peter Northup, Philip Pettit, Mario Rizzo, Jay Rosen, David Rothman, Ekkehart Schlicht, Bart Schultz, Kenneth Shepsle, Charles Silver, Perri 6, Paul Sniderman, Kate Stimpson, Stephen Turner, Edna Ullmann-Margalit, Barry Weingast, Tom Weisner, William Wimsatt, and Alison Wylie for various contributions, including careful critical readings and even written commentaries on various parts of this work. More than one can make clear, I owe a great debt to Huan Wang for his energetic and creative research support in recent years, and to Mariel Ettinger and Larisa Satara for research assistance in earlier years.

Some of the chapters were published in earlier versions. I thank the editors and publishers for permission to reprint them in revised form here. (As they appear in the present volume, the chapters carry somewhat revised titles.)

Chapter 2: "If It Rained Knowledge." *Philosophy of the Social Sciences* 33 (no. 1, March 2003): 3–23.

Chapter 3: "The Street-Level Epistemology of Democratic Participation." *Journal of Political Philosophy* 10 (no. 2, 2002): 212–29; reprinted in James Fishkin and Peter Laslett, eds., *Philosophy, Politics and Society* vol. 7. London: Blackwell, 2003: 163–81.

Chapter 4: "Seeing Like Hayek." *The Good Society* 10 (no. 2, 2001): 36–39.

Chapter 5: "The Economics of Knowledge and Utilitarian Morality." In Brad Hooker, ed., *Rationality, Rules, and Utility: Essays on Richard Brandt's Moral Philosophy.* Boulder, Colo.: Westview Press, 1993: 127–47; and "Commonsense at the Foundations." In Bart Schultz, ed., *Essays on Henry Sidgwick.* Cambridge: Cambridge University Press, 1992: 143–60.

Chapter 7: "The Economics of Religious Belief." *Journal of Institutional and Theoretical Economics* 153 (March 1997): 259–78.

Chapter 9: "The Crippled Epistemology of Extremism." In Albert Breton, Gianluigi Galeotti, Pierre Salmon, and Ronald Wintrobe, eds., *Political Extremism and Rationality,* Cambridge: Cambridge University Press, 2002.

How Do You Know? is dedicated to Gary Becker, my sorely missed colleague at the University of Chicago. Gary is emblematic of the intellectual power and energy of Chicago. He causes great things to happen and stimulates everyone in his presence to do better and more interesting work than they would otherwise do. I cannot imagine that anyone has benefited more from his presence in their intellectual lives than I have.

CHAPTER 1

Ordinary Knowledge

WHILE SAMUEL JOHNSON [1709–1784] was working on his book on the lives of the English poets, James Boswell [1740–1795] volunteered his assistance in lining up a conversation with Lord Marchmont about Alexander Pope, one of the poets discussed in the volume. Johnson dismissed the offer, saying, "If it rained knowledge I'd hold out my hand; but I would not give myself the trouble to go in quest of it" (Boswell [1791] 1976, 989).[1] (Pope was, of course, the same Alexander Pope who noted that a little learning is a dangerous thing.) Johnson's perhaps dyspeptic attitude captures a large part of the difference between ordinary and scientific knowledge, and I will use his two metaphors—raining knowledge and going in quest of it—to characterize the difference. Ordinary knowledge is almost entirely grounded in hearsay from a supposedly credible or even authoritative source, although commonly the credentials of the source are not compelling and perhaps even more commonly we can no longer remember the source or its quality. Psychologists refer to "source memory" and they commonly find that we remember a fact but have no memory of how we came by it. We will typically not double check what our newspaper or encyclopedia may once have said; we will stop our inquiry sooner rather than later.

Johnson lived in an age that we think of as having been shaped by Isaac Newton [1642–1727], the archetypical scientist, all of whose science was done well before Johnson was born.[2] But as a rule, Johnson no more thought scientifically than did anyone else who lived centuries earlier—or since. If he had been a poor farmer, he might have given more thought to explanations of natural phenomena than he did as a remarkably educated and urbane man. Newton's revolutionary scientific thinking did not

---

[1] The full exchange has the quick charm of many of Boswell's reports. When told that Boswell ([1791] 1976, 988–89) had arranged for Marchmont to call on him the next day, Johnson retorted, "I don't care to know about Pope." Mrs. Thrale took Boswell's side and chided Johnson, "I suppose . . . that as you are to write Pope's *Life*, you would wish to know about him." Johnson said, "Wish! Why yes, if it rained. . . ." Perhaps Johnson was merely in one of his sour moods (Boswell refers to "something morbid in his constitution"). In any case, a year later he did speak with Marchmont.

[2] In the morality tale for children, Newton's understanding of gravity began when an apple rained down on his head as he sat lazily beneath a tree. He did not even put out his hand for it.

have great influence on the way ordinary people thought in his time. Indeed, it did not affect Newton's own astonishing defenses of certain religious beliefs about the date of the creation of the universe in 4004 B.C.E., an issue that alone may have occupied more years of his long life than did all of his scientific investigations. Even today, scientific thinking has far less influence on daily thinking than some might wish. I will argue that *this fact reflects rationally correct views and is commonly even a good, not bad, thing. Recognizing this fact is not to criticize ordinary knowledge or ordinary people.*

A beauty of Johnson's comment is that it shows how well he understood the nature of his knowledge. He might not have known very well how the knowledge of scientists in their specialized realms differed from ordinary knowledge, but he clearly knew that most of his bits of knowledge had a somewhat laconic quality. He happened upon them or they happened upon him, and he perhaps occasionally held out his hand to catch bits of knowledge. Most of them were not a matter of his craft but only of his experience. Most of us might not have even so much as Johnson's self-understanding that our knowledge is similarly happenstance. We are often as sure of our casual, happenstance knowledge as any scientist is of the results of some massive, careful study, whether experimental or merely observational.

Philosophical theory of knowledge is largely about a kind of public, not personal knowledge. What must interest anyone who wishes to explain behavior is the knowledge or beliefs of actual people. An *economic* theory of knowledge would address this issue. Such a theory would not focus on the objects of belief but on the ways people come to hold their beliefs, and on the overall structure of their beliefs. By an economic theory, I mean merely a theory that focuses on the costs and benefits of having and coming to have knowledge, or to correct what knowledge one has. It must fundamentally be a theory of trade-offs between gaining any kind of knowledge and doing other things, such as living well.

An economic theory of knowledge would be grounded in three quite distinct facts, all of which matter to anyone whose knowledge we wish to explain. First, knowledge has value as a resource and is therefore an economic good; hence, people will seek it. Sometimes we seek it at a very general level, as when we absorb what we can of a general education. In this case, we may have little idea of how we are ever going to use the knowledge, and we may not know in advance much about the range of the knowledge we will be acquiring. Sometimes we seek it for a very specific matter, as when we seek mortgage rates when buying a home. In this case, we know very well what we want the knowledge for, and we know reasonably well where to get it and when we have gathered enough of it.

Second, the acquisition of knowledge often entails costs, so that its value trades off against the values of other things, such as resources, time, and consumptions. Moreover, these costs are often very high. For example, the costs of gaining enough information to judge the political candidates in an election are thought commonly to be far too high for most voters in the United States to be able to justify the expenditure, especially given that they have little to gain from voting anyway (see chapter 3 on democratic participation). Instead, they vote on the strength of relatively vague signals about issues they do not adequately comprehend.

And third, a lot of our knowledge, which we may call "happenstance knowledge," is in various ways fortuitously available when we have occasion to use it. Some knowledge comes to us more or less as a by-product of activities undertaken for purposes other than acquiring the knowledge, so that in a meaningful sense we gain that knowledge without investing in it—we do not trade off other opportunities for the sake of that knowledge. For example, you know a language because you grew up in human society. Much of what is loosely called social capital is such by-product knowledge. If you grew up in a bilingual or multilingual community, you likely know more than one language. By-product knowledge may simply be available to us essentially without cost when we face choices. Some knowledge may even come to us as virtually a consumption good. For example, your love of gossip may lead to knowledge that is quite valuable to you. Finally, the knowledge in which you deliberately invested yesterday for making a specific choice may still be available to you today when you face some other choice to which it might be relevant.

Again, the account that follows is of subjective, not public knowledge. It is not concerned with what counts as knowledge in, say, physics, but rather with your knowledge, my knowledge, any specific individual's knowledge. The principal interest here is not in the theory of knowledge itself but with how this account of knowledge informs analyses of various kinds of belief and behavior, such as ordinary moral choice, religious belief and practice, political participation, liberalism, extremism, popular understandings of science, and cultural commitments.

There is an important category of knowledge that is not at issue in the discussion here. Gilbert Ryle ([1946] 1971) distinguished between knowing that and knowing how. I know that the height of Mont Blanc is about 5,000 meters. I know how to ride a bicycle.[3] The latter kind of knowledge is experiential. The former kind is typically not experiential for most of what ordinary people know—and we are all ordinary people in most realms. But our capacity for knowing that may turn on our knowing how. For example, it surely depends on our mastery of language, which is partly

---

[3]Indeed, if you rode one as a child but then not again for decades, you would almost instantly reacquire the motor skill of cycling. In scientific terminology, this phenomenon is called 'savings.'

a matter of knowing how, in the strong sense that most of us could not begin to articulate our knowledge of language and how it works for us, anymore than most of us, or even the best scientist in the field, could articulate how we manage to keep a bicycle underway without falling over (Wilson [1974] 2004, esp. chap. 8). The central concern of this work is with cognitive knowledge, or knowing that.

The theory of knowledge we need here is pragmatic; it has closest affinities with recent social epistemology (see contributions to Schmitt 1994). Social epistemologists agree that much of even scientific knowledge depends on testimony, rather than on direct investigation. They wish to establish criteria according to which testimony can yield justified true beliefs. The focus of an account of pragmatic street-level knowledge and belief is on the use and subjectivity of knowledge, not on justification of any claim that it is "true" knowledge. It is subjective because it is about *your* knowledge or *my* knowledge, not about knowledge per se.

AN ECONOMIC THEORY OF KNOWLEDGE

What we need for understanding knowledge at the level of the individual, and not merely at the level of a super knower who does not suffer human limitations, is an explanatory theory, not merely a definitional or essentialist theory. I propose a pragmatic theory that can be characterized as economic. It is economic in the sense that we can explain bits of knowledge that a given person has as being substantially affected by the costs and benefits of obtaining and using those various bits. Moreover, we can explain the retention of bits of knowledge in the face of competing knowledge by the seeming costs and benefits of retaining them, balanced against the costs and benefits of revising or rejecting them. In a widely quoted remark, F. Scott Fitzgerald (1945, 2) says that "The test of a first-rate intelligence is the ability to hold two opposed ideas in the mind at the same time, and still retain the ability to function." As is true of much of Fitzgerald, the remark is clever, but misguided. Everyone who functions at all manages to do so while holding many opposed ideas in the mind at the same time, from sunup to sundown. Surely, however, not everyone who functions at all has a first-rate intelligence.

For the understanding of human behavior—normative or merely factual—we require not a philosophically general theory of knowledge, but a street-level account, a theory of the general pattern of individuals' available knowledge. To assess knowledge that is practical, that is actually put to use by ordinary people, our account must be subjective. That is, it must be grounded in the particular individual whose knowledge it is. To speak of knowledge is to speak of someone's knowledge. Otherwise, it is the knowledge that exists somewhere, even out in the ether, as, at the extreme, in the noosphere of Teilhard de Chardin. If we wish to understand knowledge at the practical level of those who have it, we must first ask why they come to know what they know. For much but not all of knowledge, this is to ask what good it does them to know it, which is in some rough sense the sum of the costs and benefits of their knowing it.

Of course, the assessment of costs and benefits depends itself on knowledge that must be subjected to the economic test. This means, of course, that the costs and benefits may be neither precise nor confidently measured. Rather, they are partly, even largely, guessed. In particular, one cannot typically know the full costs or benefits of trying out a new bit of knowledge, although one might have little choice but either to try it or not to try it, on the strength of a poorly grounded estimate of those costs and benefits. Note that, although the pragmatic or street-level account of knowledge is an economic theory, it is not the sort of economic theory that presumes full knowledge, as in the economists' rational expectations theory or much of game theory. And it is not merely about the costs of information, as it is in some economic accounts of, for example, George Stigler (1961). It is economic in the sense that the value of any bit of knowledge is how it would matter to us and our behavior, with consequences broadly defined to include the full range of costs and benefits of coming to know that bit of knowledge and of putting it to use.

The general tenor of an economic theory of knowledge is pragmatic. The central import of pragmatism in this context is roughly a combination of the following visions:

1. Wittgenstein's (1969) view that there are no foundations for much of knowledge;
2. Dewey's ([1920] 1948, 161; see also [1929] 1984) view that there is no final or best state of affairs in personal and social life, so that choices are not about reaching a maximum of some kind but about making things better; and
3. The contemporary view that much of an individual's knowledge is socially generated.

The first two of these visions are presumably clear enough without further elaboration. It might be hard to be at ease with these views, but their content is not unclear. The third vision is similarly simple enough. But the meaning that the term "socially generated" often is taken to convey is that the very fact of the matter, and not merely our knowledge of it, is socially determined. For social facts, this can be true. For the account here, all that is wanted is that much of our knowledge is grounded in social systems. That is, an individual acting alone could not have established it. The contributions of many people and even whole industries were required to establish much of our knowledge. This vision will be spelled out further below.

It may be useful to note some caveats on what follows. First, for the problem of any practical knowledge, one must focus on the computational limits of the human agent, and on the incentives that agent may have to acquire knowledge, given that there are severe limits of capacity and cost in the acquisition of knowledge. My account here is not driven by an especially articulated theory of mental capacities, but only by a more-or-less commonsense view of limits on such capacities. Often, the main limit is time; we do not have the time to do all that we would like to do. Given that there are severe limits, we must be concerned with the ways in which bits of knowledge are acquired, and with the reasons or incentives for acquiring any bit of knowledge.

Second, on the view that there is no generally privileged position from which to judge whether someone's beliefs are true, there is no clear general distinction between beliefs and knowledge. The standard philosophers' category of justified true beliefs does not play an important role in a pragmatic theory of ordinary knowledge. Many philosophers in epistemology seem to suppose that they own the rights to usage of the terms 'knowledge' and 'belief.' Such philosophers are vastly outnumbered by ordinary people who are not impressed by claims to trademark these terms. My account is of the knowledge and beliefs of these vast numbers, and I will generally use the two terms as they are used in the vernacular.

Finally, moral and factual knowledge may not generally be distinguishable for anyone who has not been impressed with the theoretical distinction between them. The economic theory advanced here suggests that there need be no such distinction for a particular individual, because action on either kind of knowledge can entail costs and benefits that affect the content of the knowledge. Hence, for example, people seem commonly to moralize mere conventions, such as the conventions of table manners or those of tastes, that are place- or time- or culture-specific. For conventional reasons, we may refer to some bits of knowledge as beliefs, as in the case of religious beliefs. But these may be subject to the same account as any other knowledge, and may be distinguished from other knowledge in no way other than their subject matter.

Calling a theory of knowledge 'economic' implies essentially that there are choices to be made, in the sense that I must trade off other possibilities in order to invest in better knowledge. Hence, getting better knowledge does not automatically trump remaining ignorant should we choose to put our effort into other things. There is a corrupted, vernacular sense of "economic" that is not relevant to the discussion here: *An economic theory is not a theory about prices or money,* but is only about choice in the face of constraints on resources, time, and so forth. Similarly, costs and benefits need not be tabulated in monetary terms nor assigned prices in order for us to make compelling sense of them. There are costs to you of enjoying some wonderful bit of food that are independent of the monetary price to be paid for it. Those costs include effects on your health, your wakefulness this afternoon, and your appetite for dinner with a friend later, none of which you might ever price monetarily. *Every credible theory of general choice is at least partly an economic theory in the sense used here.*

On the economic theory, we come by our knowledge in at least three quite different ways:

1. Sometimes we deliberately seek knowledge. We go in quest of it to be able to put it to use because we suppose that it will have value for us. Some of the knowledge we might deliberately seek is very specific, as is knowledge of current mortgage rates when we are buying a home. Some of it may be very general, as is the knowledge we will gain from going to university or that our children will gain from attending school, all as part of a larger plan of education for general or specific purposes. It is a distinctive aspect of modernity that education is quite general up to a fairly advanced age. In industrial society, education is typically generic (Gellner 1983, 27).

2. Sometimes we merely happen onto knowledge. It rains on us while we are engaged in some other enterprise. In this sense, much knowledge is an opportunistic by-product. In this category we may include knowledge that is a consumption good, such as the knowledge you gain from the pleasure you take in reading a newspaper or magazine. You often may gain such knowledge because it gives you pleasure to do so, and not because you think it is likely to be of any practical value to you.

3. Sometimes knowledge is imposed on us. Many people think of their schooling or their religious training as having been imposed. Indeed, the very word "training" is a peculiar term with somewhat odious implications of imposition. This is a complex issue, because the imposition cannot be simply by diktat. The Ayatollahs have massively affected the beliefs of Iranians since 1979, but to explicate the ways that that has happened is not a simple matter.

All of the knowledge you now have when you face a decision may be knowledge gained in these ways *in the past.* It is therefore, in a meaningful sense, *happenstance* with respect to the decision you now face. Most of your knowledge is a residue of the past in some sense. You might, of course, seek out some bits of additional knowledge, such as the current mortgage rates, but the bulk of your knowledge, even virtually all of it, may be happenstance in this sense for most of the decisions you ever make. Your choices of what to know at various times in the past plus your opportunistically gained knowledge determine what you know now when you have to decide something. We cannot usually speak of *our* knowledge as though to imply we all have it. Our knowledge is simply your, my, his, or her knowledge. (Even less can we sensibly speak, as many intuitionist moral philosophers do, of *our* moral intuitions, whose Venn diagram is likely to be an empty set.)

Consider an example of a relatively trivial bit of knowledge that is, as argued below, nevertheless extremely complex. In the book *On Certainty*, Wittgenstein (1969, §170) says Mont Blanc is 4,000 meters high. It is actually nearer 5,000 meters. A standard philosophical analysis of these claims would focus on whether there are grounds for believing, for example, that the height of Mont Blanc is nearly 5,000 meters (or 15,728 feet). It would focus on the *matter* of belief or knowledge in question. The economic theory of belief focuses on the individual believer, not on the matter of belief, and on the costs and benefits to the individual of coming to have various beliefs. In such a theory we cannot speak of the justification of a particular belief *tout court;* rather, we must speak of the justification of that belief by some person in the larger framework of that individual's knowledge and experience. For this we require a theory that focuses on the individual and on the ways the individual comes to know or believe relevant things, such as how trustworthy another person, a book, or an agency is as a supposed authority on some bit of knowledge.

The economic theory has numerous implications, some of which may seem perverse on a standard philosophical account of knowledge. For example, my current knowledge is path dependent: it depends on the life I have led up to now. Indeed, even what I would count as knowledge is largely path dependent. I may, of course, come to correct part of my past knowledge, but in doing so I may not be able or may not think to correct other knowledge that is strongly connected to it. Hence, path dependence might contribute to the incoherence of beliefs. Moreover, if one has any concern with the coherence of the set of one's beliefs, path dependence might commend the rejection of new knowledge more readily than of old knowledge, for the reason that it is mentally cheaper to question a bit of new knowledge than to jettison a lot of old knowledge with the consequence of then having to restructure the broken remainder of old knowledge. A new fact might not merely challenge a particular old fact but also much that is inferentially based on the old fact. Those inferences from the old fact might be hard to track down, because they might not be mentally keyed to the fact from which they were inferred.

Hence, we may have some incentive to be conservative in our knowledge commitments. At the extreme of the very risk averse who wish to conserve limited mental and other energy, some people might be utterly blockheaded in refusing to consider revision of any of their knowledge. One who seldom does reconsider might have little experience of the potential value of reconsideration, and might therefore become almost entirely embedded in stubborn beliefs from a dreadfully limited past experience. This is virtually a definitive condition of very traditional societies (Lévy-Bruhl [1910] 1926), if not to some degree of all societies.

David Hume ([1739–40] 2000, Appendix, §1) states the scientific creed with perhaps excessive enthusiasm: "There is nothing I wou'd more willingly lay hold of, than an opportunity of confessing my errors; and shou'd esteem such a return to truth and reason to be more honourable than the most unerring judgment. A man, who is free from mistakes, can pretend to no praises, except from the justness of his understanding: But a man, who corrects his mistakes, shews at once the justness of his understanding, and the candour and ingenuity of his temper." (He adds, a bit less modestly, that "I have not yet been so fortunate as to discover any very considerable mistakes in the reasonings deliver'd in the preceding volumes, except on one article. . . .")[4]

Again, on the economic theory the blurring of moral and factual knowledge can make sense. The incentive for gaining knowledge may, however, typically favor gaining practical knowledge over moral knowledge, because occasions for gaining such knowledge may be more frequent than those for gaining moral knowledge. For most of us, solving pragmatic problems is daily more common in our lives than is resolving moral issues. Hence, we may become better at factual than at moral knowledge, and may tend to bias our actions toward our own interests not because we are especially amoral but merely because we can be surer of making good self-interested choices than of making good moral or altruistic choices. On a related point, a moral theorist who is not a moral skeptic may rightly be held accountable on her own theory to higher standards of moral conduct, for the simple reason that she knows better than most people, who are not moral specialists, can be expected to know.

The economic theory also has strong implications for differences between institutional and individual capacities. Hence, pragmatic and moral considerations recommend use of institutions in some contexts just because institutions have special capacities for mastery of some kinds of knowledge. In other contexts, individuals often have advantages over institutions. To fill out the economic account of individual knowledge, let us address several topics: the social generation of knowledge, knowledge from authority, the division of labor and individual knowledge, and the internalization of norms.

[4]Stephen J. Gould (1993, 452) says virtually the same thing: "The factual correction of error may be the most sublime event in intellectual life, the ultimate sign of our necessary obedience to a larger reality and our inability to construct the world according to our desires."

The Social Generation of Knowledge

Much of the knowledge that you or I have is knowledge that no individual alone could have established. Rather, the knowledge is generated by a social system to which many individuals and, often, institutions contribute. Again, this is not to say that the knowledge is socially constructed in the sense that we determine the underlying reality, as is sometimes argued of social knowledge and as might be true of some knowledge. As in Hume's and Smith's view of the greater productivity of the division of labor,[5] discussed further below, knowledge grows faster if you pursue some things and I pursue others, rather than having all of us pursue everything together. But division of labor in the production of knowledge requires acceptance on faith of what others have come to know, if the advantage of division is not to be lost.

As an example of socially generated knowledge, consider again the knowledge of the height of Mont Blanc. How does one come to know such numbers as Wittgenstein's 4,000 meters—or the more widely accepted figure that is nearer 5,000 meters? Satellite measurements once suggested that K2 reaches higher than Mount Everest (Krakauer 1990, chap. 9). We have thought for about a century that Everest is the highest mountain on earth. But we might have been wrong. Suppose we eventually find that all measures corroborate the greater height of K2. What did we have to get wrong to get the particular bit of knowledge that Everest is highest wrong? These are all bits of knowledge that are not merely pieces of a system of knowledge—they are knowledge that could only be generated by a *social* system. To be confident in such pieces of knowledge is to be confident in the system that generates them. Hence, we might be able to assess these facts—but not my knowledge of them—according to the procedures followed in measuring them.

In the measurement of the height of a mountain, various tools are used, including surveyor's instruments. The users of these tools might have little understanding of the technology required to manufacture them to the fine tolerances required for their giving accurate measurements.[6] The users must correct for the distorting effects of temperature on their tools, and also for the curvature of the Earth in measuring a mountain from which they must, of necessity, stand at a distance, and even the distorting effects of gravity from the mountain itself. They typically will not themselves have determined that curvature and might not even know how to mea-

---

[5]Poor Hume ([1739–40] 2000, book 3, pt. 2, sec. 2, ¶3) maladroitly speaks of "the partition of employments" and therefore loses paternity for our contemporary phrasing to Smith.

[6]This is a difficult problem. See Lehrer 1995.

sure it. Indeed, many of these things—the various technologies for manufacturing the equipment, the correction factors to control for the effects of variant temperatures on the instruments, and the correction factor for the curvature of the Earth—may all be essentially socially generated in the sense that they are the aggregate of many experiences that no individual could possibly replicate. Everyone must take at least many of these facts on faith in assuming that they have been determined correctly by a large number of contributing authorities.

Consider an example. In 1999, a German team scaled Mt. Kilimanjaro in Tanzania to measure its height. They used several global positioning system (GPS) receivers, to time and triangulate signals from satellites (whose elevations are highly calibrated). Their measurements, to within a few centimeters, at 5,892 meters, shaved 3 meters off the previously established height, as measured from atmospheric pressure ("Random Samples," *Science* 286, 15 October 1999: 401). The 1852 measurement that proclaimed Mt. Everest the world's tallest was carried out by the British Great Trigonometical Survey of India with traditional surveyors' instruments. These are dramatically different technologies all put to the same purpose. An even more massive task was the measurement of the Earth itself (Danson 2006).

KNOWLEDGE FROM AUTHORITY

We are still left with the individual-level question: How did you and I come to have whatever knowledge or beliefs *we* have of the heights of Mont Blanc, K2, and Everest? Many of us followed the second device discussed above, coming to it as a by-product of doing other things. Or rather, we didn't follow any device at all, we merely happened onto the knowledge at some point and in some way that we might not even recall. We largely took it on authority, such as the authority of an encyclopedia or a newspaper story. And of course the encyclopedia editor or news writer most likely took it on authority from a geographer or other supposed expert.

Note one of the peculiarities of our presumptive knowledge of the height of Everest. We first have to judge a particular authority, and then we infer the truth of the authority's claim. Most of our knowledge has this structure—it depends on reliance on some authority. Only rarely do we genuinely investigate for ourselves. But some of our authorities are now superseded in our judgments—although the facts we got from them may still linger in our minds as though they were correct. This character of our knowledge is especially important in moral judgments, because our moral beliefs may largely have been determined by the impositions of past authorities, some of whom we would discount heavily today. But it afflicts much of our factual knowledge as well.

Ideally, each bit of our knowledge would carry a subscript to weight the quality of the source of that bit. Although much of our knowledge does not come to us associated with such weights, some of it does. Indeed, our ordinary language includes qualifications on our claims: I know, surely, more than likely, I think, the *Times* said, I've heard, maybe. In Tzotzil, a Mayan language spoken by about 200,000 Guatemalan Indians, there is a clitic, "la," that must be inserted in every statement that reports mere hearsay as opposed to what one has personally witnessed or experienced. This hearsay clitic is in the class of "evidentials," which qualify the commitment of the speaker to the claim being made. In English one can make similar qualifications, but it is not obligatory to do so. In Tzotzil, it is obligatory (Judith Aissen, personal communication, 27 December 2005). In the present world, in which we rely almost entirely on other sources for our knowledge, we would have to include a hearsay clitic in almost every sentence. That is a pervasive characteristic of our knowledge.

Might we ever follow the first device discussed above—deliberately seeking knowledge—in improving our knowledge? At least someone might. For example, someone working with satellite data might have tried to get the heights of all the Himalayas right. But even this person would depend inescapably on accepting knowledge from others without testing it—for example, knowledge of the solid state physics and the laser technology that lie behind the electronic measurements of height. Hence, even this expert seeker after these particular facts must have relied in large part on happenstance and personally uninvestigated knowledge. That is inherent in depending on *the system of knowledge,* as opposed merely to bits of knowledge in isolation.

Indeed, in the end it is hard even to imagine a single bit of knowledge in many areas of our seeming competence so that the problem of socially generated systemic knowledge pervades our lives. I compose these sentences at a computer whose structure is the result of millions of inputs by uncounted individuals, some of them expert on slight pieces of it and others expert on other slight pieces. The whole to which their expertise contributes is surely beyond the real comprehension of any of them or anyone else. Yet even I, who understand little of my computer's working, can presumably rely on it to radically improve my life in certain respects. My knowledge of that computer is fundamentally pragmatically determined: it works—although it sometimes fails, either because of its hardware, its software, or my errors in using these. In this case, I can try out alternative equipment to decide intelligently that some other set of machines is reasonably suitable for my task. Moreover, I can depend on social selection to have produced relatively good devices, because social selection through market and other forces puts alternative devices to much better test than I can, and because I can expect the incentives of many of the people involved in the social selection to fit my own interests. I can also depend on social selection to have produced a lot of information on these devices, so that I may avoid testing everything or starting completely blind in my tests.

The paths to most bits of my knowledge have long been forgotten and could not plausibly be reconstructed. The overwhelming bulk has been accepted on authority of some kind, often of a questionable kind and often of a completely forgotten kind. There is a compelling sense in which it is useful to us to rely on the authority of others, because it enables us to make better choices for ourselves than we could if we had to rely only on what truths we had demonstrated in some way entirely by ourselves. It is thus deeply in our interest to rely on others. In our early years, indeed, it is a matter of life and death to rely on others and their knowledge. Throughout our lives, we would be foolish even to reject much of the knowledge we have that is probably grounded in dubious authorities, knowledge that we might even *know* to be grounded in dubious authorities.

Most of us have been stopped short on occasion by the question: How do you know that? Often the point of the question is to elicit information out of curiosity about our experience or our capacity to remember odd facts. But sometimes the query is an implicit statement of doubt, as though it were really the question: How *could* you know that?[7] In either case, the questioner would often be satisfied by such simple answers as, I read it in the newspaper, my mother was a dentist, or I studied history. The question is then commonly not further directed at the authorities implicated in these answers, as it perhaps often should be. Nor is it so often followed by the relevant question, Are you sure that's what was claimed? For most bits of knowledge, the buck stops long before the end of the chain of authority. We typically do not seek out a first knower of any fact.

Given our radically defective reliance on authorities that are essentially unknown to us in the moment we put most knowledge to use, we take inordinately much knowledge on only a little more than blind faith. Why? Presumably because it seems to work well enough. That is the sense in which it is at least a little more than blind faith. We sweep vast quantities of putative knowledge into the maw of our minds with hardly a second glance. And we do it because we need to have enormous lots of knowledge but cannot plausibly take the time to check out the authoritative sources from which we take it to be true knowledge. I have a friend who often asks me, How do you know that? She invariably means it in the

---

[7]This question could be phrased with the emphasis on any of its words, or on various combinations of them, to alter its sense.

curious sense, and she seems almost as invariably to accept what I say as true, even though often I honestly can no longer say how I know whatever it is that is at stake. She, I, and no doubt you live by such knowledge, and we typically live reasonably well by it.

THE DIVISION OF LABOR AND INDIVIDUAL KNOWLEDGE

The constructive division of labor gives value to our social product. The division of labor is commonly seen from the perspective of its value to the larger society: it reduces costs and increases production. In these functions, it works in at least three ways. One, it allows you to specialize in the use of your time so that you work more efficiently with, say, a single tool rather than by switching from one tool to another as you perform the many very different tasks in producing a particular kind of object. Two, it allows you to specialize in the development of your talents to do some one thing especially well. And, finally, it allows us collectively to select from among us the one most capable of doing some difficult task: a Maria Callas can be selected to sing, a Michael Jordan to play basketball, and an Adam Smith to study the division of labor and its implications.

But the division of labor has another great value for an individual: it reduces the investment that the individual must make in understanding the world. You can generally rely on specialists who have already mastered parts of that world at least as well as you could expect to do. Those specialists might often be wrong, but they might still, on average, be less wrong than you would be if you had to rely only on your own wisdom and experience. Just as you rely on others to produce cars that work, so also you rely on others more generally to produce knowledge that works. In the social generation of knowledge, *we engage in division of labor— and this implies reliance on authority or testimony* (Coady 1992; Audi 1997; Adler 2002, chapter 5).

How does the individual detect error on the part of knowledge specialists? Primarily by having it pointed out by others. You learn that the ignition system on your car is prone to catching fire not by experience, testing, or deliberate personal investment in finding out the fact, but by reading of the problem in the newspaper. De facto, you rely on someone who has invested in finding out the facts of the matter, or in collating what many others have found out. Indeed, even if you had the experience of a fire in your car's ignition, you might still not know enough to judge the cause of or the responsibility for it. Such knowledge can come only from a larger canvass of the problems of that car's design and experience. You are spared the need to invest very substantially to learn either the fact or the nature of the problem, because you get the knowledge more or less by chance from a credible source. That source might be very different in qualifications and in the incentives it faces than the company that made the cars, or than the individuals who own the cars; and that source might also be expected to have specialized in collecting the relevant knowledge. Competition in the production of knowledge is as valuable for productivity as competition in the production of goods is.

If we are in a traditional or small society, the prospects of our gaining insight into errors in the society's knowledge may be relatively poor. There may seldom be alternative sources of information beyond our collective social knowledge, configured more or less as it has been received from the past (Lévy-Bruhl [1910] 1926). The apparent conservatism of such societies need not, however, be a matter of psychological disposition but merely of lack of opportunity to learn on the cheap that their ways are not as effective as they might be. One of the great advantages of large, plural societies is that they offer up criticism of practices and knowledge very much on the cheap. The mass of criticism might often be disconcerting, but it is also very often enormously useful. In such a society, on many issues we may come to have no standard for what is normal, and we may be spared the normative challenges of people who might otherwise attempt to hold us to the "normal."

Appeal to authority is just a part of the division of labor for the creation and judgment of knowledge. We benefit from having specialists to assess auto safety, weather, and the truth of various matters. It is only an extension of normal reasoning to let specialists assess religious matters and moral matters of right and wrong, as will be argued in later chapters.

The Internalization of Norms

One of the most remarkable moves in ordinary understandings of the world is the internalization of norms, meaning adopting them to such an extent as to permit one to act on them without need of external sanction to motivate the action. But there are two forms of internalization of norms that are against one's interest. One is religious sanctions (exercised by the self) and the other is hierarchical social norms, such as a caste system, sexism, or racism, which some people internalize deeply enough to judge themselves inferior. Both kinds of norms have substantial social backing or enforcement, but they also seem to have internal reinforcement, which prima facie seems irrational. I strive charitably to show that the internalization in these cases can be arguably rational.

Many scholars think that the internalization of norms is an incoherent idea. Others think it is a real phenomenon, but one that requires complex and somewhat esoteric explanation as a product of psychoanalytic processes that are not directly observable (Scott 1971). From the perspective of ordinary knowledge, however, it appears to be a fairly straightforward, even simple, phenomenon. First, let us start with the recognition that we can internalize lots of factual knowledge, and that this capacity or phenomenon is not unlike internalizing norms. Moreover, others can confirm that you have internalized such knowledge, so there is no insuperable difficulty in showing that the knowledge is in the black-box brain, even though we cannot directly observe the contents of that brain.

We commonly think of norms as action-guiding, as though this were a distinctive feature of them. But objective facts can also be action-guiding. I know that turning the key in the ignition will start my car. If I want to start the car, I turn the key. The more important characteristic of norms is that they are often motivating. What is of special interest to us in the internalization of norms is this fact that they are motivating.

Recall Ryle's distinction between two kinds of knowledge: knowing how and knowing that. These two may overlap. Suppose you have mastered the piano, or the technique for doing anything at all. The rest of us can know that you have internalized that knowledge from the way in which you put it to use in relevant contexts, when using it well would benefit you in some way. If one plays the piano, that might be almost entirely in the category of knowing how. But a Mozart, who can put musical theory to work, might also use a lot of knowledge-that when he plays.

Similarly, we might even say you have internalized knowledge of arithmetic, although some might insist that this is somehow hard-wired in the logic of the brain. Clearly, however, some people are very good at arithmetic, mathematics, and other logical fields and others are so poor at these things that they can hardly go beyond what they have learned, as in the rote learning of the simplest multiplication tables. The former people have come to do arithmetic with great ease and seeming natural mastery as a form of knowledge-how. The latter people, by contrast, seem to have done little more than internalize simple arithmetic through the rote learning of early schooling; they have only knowledge-that, for example that 2 times 3 is 6 and so forth.

The mastery of knowledge and techniques for doing things in the world is of course not the internalization of norms in the sense of moral norms that can guide behavior. But note that we smear the boundaries between normative beliefs that cannot be tested in the world and quasi-technological or scientific beliefs that *can* be tested. For example, many people think that their religious beliefs are matters of objective fact. We can therefore internalize such normative beliefs just as we internalize objective beliefs. They may in fact seem objective to many of us. Moreover, they may be reinforced by the reactions of other people to our behavior when those reactions either conform or fail to conform to these norms. This differs from reinforcement of the belief that something like gravity is at work in our physical lives, but it is reinforcement nevertheless.

Moreover, we seldom attempt to test any of our beliefs, but merely accept them and sometimes act on them. Acting on a false belief that has objective consequences may de facto test the belief for us, and we might be given sufficient evidence to reject that belief. It is a peculiar characteristic of normative beliefs that they commonly do have consequences for us when we act on them, but are often held to have further consequences that cannot yet be seen. An extreme version of this is religious belief that one will be rewarded in an afterlife.

So far, we have established that internalization is a plausible and indeed likely commonplace in our lives, and that there is ample empirical evidence that many facts and techniques are internalized, evidence sufficient for others to know that you have internalized some fact or technique. Even some more or less normative beliefs may be internalized. But the hard issue to address here is whether we can internalize beliefs that are not in our interest. These include moral beliefs that lead us to act in ways that are not in our interest. They also include inferiority beliefs, such as beliefs by the proletariat that they are inferior to the higher classes, or beliefs by those in a low caste, by women, by an ethnic minority, or by many other groups that they are inferior in status to some other group.

Let us go back to arithmetic for a moment. We know that there are cultures in which arithmetic has not developed very far. Indeed, in one Amazonian culture, there is no counting beyond something roughly like a little and a lot (Everett 2005; Gelman and Gallistel 2004).[8] In some of these cultures it is very hard to teach older people to do ordinary counting, although presumably the children could be taught readily.[9] This means that even counting has to be taught in order for it to be internalized. Suppose you are one of the dullards who have to remind themselves of the multiplication tables to do some simple arithmetical calculations, and even have to rehearse the numbers in order to get counting right. You do this now not because you can independently believe that these moves work *but only because someone else has forced it into your head that these are the ways to do certain things.* At an age at which you are taught arithmetic, or even before that, you are also taught various moral principles and rules for behavior. In neither case—neither arithmetic nor moral norms—do you have independent proofs of your beliefs, as you might have of the relevance of your techniques for accomplishing various things, or of your knowledge of many objective facts.

---

[8]Some reports on the research findings say that the tribe counts only one, two. Daniel Everett (2005) claims they do not even have *these* two numbers.

[9]Hence, there may be an ethological constraint on the intellectual developments necessary for counting, just as there is for learning language (Lane 1976; Bretherton 1992, 762).

The moral principles that you are taught may come to you as facts no different in kind from other facts, such as that the moon goes through its various phases. You need not understand any of these bits of knowledge in any meaningful sense, beyond believing that they are true. For example, some of the things you believe might require that you go through various rituals in which you destroy perfectly good food, even though you are often hungry and could well use the food. Of course, you might sometimes have conflicting bits of knowledge and desires. In a state of severe hunger you might therefore cheat on the ritual you believe to be necessary for receiving more food. One might have no beliefs or norms that always trump all others or all conflicting desires.

It is not a big step now to believing, from having it drummed into one's head at an early age, that one is of an inferior caste, and that it is right that one should be badly treated as members of that caste are. Discovering that there are societies that are not organized into a hierarchy of castes might bring doubt to one's beliefs about the rightness of the caste system in which you live, but your ignorance of alternatives might otherwise characterize your life, and you might never doubt the rightness of how you are treated. If you explain all of this to your children, you might speak in moral or objective terms, you might invoke both, or you might not even draw a distinction between the two. But you and they might think that the ugly system of discrimination is fundamentally right, or is the way the world is naturally organized, just as it is organized to have monsoons and floods and droughts. Perhaps the most dramatic case of such internalization of norms of inferiority is the internalization of the so-called basic values of Stalin's Soviet Union, even to the point of accepting that it is reasonable that one should be horribly abused in the Gulag (Figes 2007).

That beliefs are internalized helps to make sense of behaviors when one has lost an earlier religious belief. Many lapsed religious believers still react to symbols and contexts that evoke earlier religious responses. If they have rejected their basic religious belief in, say, Catholic doctrine, there is no longer ground for the emotions formerly stirred by these symbols, such as the cross, or a consecrated and therefore supposedly holy wafer. Suppose you have lost your beliefs in the fundamental tenets of Catholicism. You might still not have hunted down in your mind and corrected or erased all of the minor associations of those earlier beliefs and practices. Perhaps they linger in the way memories of a lost lover or a dead friend linger in scattered places, and thus are not logically dependent on the greater beliefs in the falsity of Catholicism, the loss of the lover, or the grievous loss of the friend. Hence, you might, for example, go on a picnic where you had once gone with the lost lover or friend and find that the experience has evoked positive memories that then bring renewed sadness at the loss, even though you might well have got over the loss before the moment of the picnic. In any case, the force of the associations of the past religious beliefs makes sense now only if those beliefs and certain consequences entailed by them (if they are true) had been internalized in the mind in ways that make them available for evocation now.

STANDARD PHILOSOPHICAL THEORIES OF KNOWLEDGE

The philosophy of knowledge, or epistemology, is a highly developed inquiry. Much of it focuses on particular beliefs or types of belief and the criteria for truth or "justified true belief." But the knowledge of people on the street bears little relation to the theories of knowledge of those in ivory towers. Ivory tower epistemology is about justification, about the truth conditions for counting some putative fact as known, rather than merely falsely believed. There are varied ways in which standard philosophical epistemology is divided into particular theories. Let us consider one of these, due to Keith Lehrer.

Lehrer (1990, 9 and 12; see also Kitcher 1994, 113) accepts the following conditionals for a theory of knowledge. If S knows that p, then it is true that p. And, if S knows that p, then S is completely justified in accepting that p. The odd quality of these conditionals is that they have no practical import. *There is no super knower who can attest to whether S meets them.* Without starting an infinite chain of queries, we can stop at one and ask, How does S know that it is true that p? Indeed, for much of life, perhaps arguably most of life, the only knower who might be concerned to attest whether S meets these conditionals is S, in which case the criteria are question-begging. Much of the theory of knowledge reads this way, as though somewhere out in the ether there were a super knower whose judgment is knowable to the epistemologist or even, illogically, the knower. But actual epistemologists are themselves merely other S's who need have no special qualification to assess knowledge in general outside their own domains. Your local epistemologist is not a super knower, and cannot usefully judge your knowledge of most of the things that might affect what you must decide in your own life. The burden of finding competent judges of the bits of that knowledge is itself merely part of the burden of the formation of the knowledge—it is not a separate enterprise undertaken retrospectively or on the side, in order to judge the truth of the knowledge.

For a practical account, therefore, characterizations of and conditions for knowledge must finally be reduced to the perspective of S. Standard epistemology, however, is not subjective in this way but is essentially public. We can judge the knowledge of a *field* of science by the criteria of standard epistemology. It is not feasible that we judge the knowledge of an individual *person* by these criteria. Briefly consider five visions of epistemology to assess their relevance to ordinary knowing by ordinary people: fundamentalism, coherentism, externalism, proceduralism, and communalism.[10]

(1) In fundamentalist epistemology, there are some things that are simply known directly. All other things are then known by their deductive fit with these directly known things. One need hardly show that this is an implausible description of the knowledge that you or I have, although one might suppose that some science could be characterized in this way. Suppose that an epistemologist could know what you know, and could therefore attempt to assess it. She might be able to show that parts of your knowledge do fit the model of deduction from fundamentals. But it would be utterly startling if she could do that generally, because your knowledge has been acquired in such a messy agglomeration of ways. The ways in which we acquire knowledge—most of it through accepting the views of manifold "authorities" or "experts" or merely sources—suggest that it is implausible that our knowledge can have happened to be deductively related to some fund of direct knowledge. We surely did not *adopt* much of our individual knowledge by personal deduction from any foundational beliefs. In any case, most of us might not have any foundational beliefs.

(2) In coherentist epistemology, each piece of possible knowledge is judged to be actual knowledge if it fits coherently with the rest of accepted knowledge. There might be a problem of circularity in determining some initial set of known facts against which to test any putative new fact. But at some point, one might settle for supposing that I just do have a coherent body of beliefs to which I can now fit new facts. However that might be, I am quite sure that my own knowledge is not coherent enough to pass a serious coherentist test.[11] Some of it—especially much of my professional academic knowledge—may be block-coherent. For example, my knowledge and understanding of the sociopolitical problem of collective action may all be coherent in the sense that any of the propositions I would make about it or within it fit with the other propositions I would make about it, both logically and empirically.

Much of my knowledge may seem to be unrelated to much other knowledge I have, and some distressingly large part of it may seem plausibly inconsistent with much of my other knowledge. We can readily justify living with such inconsistency, even at the base of our knowledge. Willingness to live with such inconsistency allows us to do many things other than getting our knowledge right or consistent.

---

[10]Lehrer (1990) presents a clear and careful account of the first three of these. The fourth, proceduralism, is a pragmatic theory of knowledge that fits the activities of many scientists and of many institutions. Although there are hints of it in earlier times, communalism is a relatively recent vision, except as it relates to religious and cultural knowledge.

[11]A coherentist might rudely say that this is merely my problem—but it is inconceivable that anyone has genuinely coherent knowledge in general.

For example, consider the physicist who believes in the laws of physics and also in the basic principles of some religion, including an intervening god who manipulates outcomes. That physicist might have great difficulty supposing that these two bodies of knowledge fit together. Many people seem to suffer from superstitious reactions to many things while also formally believing that the causal connections necessary for the superstitious beliefs to work are false. (Stuart Vyse [1997] chronicles many standard superstitions.) Even the best of decision theorists might suffer from probabilistic instincts that they can formally demonstrate to be false. Again, the varieties of acquisitions of anyone's knowledge (as above, much of it from a huge number of authorities) make it implausible that it is all coherent.

Moreover, knowledge must be to some substantial extent spatially organized in the brain, and the different parts of the brain may not communicate well enough to keep all of the bits coherent. For example, consider a plausible account of why grief over the loss of a close loved one lasts as long as it sometimes does (Hardin 1988b: 181–82). My knowledge of the newly deceased person is recorded in many contexts—all those contexts in which she played an important part in my life. Her death now, however, does not instantly get recorded in all of those contexts, which therefore remain potentially live to jump to my attention with the freshness of richly lived experience that still has prospects of continuing. I have to read her death into each of these memories when they are evoked, and this is not unlike discovering her death anew on numerous occasions, over a long period of time, until finally her death informs almost all of my memories of her, and I cease encountering her alive and vibrant. If a fact of some other kind is similarly implicated in many aspects or moments of my life, I may similarly find it cropping up anew even after I have discovered it to be false. Moreover, I may find it particularly difficult (even unnatural) to purge not only the false fact but also the false inferences from it that inform my understanding of various things.

A deep problem for applying a coherentist theory of knowledge to an ordinary person is that the person is likely to have diverse blocks of knowledge, each of which might seem to be blockwise coherent, but pieces of any of which would not be coherent with other blocks. For example, your knowledge of different areas might come, respectively, from childhood teaching by long forgotten people, from your own somewhat random experience, or from instruction by masters in those areas. When you now acquire a new bit of putative knowledge, to which of these blocks are you to test it for coherence?

(3) In externalist epistemology, it is supposed that "what must be added to true belief to obtain knowledge is the appropriate connection" (Lehrer 1990, 153). That connection might be causal, or might simply be unknown so long as there is a connection. Actually, to conclude that someone

has knowledge under this epistemology requires a move different from the move the someone makes to have the knowledge. It requires something like the super knower above to conclude that the appropriate connection is there. Hence, externalist epistemology is simply irrelevant to the judgment of a subject about the subject's own knowledge. There is a version of externalist epistemology that is not so clearly afflicted with this problem, and I will discuss it separately as proceduralist epistemology.

(4) Proceduralist epistemology counts as true those facts that have been tested or established through following relevant procedures, such as experimental or other procedures of inquiry. This epistemology might well fit much of the knowledge of a well-developed, open, critical science. Historically important experiments in many sciences seem to meet routinized procedural requirements. For example, more than a century ago, the German bacteriologist Robert Koch proposed a procedural test of whether a disease is caused by a specific microbe. First, it must be possible to isolate the microbe from the diseased organism. Second, that microbe must be able to infect a healthy new host, in which it must cause the same disease. Then the microbe must be isolated from the newly infected host. For testing a human disease, for obvious reasons, the second step here usually requires an animal that is subject to the disease. In the demonstration that a microbe causes most cases of stomach ulcers, one of the proponents of the theory made himself the test host. He was massively criticized for that risky action, but his demonstration largely ended debate, and he eventually shared a Nobel Prize for demonstrating the bacterial role in causing ulcers and therefore an easy cure for them.[12]

Because AIDS has not been shown to afflict other animals, the Koch test of the causal role of HIV is said not to have been carried out. Peter Duesberg and others have therefore argued that AIDS is not an instance of retroviral infection from HIV but depends on several other factors, including lifestyle (Duesberg 1988, 1996; see, further, Horton 1996). Unfortunately, three lab workers were accidentally infected with HIV from a cloned strain (that was therefore free of AIDS infection), and they went on to develop symptoms of AIDS. Their grim misfortune completed the Koch test of the role of HIV in causing AIDS (Cohen 1994, 1647).[13] One

---

[12]More than 90 percent of peptic ulcers are caused by a bacterial infection (*Helicobacter pylori*) and are therefore almost instantly curable with antibiotics. Australians Barry J. Marshall and J. Robin Warren received the Nobel Prize in physiology or medicine in 2005 after earlier enduring scorn from established medical authorities who dismissed their claim. As a major side benefit, their work may also reduce the incidence of stomach cancer, the second worst killer among cancers worldwide. Press Release from the Nobel Assembly at Karolinska Institutet, 3 October 2005. URL: http://nobelprize.org/medicine/laureates/2005/press.html.

[13]This is a fundamentally important finding, because by 1998 AIDS had become the fourth leading cause of death in the world (*Science* 284: 14 May 1999, p, 1101). Unlike some of the killers, it *tends* to strike people in their most active years.

might still insist that the Koch test is inadequate for establishing a causal relation here.

In the realm of social choice, we often expect institutions to apply standard procedures for reaching conclusions, as for example we require the justice system to follow standard procedures in reaching conclusions about whom to penalize for apparent crimes. The knowledge that courts "discover" is in part procedurally determined. But it is implausible to the point of being laughable to suppose that the knowledge of an ordinary individual can substantially be accounted for as the result of following some reasonable set or even sets of procedures.

(5) In addition to these four standard epistemologies, there is another that is currently developing. It is focused centrally on the social construction of knowledge, rather than on the knowledge itself. Hence, it is similar to the other epistemologies in its focus on public knowledge, although it has a strong subjective element. This epistemology can be called *communalism*. According to communalism, knowledge is what is grounded in a particular community of knowers, as in Thomas Kuhn's ([1962] 1996) account of scientific knowledge for a particular research paradigm, in David Hull's (1988) account of science itself as an evolutionary process, or in the contemporary literature on communitarianism, in which all of a person's knowledge might be supposed to depend on her community (for fuller discussion, see Hardin 1995, chapter 7).

On some readings, communalism might be taken as a variant of externalism or, especially, of proceduralism. On alternative readings, it is a full-scale rejection of externalism, as in some of the writings of Richard Rorty ([1985] 1991). In the strongest positions, communalists deny the meaning of truth as a standard independent of what a particular community knows. They do not merely deny the pragmatic relevance of such a standard to a given community; rather, they assert its utter meaninglessness and inaccessibility. At the most extreme, some postmodernists evidently hold that all knowledge is merely the conventional product of communities, that there is no genuinely general truth independent of communities and ideologies (for criticisms, see contributions to Koertge 1998). In the hoax of Alan Sokal (1996a; 1996b: 62–64), the value of pi (the ratio of the circumference of a circle to its diameter) was asserted to be a social construct rather than a mathematical constant, and his deliberately silly assertion was honored with publication in *Social Text,* a prestigious postmodern journal.[14]

For present purposes, the problem with all of these epistemologies is that they are not applicable to the way we acquire most of our knowledge. *They do what they are intended to do,* which is to assess claims of

[14]See the collection of contributions to this debate: *The Sokal Hoax,* edited by the Editors of *Lingua Franca* 2000.

truth, but they do not explain our ordinary knowledge, as I wish to do. The pragmatic theory of individual knowledge has closest affinities with recent social epistemology (see, for example, contributions to Schmitt 1994 and to *Synthese* vol. 73, 1987; and Goldman [1992] 1993). Social epistemologists insist that much of even scientific knowledge depends on testimony (Coady 1992; Foley 1994). Without much if any investigation, scientists rely on the findings—the testimony—of others. Social epistemologists wish to establish criteria according to which testimony can yield justified true beliefs. Ironically, they reverse the move of Descartes, Locke, et al., who wanted to break the destructive hold of the supposedly authoritative views of Aristotle on science.

One might suppose that usefulness and how we discover our knowledge are merely prior questions, and that the usual questions of epistemology follow once we conclude that some bit of knowledge is useful. There are at least three problems with this view. First, people are typically not concerned with the central point of standard epistemology, which is justification. For the bulk of learned knowledge, people simply accept its truth; they do not attempt to establish it or test it. In ordinary affairs we might occasionally wish to check to be sure that some putative fact is actually true. For example, if I am told that some close associate or relative has violated my trust, I might strive to get the facts right. As Othello struggled with the (false) claim of Iago that Desdemona was deceiving him, he required substantial evidence before he accepted the claim. About the loyalty or trustworthiness of most people around him, the same Othello might have accepted relatively loosely grounded claims without substantially checking them, especially if they came from a source he trusted, as he mistakenly trusted Iago.

Second, as discussed further below, the criteria of standard philosophical epistemology are what could be called public criteria, rather than the personal criteria that the actual knower might apply. They are relatively esoteric criteria that the typical person does not command, and they are recent inventions that could not have governed, say, Aristotle's assessments of truth. They are public the way the contemporary laws of physics are public, and they are esoteric in the way that these laws, which a very tiny number of people know at all, are esoteric. They are decidedly not the criteria of ordinary knowledge, which cannot plausibly be said to meet them. Hence, it is of only academic interest that a philosophical epistemologist might say that John and Mary Doe's "knowledge" is not philosophically sound enough to be knowledge, even though their knowledge governs the choices they make.

And third, the criteria that a person applies to judging a bit of knowledge are not necessarily criteria for truth, but merely and genuinely criteria for usefulness. Individuals cannot typically know much about whether their knowledge is true, but they can commonly grasp whether it is useful, whether it works in some sense. For knowledge, use is what matters to most of us most of the time, apart from when we might be doing science or philosophy. Truth might very often happen to be part of what makes some bit of knowledge useful, but it is not the same as usefulness and need not be a part of what makes for usefulness. Some bit of knowledge that would be false by any standard epistemological criteria—as arguably most of a typical person's knowledge is—might nevertheless be very useful. Indeed, much of the knowledge we accept and act on is merely satisficing knowledge, that is, good enough.[15] It is adequate for the relevant tasks and it need not be useful for us to invest the effort needed to improve the knowledge. One might say that such knowledge is "true enough" for its purpose, but that is an odd locution. In any case, it is instructively a locution misfit in the realm of standard philosophical accounts of knowledge.

Ideal knowledge is of interest only academically, not practically. When we turn to practical knowledge, we must inherently be interested in knowledge that is put to use by someone, such as you or me. But, then, what is knowledge for me might well not be knowledge for you. This is conspicuously true for knowledge of any kind, even philosophically sound knowledge, that I have acquired that you have not acquired. But the point here is even more far reaching than this. I might even know a physics that is different from your physics, and I might act on it while you act on yours. Arguably more important in our lives than different knowledge of physics is different knowledge of social causation and of social facts, both of which play far more important conscious roles in our actual choices from day to day than does any articulate knowledge of physics.

CONCLUDING REMARKS

In standard philosophical epistemology, it would commonly be thought incoherent to speak of my mistaken knowledge. Knowledge is, in some epistemologies, "justified true belief." If I am mistaken in my belief, then I most likely lack justification for the belief. Hence, it is not knowledge. And in any case, the category of justified true belief is a category of somehow public knowledge, not personal knowledge. For most of us, most of the time, there may be no ground for claiming in general that our knowledge is philosophically justified in any such sense. There is commonly only a story to be told of how we have come to have our beliefs. There is

[15]This term is due to Herbert Simon (1955).

therefore little or no point, for present purposes, in distinguishing between belief and knowledge. Typically, at the street level of ordinary people, who are not philosophical epistemologists, the term "belief" is commonly used when the substance of the knowledge is a particular kind, such as religious knowledge. There is often no other systematic difference in degree of confidence in knowing those things that are labeled as knowledge and those that are labeled as belief. Indeed, people with strong religious convictions commonly claim to know the truth of the things they believe religiously far more confidently than the truth of many simple, objective things they might also claim to know. It is true that we sometimes use the term 'belief' to allow for doubt, as when we say, "I believe that's the way it happened, but I might be wrong." But this hedge applies to virtually all our knowledge.

Standard philosophy of knowledge is concerned with justification, that is, justification of any claim that some piece of putative knowledge is actually true. The ordinary person's economic theory is economic in the sense that it is not generally about justification but about usefulness. It follows Dewey's ([1920] 1948, 163) "pragmatic rule": the meaning of an idea is its consequences. In essence, the theory here applies this rule to the idea of knowledge, with consequences broadly defined to include the full costs and benefits of coming to know and using knowledge.

Trudy Govier (1997, 51–76) argues that our knowledge therefore depends on trust. It might be better to say that it depends on the trustworthiness of our authoritative sources, although even this is saying too much. Very little of our knowledge seems likely to depend on anything vaguely like an ordinary trust relationship. I personally know none of the authoritative sources for much of what I would think is my knowledge in many areas. It is not so much that I take that knowledge on trust as that I have little choice but to take it. If I do not take it, I will be virtually catatonic. I am quite confident that much of what I think I know is false, but still I rely on what I know to get me through life, because I have to.

The concern of an economic theory of knowledge is, again, the problem of *a choosing agent's knowledge* as opposed to a theorist's or critic's knowledge. We commonly have no recourse to a super knower when we are making life decisions, whether minor or major. Occasionally, we may turn to supposed experts for assistance, although it is we who must judge whether someone or some source is a relevant expert (see further, chapter 2 on science). Tony Coady (1994) goes so far as to ask how the lay person can distinguish between communication from an expert and communication from a spirit in the spirit world.

We ground our lives in putative but philosophically ungrounded knowledge. The task of clearing out the Augean stables in our heads would dominate our lives for decades and would get in the way of our living, not to speak of living well. Actually completing the task might well disable us almost entirely. Wittgenstein (1969: §344) says: "My life consists in my being content to accept many things." These are de facto *my* foundations for going on to consider other things.[16]

In the end, if we did attempt to clear the fouled and cluttered stables in our heads in a Herculean commitment to some epistemology, we would plausibly have so little left that we could scarcely have grounds on which to choose at all in most contexts. If we finally cleared out everything that did not fit one of the standard epistemologies, we would be very nearly catatonically incapacitated. Any of those epistemologies would arguably be pragmatically disastrous for most people. Since the principal value of knowing at all is to enable us to choose and live well, it therefore follows that we should—at least most of the time—pragmatically reject the demands of those epistemologies as deleterious to our prospects. Most of the time, we should join Samuel Johnson in not going in quest of knowledge.

Philosophers sensibly pursue the enterprise of standard epistemology, the enterprise of the justification of knowledge, but ordinary people can rightly forgo it for most of their own lives. This is, of course, merely a claim from the economic theory of knowledge, with its pragmatic focus, and is only a practical, not a theoretical claim. That economic theory of knowledge would fail the truth-tests of all the standard epistemologies, and the relevant epistemologists would dismiss it in turn. Nevertheless, although there may be good reasons for doing or knowing philosophical epistemology, those reasons are not among the practical reasons that should inform the reasoning of ordinary people when they are making decisions about their lives. For much of knowledge, if we ask "Why know?" we surely must answer "Because it is useful." But if that is our answer, it follows that we should assess such knowledge by its utility—which is to say, by an economic theory of knowledge.

A frequently cited legal standard of rationality says that "the reasonable observer is an informed citizen who is more knowledgeable than the average passerby" (*Modrovich v. Allegheny County,* p. 407). This already sets the standard above the average, and is therefore too demanding for most people. We would live much less fulfilled lives if we were far more demanding in the standards to which we subject the flow of knowledge into our minds. This is the vague, pragmatic test to which we subject putative knowledge. Moreover, it seems clearly to be the correct test for real life. That is to say, if we are commending a practice to someone else, we should rightly commend this practice to them. We would commend rigorously following any of the standard epistemologies only if we were foolish or mean-spirited. That is, in any case, not the point of philosophical epistemology.

---

[16]Indeed, "propositions of the form of empirical propositions, and not only propositions of logic, form the foundation of all operating with thoughts" (Wittgenstein 1969: §401).

CHAPTER 2

Popular Knowledge of Science

SCIENTIFIC KNOWLEDGE, in each instance of it, is usually something that someone has gone in quest of. If I am, say, a geneticist, I will not have gone in quest of all knowledge in my field; I will merely have held out my hand to receive much of it from others who supposedly did go in quest of it, or who report what someone else who went in quest of it has told us. But part of it will genuinely be mine, in the sense that I will have sought it out. Indeed, I may even have discovered some of it. Even then, of course, I will take many of the elements of my own search in essence on faith from others. I will not make sure that my chemicals are what their labels say they are; I will not test to see that my instruments actually do what they are supposed to do—I may not even know how they work; I will not become an expert in understanding the statistical methods I use; I will not check the code of my software; and I will generally not master translation from the original languages of all of the texts I might hope to use.[1] I will almost entirely rely on authorities for such things.

But note two important points. First, I do not mean here to characterize some people as scientists and others as nonscientists, as though individuals in either of these categories always reason in one way rather than the other. The argument is not about ordinary people versus scientists but about *ordinary versus scientific knowledge*. It is about two very general ways of knowing. Both ordinary people and scientists come to both kinds of knowledge, but both are far more governed in their lives by ordinary knowledge than by scientific knowledge. Hobbes ([1651] 1994, ch. 13, ¶2) says, science is "not a native faculty (born with us), nor attained (as prudence) while we look after somewhat else. . . ." It takes deliberate effort to think scientifically, and it is a skill "which very few have, *and in but few things*."

Second, I am also not concerned to pose scientific knowledge as a standard to which to compare ordinary knowledge, except in the very limited sense that I wish to give an account of how ordinary people deal with contemporary science and its understanding. Against any claim for the gen-

---

[1] These are not idle problems. They have led to massive failures, ranging from a recent space probe's confusion between metric and English measurements to a software glitch that badly affected a massive study of the risks of excess deaths from soot in the air (Kaiser 2002).

eral superiority of scientific knowledge, ordinary knowledge is defensible as the best way to go most of the time, very nearly all of the time. To follow assiduously the most demanding canons of science would likely be disastrous for our daily lives.

One should not be very harsh with the lack of scientific foundations for most of our thinking, because there is simply no time for us to investigate the truth of even a small fraction of the things we know. John Stuart Mill ([1861] 1977, chap. 3, ¶2) says that a "person must have a very unusual taste for intellectual exercise in and of itself, who will put himself to the trouble of thought when it is to have no outward effect. . . . The only sufficient incitement to mental exertion, in any but a few minds in a generation, is the prospect of some practical use to be made of its results." Often, however, the failure of ordinary thinking to investigate is troubling and, in any case, it undercuts the possibility that we might get certain important things right, things that would matter to us. Our task is either by instinct or by deliberate judgment to know when to investigate and when to proceed with what we already know or what some "authority" says, as all of us do most of the time.

It is commonly said that we live in the Age of Science. In fact, however, we "mostly partake of the fruits of science—technology—whereas fundamental principles of scientific thinking are often poorly taught and rarely employed" (Shermer 2000, 35). *If careful scientific reasoning has little payoff for us, we are unlikely ever to develop any talent or interest in such thinking.* Hence, on most issues most of the time we are unlikely to move from ordinary knowledge to scientific knowledge. Certainly we cannot do it often, even if we do develop the talent for it. But dwell for a moment on the costs, not of pursuing scientific investigation into some ordinary matter, but of ever *learning to think scientifically.* Consider, for example, doctors, who are notoriously not good at statistical inference (very few people are good at it).[2] Yet for very much of what they do in dealing with patients, statistical analysis is of fundamental importance (Swets et al. 2000). Unfortunately, statistical analysis requires large numbers of cases, but a doctor faces cases one at a time. Keeping a good subjective inventory of all of the cases one has faced, even as a very narrowly

---

[2]Dr. Roy Meadow, a renowned British pediatrician, testified on the odds that two infants in the same family could have died of sudden infant death syndrome (SIDS). He overstated the odds against, and his estimate helped in convicting a mother whose two infants had died. He is not a statistician, and he made a simple, amateurish mistake. He was censured by a panel that ruled: "You abused your position as a doctor by giving evidence that was misleading, albeit unintentionally, and . . . *you were working outside the limits of your professional competence* by straying into the area of statistics." They found him "guilty of serious medical misconduct" because his expertise was irrelevant to his testimony (*Science* 309 [22 July 2005]: 543, emphasis added).

specialized doctor, would not be easy.[3] A much more broadly focused doctor might find it virtually impossible to keep such an inventory. The only way to do it is through well maintained records—ideally across many hospitals and other medical institutions. Discovering what causes what in medicine can take years of collective effort in collating data from thousands of cases.

When a student does an experiment in chemistry, physics, or biology, or does some kinds of research in the social sciences, the results are often virtually instant and compelling—and often they are readily repeatable on the spot. When this is the case, then understanding the ways of scientific reasoning in the laboratory is relatively easy.

We hardly need any scientific thinking to use technology. Turn the key and the engine starts; open the laptop and type in a passage and it instantly appears on the screen for us to manipulate further; get on an airplane and it takes us across the ocean. Who knows how or why? As far as useful technology is concerned, we need not know much more than that it works if we do certain things properly. We get through all our days, using various bits of technology, without needing to understand why any of it works. Indeed, a strictly economic view recommends that we should not bother to know how most of it works, because it would exhaust all our efforts and all our time to understand it. It is much more useful merely to take advantage of it than it is to master its principles.

If we are to understand political behavior, religious belief, extremist commitments, or even ordinary morality, we must first understand how people come to know or believe what they know or believe, as is argued in later chapters. Here the focus is primarily on the difference between popular knowledge of physics and cosmology and popular knowledge of medicine and health care, as relatively transparent examples of the problems of ordinary knowledge. The reason for the dual focus is that ordinary persons' knowledge of physics and cosmology is unlikely to affect their behavior in any significant way, whereas their knowledge of medicine may make a great difference to their lives and their behavior. People can often use newly created medical knowledge; they cannot use newly created knowledge in physics or cosmology.

---

[3]An almost weekly feature in the *New York Times Magazine* is a column, "Diagnosis," about interesting medical cases that, usually, are eventually resolved by some doctor's clever hunch or insight. In one case, several medical specialists cannot figure out why a woman is suffering manifold problems. They perform lots of tests and confer heavily on the case. The senior physician comes in and instantly recognizes the symptoms of scurvy, which he had seen once before, twenty-five years earlier, and which does not happen often in a modern society (Sanders 2006). It afflicted sailors in the British navy until they added limes to their diet at sea (thus becoming limeys) to provide what eventually came to be known as vitamin C.

We could modify Dewey's ([1920] 1948, 163) pragmatic-rule definition of knowledge to say that the value of any bit of knowledge is how it would matter to us and our behavior. Medical knowledge has greater value to most of us than knowledge of contemporary physics has. A full economic account would weigh this value against the cost of gaining some bit of that knowledge. The economic account suggests that most people will put more effort into obtaining medical knowledge, because it could matter in affecting their own lives, *through their own actions,* whereas knowledge of modern physics could not. This is not to say that contemporary physics and cosmology have no value to any ordinary non-scientists. They might, for example, have substantial curiosity or entertainment value. For most of us, medical knowledge is like technology. We go to a doctor or a hospital and hope we can get repaired.

A striking instance of the differentiation between the pragmatic value of knowledge of medical science and the entertainment value of physics is the ways in which the contemporary press reports on medical science and physics. As noted by Edna Ullmann-Margalit (private conversation, 20 March 2002), in the weekly Tuesday "Science Times" section of the *New York Times,* the discussions of medical knowledge are generally pragmatically about how new findings might help us. They often have the flavor of medical advice. The discussions of physics are mostly razzle-dazzle reports on amazing new discoveries or theories. They concern string theory, the big bang, black holes, exploding novas, and other such wonders beyond ordinary experience. A clear example of this split focus is the "Science Times" of 13 April 2004, with its two lead stories. A wonderful graphic represents a gravity experiment to test an implication of Einstein's general theory of relativity, the implication that space and time must be warped by their proximity to massive objects, such as the Earth. The other lead story is of hope for treatment of Alzheimer's disease. Almost no one can likely understand the first story very well, despite its being well written (Overbye 2004). Actually understanding Alzheimer's is also likely restricted to few readers, but the import of the report (Kolata 2004) on potential treatments is clear, and probably of great real interest to many readers, young and old.

The economic account is, again, a theory of ordinary knowledge as acquired and used in ordinary daily life. It is usually not a close kin of philosophical epistemology, which concerns various theories, in a sense, of the abstract truth of various claims, such as that the atom is made up of electrons, protons, and neutrons. As argued earlier, ordinary knowledge is usually not a close kin of such scientific knowledge, because most of it is learned and defended in ways that bear little relation to scientific discovery, test, or corroboration. Edward Craig (1990) suggests that the way to understand knowledge is to answer the question, "Why do we have it?" For ordinary knowledge, the answer is generally that it is useful.

Some of the seeming shortcomings of ordinary knowledge are treated as psychological tricks that lead us astray.[4] Such tricks might be a major problem for ordinary knowledge, but the greater problem is essentially economic, not psychological. We have neither the time nor the resources to investigate the truth or even the coherence of our views on most matters. We can do little better than Samuel Johnson—we can happen upon bits of knowledge and put them to use, generally without going in quest of anything on behalf of our beliefs.

John Locke (1632–1704), almost an exact contemporary of Newton and one of the first and most important modern theorists of the nature of knowledge, argued forcefully against the economic theory of knowledge that I defend. He writes:

> . . . we may as rationally hope to see with other Mens Eyes, as to know by other Mens Understandings. So much as we our selves consider and comprehend of Truth and Reason, so much we possess of real and true Knowledge. The floating of other Mens Opinions in our brains makes us not one jot the more knowing, though they happen to be true. What in them was science is in us but Opiniatretry, whilst we give up our Assent only to reverend names, and do not, as they did, employ our own Reason to *understand* those *Truths,* which gave them reputation. . . . In the Sciences, every one has so much, as he really knows and comprehends: What he believes only, and takes upon trust, are but shreds; which however well in the whole piece, make no considerable addition to his stock, who gathers them. Such borrowed Wealth, like Fairymoney, though it were Gold in the hand from which he received it, will be but Leaves and Dust when it comes to use. (Locke [1689] 1975, 1.4.23. p. 101; see, further, Schmitt 1987, 43–44; Foley 1994; Shapin 1996, chap. 2)

Contrary to Locke's view, the knowledge we have that is mere opiniatretry is what we live by, and it is enormously useful to us. This is arguably the most distinctively human capacity: knowing things we haven't seen. If a monkey hasn't seen it, the monkey doesn't know it. For humans, only because knowledge is socially produced is it rich enough to enable us to live well. Locke's dictum elevates the ignorance of monkeys.

Locke's view here is very important to his argument for religious toleration, on the ground that I cannot simply adopt the religion that the state wants adopted, because I cannot simply accept the state's view in prefer-

---

[4]The body of work on nonrational decisions and thinking more generally is enormous and growing fast. Consider two mainstays: Baron [1988] 2000 and Kahnemann and Tversky 2000.

ence to my own, as Hobbes ([1651] 1994, chap. 26, §41) also claims for simple reasons of his commonsense view of how the mind works (§40, fn. 14). My belief might be wrong and the state's might be right, but the mere fact that the state holds some view need not matter to my own font of knowledge in these matters. Hence, it is irrational to attempt to coerce me to believe what I do not believe on my own account. Jean Bodin ([1576] 1606, bk. 4, chap. 7: 539) says similarly that people's minds "could by no threats or commands be constrained or bound," and Martin Luther ([1523] 1991, 25) concurs. On their view, Protestantism, with its individual doubt, is virtually a fact of the organization of the mind. One could fully accept this conclusion on religious toleration, however, without grounding it in the views that Locke and others state here.

Of course, the state can de facto strongly influence its citizens' knowledge, even on religious matters, if it starts early enough. The school board of Dover, Pennsylvania, and various boards elsewhere, including most notoriously Kansas, Arkansas, and Louisiana, and state-sponsored madrasas throughout the Middle East and Pakistan (see Dalrymple 2005) have attempted to inculcate fundamentalist religious views in very young children. An irony of the Kansas stance is that it is hostile to the use of the evolutionary theory that has made Kansas agriculture so impressively productive. The Kansas anti-evolutionists wish to stop teaching about the very basis of the state's current and presumably future economy (Hanson and Bloom 1999).

Our task in life is not to seek out all truths for ourselves, as Locke would seemingly have us do, but to judge the sources of our borrowed wealth of knowledge. We can be challenged by his railing against the floating of other men's or women's opinions in our brains, either to check out the opinions or to check out the others from whom we get the opinions. The latter might be a philosophically shabby move in comparison to the former, but it is far and away the best we can do for the vast bulk of those opinions floating in our brains, opinions that constitute most of our knowledge of our world and on which we base virtually all of our choices and actions.

Locke's vision, or the visions of Francis Bacon, Thomas Hobbes,[5] and René Descartes (see Albritton 1985, 239) before his, does not fit modern science. Standard philosophical epistemology is concerned with justification, that is, justification of any claim that some piece of putative knowledge is actually true, or that some system for generating or testing knowledge is rationally suited to its task. It focuses on the matter of belief, such

[5]Hobbes ([1651] 1994, chap. 5, ¶4) says "he that takes up conclusions on the trust of authors, and doth not fetch them from the first items in every reckoning. . . , loses his labour, and does not know anything, but only believeth."

as whether light is propagated through an ether. It deals with truth, and the justification of truth claims about such matters.

The focus of the pragmatic theory of knowledge is on the use and subjectivity of knowledge, not on justification of any claim that it is "true" knowledge. It is subjective because, again, it is about *your* knowledge or *my* knowledge, not about knowledge per se. Philosophical epistemology is generally about the criteria for claiming that some claim is true per se. It is not about your beliefs or knowledge or about mine; it is about "knowledge" as a category. *How Do You Know?* is rather an account of how ordinary people, philosophers included, come to believe what they believe, and then an effort to use that explanation to account for certain of their actions or further beliefs. There is no reason to suppose that the project here should connect to the issues of epistemological truth. It should connect to various movements in the sociology of knowledge. This latter enterprise is almost never the province of philosophers, but primarily of social scientists: economists, sociologists, psychologists, and anthropologists. I offer explanations of views; I do not offer justifications for them.

An implication of the economic theory of knowledge acquisition might be that we know those things that are likely to be useful or beneficial to us better than we do those things that will not be. I will argue, rather, that the chief implication of the economic theory is that we will tend to come to know much *more* about things for which our knowledge can affect us than about things for which our knowledge cannot affect us or is unlikely to. This does not mean that we will know *better,* only that we will know more, much of which might be scientifically unfounded and even false. But we will at least make Johnson's effort of holding out our hands to catch medical knowledge, while most of us may dismiss knowledge of modern physics much the way Sherlock Holmes dismissed knowledge of the solar system, because it was of no use to him in his professional life. Dr. Watson seemed to think Holmes should know that the Earth revolves about the sun. "What the deuce is it to me?" Holmes impatiently retorted. "You say that we go round the sun. If we went round the moon it would not make a penny-worth of difference to me or to my work." He kept his brain attic orderly by keeping it clear of such useless knowledge (Doyle [1887] 1993, 15–16).

In the economic theory we face two largely orthogonal issues. First, what are the things we know much about? And, second, what is the quality of our knowledge about any of them or about any other things? The economic theory suggests that *the typical person will come to know more about modern medical science than about modern physics*—but it need not suggest that our medical knowledge will be of high quality. High-quality knowledge in any developing scientific field is extremely costly to attain, because it would require extensive education in the relevant science, education that most of us lack and will certainly not obtain merely to help us make better choices in health care. Because medical knowledge is often very costly and may be enormously valuable to us, it poses a rich test of the economic theory of knowledge. Let us turn to it.

MEDICAL KNOWLEDGE

Given that we are not going to master medical science for the sake of our own health, what knowledge will we use? In ordinary lives the role of medical knowledge is strikingly different from the role of knowledge of modern physics. It is an area in which people actively want better knowledge than they have, and therefore they are likely to seek it to some extent, especially—but not only—if there is fairly direct evidence that investments in gathering new knowledge pay off. Again, understanding how to improve health is different from understanding physics in that the understanding itself—and not merely the technologies that are produced from that understanding—has enormous value to typical individuals, who might therefore be expected to master at least some of it. That conclusion is wrong for at least two distinctly different classes of reason. First, knowledge of health issues is collectively, not individually, produced; second, most people consume only the knowledge produced by others, so that their problem is not of judging scientific claims per se but of judging who are the right experts for reaching the right conclusions about these issues. Indeed, the first problem, of the collective creation of knowledge, is rent through by the problems of assessing who the relevant experts might be.

The economic theory suggests that we will seek medical knowledge, even go in quest of it, for the obvious reason that if we could find remedies for various common ailments, we could radically improve and even extend our lives. Unfortunately, in putting the knowledge to use, we seldom get the instant feedback that we get from using various technologies or from doing experiments in a lab. Someone who has never heard of the wonders of the computer but who writes might instantly grasp the value of the computer and its printer as a word processor. Many people of earlier generations have held out against using computers for word processing, but the market for typewriters has largely collapsed, and with very good reason. With similar alacrity, if I am told that some painkiller will stop my migraine, I might try it and discover instantly that it works. But if I am told that taking vitamin C in large doses will extend my life, I get no positive, confirming feedback, although I might have nearly immediate negative effects from dumping so much acid into my stomach.

Almost no one has a stake in the rightness or wrongness of particular scientific claims in cosmology, other than those involved, as cosmologists, in its internal debates. Hence, there is no alternative group of purveyors of scientific knowledge of cosmology, such as those who disagree about medical science. That is to say, there is no competing class of experts; there are only the standard scientists whose great hope is to get the science right. There are various nonscientists who reject certain scientific findings for religious reasons. In medicine, there is additionally an engaged class of experts who are in a heated contest with the experts of big institutional medicine. In a story set in Calcutta, Jhumpa Lahiri (1999, 158–59) gives an account of the variety of treatments of the young woman, Bibi Haldar, who suffers from an awful ailment, and who is therefore eligible to suffer further from expertise:

> Treatments offered by doctors only made matters worse. Allopaths, homeopaths, ayurvedics—over time, all branches of the medical arts had been consulted. Their advice was endless. After x-rays, probes, auscultations, and injections, some merely advised Bibi to gain weight, others to lose it. If one forbade her to sleep beyond dawn, another insisted she remain in bed till noon. This one told her to perform headstands, that one to chant Vedic verses at specified intervals throughout the day. "Take her to Calcutta for hypnosis" was a suggestion still others would offer. Shuttled from one specialist to the next, the girl had been prescribed to shun garlic, consume disproportionate quantities of bitters, meditate, drink green coconut water, and swallow raw duck's eggs beaten in milk. In short, Bibi's life was an encounter with one fruitless antidote after another.

To understand the nature of the ordinary person's medical knowledge, we must understand first how any medical knowledge is produced at all, and second how it gets transferred to the ordinary person. Both its production and its mastery are extremely complex. It is produced collectively through the efforts of vast numbers of people and many institutions. Most of us gain our knowledge of it, not through participating in its production or mastery, but by relying on various experts to guide us in our choices of medical care and prevention. These two facts of medical knowledge are obviously related. If knowledge is massively collectively produced, access to enough of it to enable us to make choices must be mediated by experts or by institutional arrangements that map the separate areas of medical science, so that although no one person might be able to oversee the whole of our condition, as Locke would have wanted, at least an organization might be able to do so.

Collective Production of Knowledge

As noted, an overwhelmingly important characteristic of medical knowledge is that it is collectively, not individually, produced. Little bits of it are, of course, very often individually produced, but the overall body of medical knowledge, even in a particular, narrow field, is collectively produced. Large numbers of medical researchers and medical providers collate their findings to produce whatever knowledge we have. That knowledge is distributed among many people and institutions, no one of whom could master the bulk of it. Many participants in these institutions may be called upon to pool their knowledge in a particular case, as graphically pictured in televised versions of emergency room activities, with many people dividing the chores according to their specializations. Even when you face an individual doctor to get advice on some condition you might have, that doctor is typically backed by lots of specialists whose separate inputs might be important for the resolution of your problem.

Individual medical knowledge, on which people often act, is very different. It is also collectively produced as the eventual product of hearsay, talk, and often a bit of reading. But much of it is applied by individuals, not by institutions, to their own cases. You may have heard from friends and others that, say, echinacea is a very good cure for head colds. You try it and maybe your cold goes away fairly soon. You now have very little, if any, evidence one way or the other that echinacea works, because colds usually go away fairly soon in any case. Or maybe you think it is a preventive, so you take it throughout the winter. You might still get colds that winter, but you might readily believe that they are the especially hardy cases that overcome your immunity. You might subjectively compare to past winters, but in all honesty, unless you have kept good records, you could not claim to know how this winter's experience with echinacea compares to last winter's without echinacea.

So what do we believe about echinacea? Some would think it not especially good, some would believe it is okay, and others might think it really good, so good that they commend it to many other sufferers. If we ask those who think echinacea to be very good, we are likely to discover that they also think numerous other popular cures are effective; and those who think echinacea largely irrelevant to health also think a host of other such cures are irrelevant. It is not strictly evidence that tips the scales for such beliefs. You believe one class of experts—those in standard medicine—and I believe another class—those who argue for homeopathic or folk medicine. Loren Israelsen, a leader of the "natural products" movement, says "This is really a belief system, almost a religion" (Specter 2004, 64–66). Others in that movement must have winced at such a claim. Science vs. religion yet again.

A medically strenuous test of echinacea would use it in controlled experiments in which the patient-subjects do not know whether they are receiving echinacea or a placebo. Of course, the experiments would involve many subjects, and not just your single experience as assessed by you. There have been at least three substantial studies, none showing echinacea to be effective in curing or reducing the severity of a cold, but inconclusive on whether a maintenance dose will reduce the incidence of colds. The genus *Echinacea* contains more than one species, and studies might need to control which species is being used. Over-the-counter echinacea is insufficiently labeled to let users know what they are taking. (See Anthony Ramirez, "Study Critical of Echinacea Fails to Faze Some Users," *New York Times,* 30 July 2005, B2; N. Seppa, "Echinacea Disappoints," *Science* 168 [30 July 2005]: 70.)

Collective production of medical knowledge often inherently involves statistical assessments of large numbers of cases. In the end, therefore, individuals usually cannot count on their own limited experience to judge medical matters, because they have insufficient data to test any cure. There is no simple test today, as there was in physics in its wonderfully simple heyday in the late nineteenth and early twentieth centuries, when Ernest Rutherford could perform an elegant experiment that showed that an atom has a tiny, dense nucleus, or Robert Millikan could do another that showed that the electron has a mass far tinier than that of the nucleus. Tests of genetically engineered antibiotics might soon be as elegant and definitive as such results in physics. Ironically, those antibiotics will then also reveal their power almost instantly in actual applications, so that individuals will be able to judge that the antibiotics are effective. Although great expertise will have gone into producing the antibiotics, assessment of their effectiveness will be accessible to virtually everyone individually. At the point of usage, a crude form of scientific testing can clearly be invoked. We have a great interest in curing our infection; strengthening our immune system with echinacea seems to work slowly if at all; the antibiotic stops the infection almost instantly.

The MIT physicist Philip Morrison once told of his effort to characterize the development of physics in the early twentieth century. As I recall his account, he interviewed older physicists to find out how they lived their science and how they taught it. One of his favorite interviewees had been a physics instructor at the Colorado School of Mines early in the twentieth century. In the local paper, that instructor had read of an experiment done the day before in Germany. The local paper had reduced its story from a wire service or a larger newspaper and had mangled the details. But even from the very brief, garbled news story, the instructor was able to intuit what the experiment had been, and that morning he had his class replicate the experiment, with virtually perfect results. The elderly former instructor told that story with great pride, adding that he and his class had been the first people to replicate the experiment in North America. Morrison said he refrained from telling the proud man that, because he had been on Mountain Time, he had been scooped by classes in many Eastern and Midwestern universities. Such was the physics of that time.[6] Knowing that something could be done was often virtually sufficient to lead any competent physicist to figure out how to do it. And the rewards of doing an experiment were often instant results, so readily corroborated that their replication became part of the standard education of generations of students, beginning already in high school.

Whose Experts?

The bulk of ordinary knowledge comes to us from hearsay: from "experts" of varying degrees of qualification, ranging from a local gossip to supposedly reliable newspapers and reference books. We do not generally investigate the accuracy of such knowledge. Rather, we simply rely on it—on some bits of it, of course, far more than on other bits of it. Hearsay of some kind is the source of most of the knowledge of everyone, including scientists, although scientists have more deliberate devices for gaining knowledge in their fields of specialization. There is essentially no alternative for most of our knowledge because we cannot possibly be deliberate about checking the truth of most of our knowledge. First and foremost, we want to use the knowledge, not to verify or justify it.

Recall the claim above that proponents of one popular cure tend to be proponents of others, and that those who reject, say, echinacea also tend to reject other popular cures. This claim is backed by only a small informal survey of many people, mostly at small dinner parties. It is only a slightly more scientifically grounded claim than are the claims of proponents of various popular cures. It may, however, lack something that those claims have, which is widespread support from many people. But if the claim is true, then it suggests that people believe *different kinds of sources* for their medical knowledge. The proponents of popular cures somehow have come to dislike and disbelieve institutional medicine and its advocates. This divergence of views raises the inescapable question of how we judge an institution or an expert to be a good source of knowledge in an area in which we are not good judges of the knowledge itself.

Answers to this question might be quite varied. Among the possible answers are that I believe particular institutions or experts because others with whom I associate believe them; that I believe in them because they have been publicly or even officially recognized; or because they seem to

---

[6]Morrison dates this era as roughly from 1890 to 1960.

be open and transparent in their views. The first of these is generally as good a source of information as any that most of us use most of the time (Margolis 1987, 135). When Supreme Court Justice Felix Frankfurter was told by the Pole Jan Karski, an eyewitness, what was happening to Jews in the concentration camps of Nazi Germany, Frankfurter seemed unmoved. Told that he should believe what he was hearing, he said the problem was not that he did not believe it but that he was *unable* to believe it (Wood and Jankowski 1994). Perhaps the Nazi death camps were so far outside the realm of experience that it was nearly impossible to suppose that there was such a murderous regime in the world. It would take far more evidence than one person's testimony to correct one's view of such a matter.

Communal "knowledge" from those with whom you associate may be a perverse source for medical beliefs. Suppose the kind of people you like and associate with happen to believe strongly in echinacea and many other wonderful cures from folk knowledge. You try them and cannot honestly claim to notice any effect. What is your individual bit of evidence against the beliefs of all these other people? In a sense, your response is more nearly like the scientific response to medical knowledge than that of your colleagues. But you are willing to let your own evidence be trumped by collective knowledge. The only issue is why you count *that* collectivity's knowledge as at all definitive or possibly right. Do you merely go along to get along, as the oldtimer's advice to newcomers to the U.S. Congress has it, or do you actually become persuaded?

Perhaps the beliefs can be understood or explained only in the larger context of what the alternative source of supposed medical knowledge may be. The chief alternative source is organized medicine. If organized medicine fails to cure, say, Steve McQueen's cancer, then he might turn to ingesting laetrile (an extract of apricot pit), not out of genuine belief that it will cure cancer but out of forlorn hope that something might. Maybe the common cold, while not so life-threatening or grim as cancer, provokes a similar response. Organized medicine seems to offer little or no help, and many people hope something else might help. People spend billions of dollars on over-the-counter drugs whose value in fighting a cold is shown to be nil in controlled tests. Despite the sound of "billions of dollars," of course, actual individuals are unlikely to spend more than a tiny fraction of their resources on these cures, and since, again, most colds get better even if left alone, they might come to believe that the cures work well enough to be worth their small cost.

Individuals choose to credit either popular medical knowledge or the knowledge purveyed by the standard, highly organized and well-funded medical establishment. They choose their own experts. Some of the time, we make such choices on the basis of some individually assessable evidence. For example, standard medicine may have rescued your child from a debilitating disease, or an antibiotic may have stopped your painful infection almost instantly. Or maybe echinacea seems to have stopped your last several colds very quickly, or to have spared you while all about you were succumbing to colds.

Or perhaps it is wrong to say we "choose." We simply come to know that one or the other kind of expert is more reliable, and we then act under the authority of that kind of expert. Knowledge is in a cognitive category with belief and trust. Commonly, knowledge, belief, and trust are not things we choose. Rather, they are things that happen to us. We may choose to put ourselves in the way of coming to know, but the knowing finally happens because for some reason, over which we have no control, the apparent fact compels us. As Hume ([1739–40] 2000, 3.1.1 ¶12) says, a mistake of fact is "perfectly involuntary." In the social sciences, we might decide that we know something with some degree of confidence because it meets some statistical test. That test might be a convention that some of us have decided more or less collectively to accept (although we might have chosen another convention), and that many of us accept simply on the authority of our teachers or other supposed experts. Ordinary knowledge, however, does not have even this much going for it. It simply grips us and we know it.

Of course, it is not only ordinary knowledge of pragmatic affairs that grips us. Religious belief has no other claim than that it somehow grips us, or some of us. Similarly, Aristotle argued that the passions are things that just happen to us. They seize us without our intending them, as patriotism or belief in some ideology sometimes does.

Estrangement from Science

The difficulties we have in understanding contemporary scientific advances are a sore point for many people. There is an especially sad strain of estrangement from modern science by intellectuals who have lost touch with science, and who openly say that they cannot understand it. Gerald Holton (1996, 51) says that contemporary intellectuals "know only two things about the basic conceptions of modern science: that they do not understand them, and that they are now so far separated from them that they may never find out their meaning." This is distinctively different from the science wars provoked by religion and by fears of technology gone wild. Both of these lead to hostility to science and technology and to policy that uses them. The estrangement is well characterized by Lionel

Trilling a generation ago ([1972] 2000, 483 and 484). The operative conceptions of science, Trilling notes,

> are alien to the mass of educated persons. They generate no cosmic speculations, they do not engage emotion or challenge imagination. Our poets are indifferent to them. . . . This exclusion of most of us from the mode of thought which is habitually said to be the characteristic achievement of the modern age is bound to be experienced as a wound given to our intellectual self-esteem. About this humiliation we all agree to be silent, but can we doubt that it has consequences, that it introduces into the life of mind a significant element of dubiety and alienation which must be taken into account in any estimate that is made of the present fortunes of mind?

Trilling does not mourn for the state of popular knowledge, but only for the state of the knowledge of dedicated intellectuals and the well educated—people like himself. He would not expect the larger public to read or understand his own literary writings, any more than they read or understand the writings of contemporary scientists. Clive James (1996, 104) broadens the range of things the well-educated commonly cannot expect to know. He says, "Most of us, when we give our opinion on such subjects as analytical philosophy and symbolic logic, are only grazing, the way we are with relativity theory, quantum mechanics, and how a mobile telephone works."

After surveying several others in Trilling's camp, Holton (1996, 57) argues that to "restore science to reciprocal contact with the concerns of most persons—to bring science into an orbit about us instead of letting it escape from our intellectual tradition—that is the challenge which scientists and all other intellectuals must now face." If he thinks there is any hope of such a restoration, however, Holton is wrong, as are Herbert Simon (1984), Stuart Vyse (1997, 211–18), and many others who want their society to escape from ignorance, superstition, and other failures of ordinary knowledge. The problem is harsher than this, as is suggested by the lack of readership even for the very accessible Trilling among the mass populace. Ignorance of science follows from the fact that personal mastery of such knowledge does not directly benefit most people, including most intellectuals. The economic theory of knowledge works forcefully against putting our thought into such issues, if we cannot then put the ideas to use in our own personal lives. And we cannot. It is only technology, the residue of science, that makes a difference to the personal lives of most of us. Much of contemporary science may never have even such a residue.[7]

[7] James Lovelock (1998, 833) pictures a survivor looking for sources of medical knowledge from the prior, failed civilization. In the face of a cholera epidemic, that survivor is more likely to find a well-worn book on aromatherapy than a competent medical text.

The plight of intellectuals partly explains the plight of ordinary people, who understand virtually none of modern science. And their plight partly explains the virulence of the ongoing science wars, because science has virtually disappeared from news coverage (Holton 1996, 41), other than in the weekly "Science Times" section of the *New York Times* and other limited-circulation venues. For those engaged in the war against science, science is an idea whose time has passed. To Trilling and his colleagues, it is an idea that has transcended understanding, an idea whose time has passed most of us by.

One might also note that the contemporary social sciences have gone the way of physics (and literary criticism) to large extent, in the sense that much of what they do is based on methods that are beyond ordinary understanding. The social sciences are even suffering their own minor variant of the science wars. These sciences are ostensibly about the very societies in which we live, and which we seemingly ought to understand. Often, critics insist that the social sciences are only so-called sciences, and that they are irrelevant or wrong. Among those who seem to think they are irrelevant are professional literary critics who have taken on social issues. Among their complaints against social science is the opacity of much of it, but their own claims are similarly opaque to the larger public, claims stated in a contrived and often incomprehensible vocabulary.

The economic theory of knowledge suggests that most of us will know little about modern physics, because we will seldom if ever be in a position to put it to use. Some of it may have entertainment value, as the big bang theory, black holes, and quasars seem to have for many people, including children, many of whom are also infatuated with dinosaurs. And some of it may have astonishing and therefore noticeable effects, as does the potential for nuclear explosives, or the threat of Earth-bound asteroids. But most people who use computers do so without the slightest knowledge of the solid-state physics that makes silicon chips do such wonders. There were people who came to understand these things and they influenced—usually—other people who put these understandings to work in designing computers. We could discuss dozens of such things that are part of the daily lives of most of the people in any advanced industrial state today. Here, the implication of the economic theory of knowledge is that we pragmatically know how to put various technologies to use, not that we understand much if anything about why they work as they do. Indeed, economic considerations halt our inquiry well before we face questions of why these technologies work.

One might suppose that people would have some interest in science, because it is so often involved in public policy issues whose resolution could matter to us. But, as argued in chapter 3, popular knowledge of politics is dismally poor. Given the difficulty of mastering contemporary science, it should therefore be no great surprise that we are as ignorant of it as we are, and that public policy on science or on issues that implicate science is largely made without popular understanding or input (see, for example, Miller 1983). In the United States, popular participation in science policy is sparked primarily by religious views and by environmental concerns.

THE SCIENCE WARS

Many people have gone beyond Trilling's estrangement and are openly hostile to science, almost at war with it. The centuries-long contest between religion and science is historically the main but not the only field of battle over science in the West. One could also cite many anti-science views of the administration of President George W. Bush, as detailed with distressing frequency in *Science* magazine (e.g., Couzin 2005), and elsewhere (Mooney 2005).[8] The range of issues is large and includes three seemingly different categories. First, there are actions that are part of the religious attack on science.

Second, there are actions that benefit certain business interests, but that run against scientific arguments on harms to the larger society, now or in the future. Both of these categories produce popular confusion and doubt that might or might not be justified. But support of certain policies commonly leads to debunking science, debunking that seems to be a crude political ploy rather than an honest statement of doubt. In virtually every economically significant case it is possible to find seeming experts who argue against the overwhelming consensus among scientists, and whose views often become policy.

A third important group who are hostile to contemporary science are those who are probably more accurately classed as hostile to current *uses* of technology, rather than to science as such. They do not rail against cosmology, for example, except perhaps insofar as research on deep space involves high-tech investments in rocketry and other equipment, including telescopes in pristine mountainous areas. These opponents of technology often think scientifically, and the best of them argue from cogent accounts of the effects of technological interventions. For example, they can cite

---

[8] To cite only three perverse actions, in its first four years, the Bush administration apparently pushed the National Cancer Institute to say that abortion may cause breast cancer; it had the Centers for Disease Control and Prevention remove information about condom use and efficacy from its website (Mooney 2005, 214, 236–37); and it canceled a relatively inexpensive and ready-to-launch climate observatory to determine whether the apparent warming of the earth is caused by variations in sunlight or by activities on Earth (Park 2006). As if to add insult to injury, Bush was awarded an honorary doctorate of science by Louisiana State University in 2004.

the incidence of genetic manipulations of foodstuffs that have evidently been propagated into the wild, so that natural stocks of, say, corn may adapt to the genetic manipulations. These altered genes may reduce the stock of available natural varieties, and may therefore make our corn more vulnerable to a disease that would destroy far more—maybe even all—of it than if it were allowed to remain genetically more varied.[9] The opponents of technology can also point to genuine disasters in the generation of nuclear energy, and to the use of various hazardous chemicals. Some of the backing for these criticisms comes from the NIMBY (not in my backyard) movement (Portney 1991; Piller 1991).

Two of these groups—those who object to some technologies on scientific grounds and those who object to progress in the modern world on religious grounds—join in opposing certain kinds of medical research, such as genetic manipulation and stem-cell research on cures for grim diseases. The opposition of fundamentalist religious true believers is not subject to ordinary debate. Their stance on science is almost entirely hostile and, virtually by immediate inference, not articulately grounded in serious understanding of the science. When they go up against opponents whose whole professional lives have been spent formulating good causal arguments and explanations, the anti-scientists are therefore at a severe argumentative disadvantage.

RELIGION VERSUS SCIENCE

Those stances against science and technology are not uniquely American. Indeed, green opposition to technology is more strongly ensconced in much of Europe than in the United States. Among advanced democratic societies, however, the United States seems to go to extremes in its religious objections to science. Still, the United States is not alone. In 2005, Dutch science minister Maria van der Hoeven proposed serious debate on intelligent design (Martin (Enserink, 2005).[10] She was roundly criticized by members of the Dutch parliament and by Dutch scientists. In the United

[9]Although the claim has been hotly disputed, some scientists thought that genetically altered maize was introduced into Mexico from the United States by natural spreading from one area to another, including into one of the major areas for cultivation of diverse strains to protect their diversity (on the debate, see Mann 2002). A NAFTA study panel concluded that the foreign corn was planted by local farmers (Elisabeth Malkin, "Science vs. Culture in Mexico's Corn Staple," *New York Times* 27 March 2005, 1.10). But apparently pollen from genetically modified crops can spread its genes to other crops and plants (Stokstad 2002; Rieger et al. 2002).

[10]On the war between science and religion in various times and places more generally, see Harris 2004.

States, active proponents of religious views—not merely content to debate scientific issues—get appointed to high policy-making positions.

Pascal Boyer (2001, 320) supposes that the reason there is such deep conflict between religion and science in the West is that the religiously and politically long-dominant Catholic church "made the crucial mistake of meddling in empirical statements of fact, providing us with a long list of particularly precise, official and officially compelling statements about the cosmos and biology, supposedly guaranteed by Revelation, that we now know to be false." His "we" is perhaps too inclusive.

Among its attempts to control the content of science was the church's outrageous trial of Galileo, one of the most disgraceful episodes in the church's long history (Finocchiaro 2005).[11] In 1990, alas for the broader credibility of the church, then Cardinal Joseph Ratzinger, the future Pope Benedict XVI, continued to defend the church's brutal treatment of Galileo and Galileo's science, which said that the Earth circles the sun rather than the sun circling the Earth. Ratzinger said, "At the time of Galileo the church remained much more faithful to reason than Galileo himself. The process against Galileo was reasonable and just" (quoted in Machamer 2005 from the *Corriere della Sera,* 30 March 1990).[12] Eppur la chiesa non si muove.

Mario Biagioli (1993, 10) argues that Galileo's fall was largely the result of the instabilities of living under a patron who might die or change his views at any moment. He says:

> I suggest that the events of 1633 [Galileo's trial] were as much the result of a clash between the dynamics and tensions of baroque court society and culture as they were caused by a clash between Thomistic theology and modern cosmology. In short, Galileo's career and his at-

[11]Reaction to that trial is commonly said to have ended the Italian Renaissance. Ironically, reaction to the execution of Thomas Aikenhead in 1697 in Edinburgh may have been the beginning of the Scottish Enlightenment (see Buchan 2003, 56–58). Aikenhead, a teenager, was executed for blasphemy. Today, that is possible only in much of the world of Islam.

[12]Benedict's papacy seems to have inspired other powerful figures to speak out against the theory of evolution. Cardinal Christoph Schönborn (2005), archbishop of Vienna, says he was authorized by Benedict to write for a wide audience in a *New York Times* op-ed article. Some proponents of ID declare that they are "very excited" by Schönborn's article. He specifically dismisses the statement of the late Pope John Paul II that "the church does not need to fear the teaching of evolution as long as it is understood as a scientific account of the physical origins and development of the universe." Schönborn says this statement is "rather vague and unimportant." He perversely calls scientists who support evolution ideologues while claiming that "the Catholic Church is in the odd position of standing in firm defense of reason." In his view, apparently, the church has been the firm defender of reason throughout its centuries of warfare on science, from Galileo to today. (See, further, Cornelia Dean and Laurie Goodstein, "Leading Cardinal Redefines Church's View on Evolution," *New York Times,* 9 July 2005, A1.)

tempts to legitimate Copernican astronomy were terminated by those same processes that made it possible to begin with.

Unfortunately, Biagioli's story is severely marred by Ratzinger's very recent and pointless intervention. Ratzinger takes what must be called a 'position' in the intellectual conflict between theology and cosmology, but he is not concerned with or implicated in the seventeenth-century system of patronage.

Popes have all too often been arrogant about the infallibility of their ungrounded personal insights into science, proceeding merely from an interpretation of scripture or an advice from Vatican officials, virtually none of them credible scientists. Yet their infallibility did not become official dogma until the first Vatican Council of 1870, which was bullied by Pope Pius IX to declare ex cathedra statements of the pope infallible (Wills 2000). To the church leadership, the totality of science on the origins of the universe and humans is in "Genesis." It seems not to have bothered them that this account is restricted to the Earth and its inhabitants, and that there is a massive universe that goes almost unmentioned, as though the agents of god who transcribed the Bible were kept in ignorance of that universe, or were not told to write about it. Church leaders also seldom acknowledge the complexity of the development of the Bible from numerous sources and under the direction of various church groups, with the loss of virtually all earlier versions of the texts from which the current versions were crafted. The end result is a dual account of origins in Genesis, one of which (chapter 1 through part of verse 4 of chapter 2) speaks of the six days of creation ex nihilo; while the other (the rest of verse 4 through the end of chapter 2) speaks of the creation of life in a universe that already exists, and gives no period of time for this feat. Biblical scholars label the two accounts P and J, and they suppose that the J account is much older. The two versions even use different names for god: *Elohim* and *Yahweh,* usually translated as "God" and "Lord," respectively (J. Moore 2002, 30–38).

In our time, it is ordinary people with little or no education in science who arrogantly proclaim that they know "god's truth" about cosmology and human origins. Commonly, they acknowledge none of the biblical problems, and they assert the earlier, six-day version of the genesis of humanity as the literal truth—although that assertion must make the other version a literal falsehood. They do not have the Inquisition to work for them, but they do have votes in many communities in the United States. Literalism in biblical interpretation is prima facie contradictory, in this and many other contexts.

The simplest sociology of organizations, some of it from Italian scholars early in the twentieth century, suggests that when religion or any broad ideology becomes institutionalized, officials of the institution tend toward professional deformation and the defense of every action of the institution[13]—even such actions as the brutality of the Vatican hierarchy in attempting to suppress Galileo and his science, and of burning Giordano Bruno at the stake when Galileo was 36. They evidently thought they could overrule Galileo's science as they had overruled Bruno's. They could not, although they could keep many Catholics ignorant, could wreck the remaining eight years of Galileo's life, and could bring the Italian Renaissance to a virtual close while watching northern Europe assume the honor of leading the world into modernity, thereby strengthening the hold of Protestantism. Now, although Galileo's science could not diminish the church's power and influence today, Ratzinger lowers its credibility with his insistence that the Inquisition was "reasonable and just" to suppress Galileo.[14]

Galileo, a deeply religious Catholic, saw his work as showing the fuller glory of god. In response to the continuing church opposition to the theory of evolution, George Coyne (2005; see also *Science* 309, 12 August 2005: 996–97), a priest and formerly the Vatican's chief astronomer, writing in a British Catholic magazine, agrees with Galileo's religious stance and defends the standard scientific views of the history of the universe and the life within it. "Creationist notions of intelligent design diminish God," Coyne writes. "Instead we should see his love for the infinitely evolving universe as like that of a parent allowing a growing child to make its own choices and go its own way in life." Coyne implies that dismissing the sciences of cosmology and evolution in favor of a simplistic vision of a god just wishing all of the stars and life on Earth into existence makes that god seem less talented than the scientists.

The critics of Galileo's views in his day refused even to look through the newly invented telescope, one that he had improved upon in order to see the moons of Jupiter. They preferred not to have their stolid religious views polluted by facts.[15] As Howard Margolis (2002, 8) remarks, the

[13]Wills (2000) says recent popes have turned Leninist in their single-minded focus on retaining power and defending the power of the Vatican.

[14]Those trying Galileo of course refused to look through his telescope, recently invented in 1609, to see plainly that he was right to claim Jupiter had at least four moons. They presumably refused because to grant moons to Jupiter was to suggest that the Copernican vision of the solar system was correct. Planets circle the sun, moons circle planets. Before Galileo's telescope, the only known moon was that of Earth. Incidentally, the passages in the Bible (e.g., Joshua 10:13 and Isaiah 40:22) that are taken to say that the Earth is the center of the universe do not say anything of the sort in so many words. Rather, they are metaphorically read to imply this.

[15]Shapin (1996, 65–80) offers a sympathetic rationale for this position. He notes that anyone using a telescope for the first time to bring a distant terrestrial object nearer can test whether the telescope works by going to the object and checking its general features against the telescopic view. (There is no equivalent test of its working for celestial objects.)

Copernican vision that the Earth moves and is not the center of the universe, was "the most astounding scientific claim that had ever been made"; it was a profoundly difficult revision of the known. Galileo, with Coyne, thought true Catholics should want to see more of god's handiwork, not to deny it or even ridicule it, and not to damn anyone who would admire it. To reject cosmology is as if to say god knows nothing of, say, black holes, which are produced by the collapse of giant stars so massive that they are crushed by their own gravity and that, in collapsing, consume everything within their gravitational ambit. But Subrahmanyan Chandrasekhar, a mere mortal despite that elegant name, wrote the relativistic equations for the phenomenon of black holes by age 24 (A. I. Miller 2005).[16] It was a strictly speculative mathematical exercise, not backed by any data that might show that there are black holes. Surely no god would frown on such brilliance. But the Catholic god's minions in Rome and his evangelical worshipers in many U.S. school districts would, and they apparently believe they are doing so on their god's behalf.

A New Science?

Galileo's collision with the church was about cosmology. The chief U.S. science vs. religion war of our time, beginning roughly from the last quarter of the twentieth century but with roots much further back in history (see Thomson 2005), is a collision between religion and biology, especially biological evolution. Among the religious opponents of evolution, one of the most important numerically has been fundamentalist—or literalist—religious belief in the creation of the universe by a god in keeping with the six-day account in Genesis (virtually ignoring the second, very different account in that same text).

The conflict became acute at the popular level early in the period after the 1859 publication of Charles Darwin's *Origin of Species*. Darwin's idea—evolution by natural selection—is spectacular. But this idea is also hard to grasp, and many people never grasp it. Perhaps from hearsay authority, however, they do grasp that it has implications that run against the simple creation story of Genesis. Some of those who hold fundamentalist beliefs are convinced that, as Isaac Newton argued, the world was created at some virtually datable moment in the not very distant past. The Irish prelate James Ussher, whose views Newton defended, set the date at 4004 B.C.E. The arguments of Ussher and Newton were founded on genealogies in the Old Testament, genealogies that are utterly incredible to

---

[16]Arthur Eddington, a hero in the experiment showing that Einstein's mathematical conjecture that a heavy mass would deflect light beams, called Chandrasekhar's speculative mathematics "stellar buffoonery." At least he did not invoke god in his fallacious cause.

anyone who comes to them without a prior belief in the truth of the manifold documents that were selected by various supposed authorities as the word of the Hebrew god. To contemporary true believers in the vision of the creation held by Newton and Ussher, modern physics and especially cosmology and evolutionary biology are a sham and, worse, an insult to their god.

Historically, the creationist view was primarily defended on purely scriptural grounds, as by William Jennings Bryan when he argued for the prosecution in the trial of John Scopes in Tennessee for teaching evolution (Larson 1997). Henry M. Morris, an engineer, attempted to give the creationist account scientific underpinnings in his 1961 book *The Genesis Flood,* written with John C. Whitcomb, in which they argue that the geological record shows the truth of the Genesis account. Since the appearance of that book, the claim that creationism is science has been commonly asserted and commonly criticized. Court rejection of creationism has spawned so-called intelligent design (ID) as an alternative science that accords with biblical accounts without necessarily invoking biblical claims.

Let us take up this issue as an entrée to the ways science establishes truths, and the ways that ordinary people and the courts commonly work in dealing with science.[17] In the United States, the religious opponents of evolution have provoked numerous court cases, brought by parents of children in school and supporters of science education, against various public officials who, plaintiffs contend, have tried to impose the teaching of Christian beliefs about the origins of life. In an important case, *Kitzmiller et al. v. Dover Area School District, et al.* (2005), the conflict was re-framed as a collision between two different sciences: Darwinian evolution and intelligent design. Evolution was originally a hard-fought new science. Now ID is proposed as another new science. ID is the claim that much of nature and humankind is too complex to have happened accidentally (as through evolution) and must therefore have had an intelligent designer.[18]

Proponents of ID have given us a very unusual case of the asserted creation of a new science, not from arcane scientists who present us with dramatic new findings, but from more or less ordinary citizens trying to resolve a major problem. We can watch this putative new science as it unfolds, and as its proponents are even taken to court and forced to meet at least court standards of proof. When bad science is put forward, the de-

[17]My purpose here is not to grapple with how people come to have their religious views, which I shall take up in chapter 7.

[18]For the historical development of ID, see Forrest and Gross 2004; also see Orr 2005; for defenses and criticisms by leading proponents today, see Pennock 2001; for a clear defense of ID, see Beckwith 2003, chap. 3.

bate over it is confined almost entirely to scientists in the relevant fields, although in the case of cold fusion (Koertge 1998, chap. 8; Park 2000, chap. 5) the potential stakes (the unlimited supply of cheap energy) were extremely high for the public at large. In the case of ID, the debate began in the public arena and was relatively ignored by scientists. ID is therefore a good case for assessing popular understandings of science and how it works.

The thesis of ID has been put forth by Sextus Empiricus, Thomas Aquinas, Joseph Butler, William Paley, and uncounted other thinkers, going back to ancient times. The argument is often explicitly probabilistic; it is about chance versus design (Franklin 2001, 228–30). A typical example in modern versions of the thesis is the pocket watch found on the heath, as discussed by Paley (1802). The obviously implausible idea that a watch assembled itself through gradual evolutionary processes, or by the hands of a blind watchmaker, is taken by some to be a knock-down argument against the biological evolution of humans.

Hume ([1748] 2000, sect. 11; and [1779] 1976) demolishes this "argument from design" for the existence of god (see also Dawkins [1986] 1996). Hume's charge is that the argument is from effects to causes, rather than the usual reverse order. Hence, even if we accept the inference from human life that there must have been a designer, all that we can claim about this designer is that it had the capacity to create human life. We cannot add to this that the designer must be merciful, good, decent, Christian, or any other thing that might characterize some putative gods. Maybe it even had to be a large committee in a grand division of labor. We cannot say. The proponents of creationism and ID (in the United States today, the two groups are virtually identical in their memberships) take a wholly unwarranted step beyond what might be logically permitted in the inference from effect to cause. They infer that the Genesis account is true, and that less than ten thousand years ago a Christian god created our world and all that we can see.

Defenders of ID cut off their own logic one step before the realization that, if it is hard to imagine the spontaneous evolution of the universe, it is just as hard to imagine the nature of an intelligent designer of it. Defenders of ID say "science cannot answer this question. It must leave it to religion and philosophy" (*Kitzmiller*, 26). If it is a mystery how evolution could have done so much, it is equally a mystery how there could have been such a designer. Did that designer pause to give thought to the coloration of butterfly wings? to the structure of every volcano? to the fragile nature of the human knee? to the workings of cancerous tumors? In any case, even on the logic of their own vision, proponents of ID are not justified to go beyond saying that there was a designer of humans and maybe the rest of the universe. Full stop. The Dover trial should likewise have come to a full stop almost on its first day.[19]

In his judgment in *Kitzmiller*, Federal District Judge John E. Jones III enjoined the Dover, Pennsylvania, school board from maintaining their policy of requiring relevant science classes to hear a statement on ID, née creationism, and on flaws in the theory of evolution.[20] Throughout his decision, Judge Jones notes that the defenders of ID in the Dover case were duplicitous.[21] For example, in a case in which the defendants claimed to be presenting *an alternative science* and not a religious view, the chief cited reading for ID is *Of Pandas and People* (Davis and Kenyon [1993] 2004), which is published by an organization called Foundation for Thought & Ethics (FTE), which has received from the Internal Revenue Service a (Christian) religious exemption from paying taxes (*Kitzmiller*, 31).[22] An earlier edition of that book used the term "creationism" and its cognates, where the current edition substitutes the terms ID and cognates roughly 150 times (*Kitzmiller*, 32). The book had been edited to purge references to creationism after a U.S. Supreme Court case from Louisiana (*Edwards v. Aguillard*,[23] at 593; see also *Kitzmiller*, 23) ruled the teaching of creationism unconstitutional.[24] Michael Behe, a biochemist at Lehigh University and a leading academic defender of ID, asserted at trial that it "is only a scientific, as opposed to a religious project, for him." But Judge Jones notes that in a written statement Behe averred that the *"plausibility of the argument for ID depends on the ex-*

---

[19]Invoking a remarkably odd bit of logic, a Washington state lawmaker introduced a bill declaring the teaching of evolution "repugnant to the Declaration of Independence." Why? The Declaration says "all men are created" (*Science* 295 [8 February 2002]: 963). One hears the self-deprecating voices of "Saturday Night Live" or "Monty Python" defending this argument. Perversely, the lawmaker halted his quotation before Jefferson's most crucial word— "equal"—and therefore before he would have had to conclude also that race relations and the distribution of wealth in the United States are "repugnant to the Declaration of Independence."

[20]Students were to be told that evolution is a theory with many flaws, and that students might therefore wish to investigate ID, which is an "explanation" (evidently not a mere theory) of human origins. A statement of this view was to be read to students, but teachers were not to discuss the issue with their students (*Kitzmiller*, pp. 45, 127). Why? Presumably because the science teachers could be counted on to be hostile to ID.

[21]Their incompetence also led them to get the relevant prior case law wrong, and to cite later cases as precedents for earlier cases (*Kitzmiller*, p. 12).

[22]There are, of course, many other books against evolution and for creationism or ID. But many of them are overtly grounded on religious views and would be barred by the Establishment clause or *Edwards v. Aguillard* from use as textbooks for teaching an alternative science (see Wells 2000).

[23]Justices Scalia and Rehnquist dissented.

[24]It has since been edited, apparently, to speak of "sudden emergence theory" (Laurie Goldstein, "Evolution Trial in Hands of Willing Judge," *New York Times* [18 December 2005]: 1.41).

tent to which one believes in the existence of God" (28). (Also see Behe 1996.)

Of Pandas and People essentially defines ID as follows: "Intelligent design means that various forms of life began abruptly through an intelligent agency, with their distinctive features intact—fish with fins and scales, birds with feathers, beaks, and wings, etc." (quoted in Talbot 2005, 71). This statement clearly tends toward the claims of creationists. One imagines the painting of Jacopo Tintorretto, "Creation of the Animals." God, with his white hair and beard (he is very old—older than the universe) drives the animals of the Earth, air, and sea before him.[25]

Edwards outlawed the teaching of *creationism* on the ground that doing so violates the Establishment Clause of the U.S. constitution (the First Amendment says: "Congress shall make no law respecting an establishment of religion . . ."). Hence, the two sides in *Kitzmiller* (9) agreed, formally, that the test of the Dover School Board's requirements on teaching evolution is whether ID is science. (Otherwise, there could have been no case.) In essence, *Kitzmiller* rules that ID is not science, and that school endorsement of ID violates the Establishment Clause.

Judge Jones, a Republican appointed by President Bush in 2002 and a churchgoer (Laurie Goldstein, "Evolution Trial in Hands of Willing Judge," *New York Times* [18 December 2005]: 1.41), strongly chastises the board members who pushed ID. He refers to their lying about their true motivations and their "outright lies under oath" (*Kitzmiller,* 46n; see also 105, 137), their "cloaking religious beliefs in scientific sounding language" (21), their testimony as "primarily by way of bare assertion" (35),[26] one of their argumentative tactics as "at best disingenuous, and at worst a canard" (89), the repeated failure of the board chair (Alan Bonsell) "to testify in a truthful manner" about his real purposes (97) and his "largely inconsistent and non-credible testimony" (102), the "ludicrous" assertion of a secular purpose in pushing ID (131), and "the breathtaking inanity of the Board's decision" (138). The harshness of these judgments is in stark contrast to the judge's generally mild style and his good-natured demeanor in the courtroom during the trial (see Talbot 2005). He seems clearly to have been offended by the apparent dishonesty of the defenders of ID in his court. Of course, without all of this dishonesty there would have been no need for trial, because Jones could simply have given a summary judgment against teaching religion in the public schools. Essentially, what was on trial was the tendentious claim that ID is science, a topic on which the defendants actually had almost nothing to say beyond its being a "bare assertion."

[25]This painting graces the dust jacket of Thomson 2005.
[26]This would be standard for claims of faith, but not of science.

54 · Chapter 2

The disingenuous tactic that offended Judge Jones was to shift to "advocating that the *controversy,* not ID itself, should be taught in science class" (*Kitzmiller,* 89; see also 99–100). Yet the Dover school board disallowed teachers from discussing ID with students (45, 127). That meant that theirs would be the unusual pedagogical case of a silent controversy. But in any case a scientific controversy is a disagreement between scientists. It is not a dispute between scientists, on the one side, and school board members, publicists, or preachers, on the other. In the cold fusion controversy, the public was largely absent. Stanley Pons and Martin Fleischmann were knocked down by other physicists who could not replicate cold fusion on a lab table even when they followed the experiments of Pons and Fleischmann to the letter.

Deceit and dishonesty are the core of the Dover defense because the defendants are constitutionally barred from advocating what apparently they actually want, which is mandated Christian religious education in the Dover schools. The attempt to package this as science is hopeless. Science is rigorously naturalist; ID is assertedly supernaturalist. ID therefore cannot be science without a radical re-conception of the idea of science. The two therefore cannot be compared, and the so-called controversy can be little more articulate than a shouting match or warfare.

Suppose we agree with the conclusion of Judge Jones that the proponents of ID in Dover were lying about their religious motivations. This suggests three possibilities for the popular understanding of science in this case. First, the Dover school board proponents may commonly have little to no knowledge of the issues in evolutionary theory.[27] That would make eminently good sense for them, because they have little prior interest in mastering that difficult body of scientific argument. They are not blameworthy for not knowing more science. Judge Jones says, "Board members somewhat candidly conceded that they lacked sufficient background in science to judge ID" (*Kitzmiller,* 121; also 131).[28] Moreover, most of them probably cannot make a scientific argument for ID, because they cannot make a scientific argument about any complex theory in any field (it seems likely that this is true of the overwhelming majority of people more generally, even outside Dover). Some of them nevertheless voted for curriculum changes to include ID in science teaching (requiring that students hear a disclaimer on the theory of evolution). They basically set themselves up for the dismissal of their views. Their actual view appears to have been that the children of Dover should be taught a Christian version of human origins. Forced by the constitutional bar against acting on such

[27]Behe, Dembski, and some other proponents of ID, such as various contributors to Pennock (2001) presumably do have such knowledge. Such knowledge can be dangerous.

[28]One board member repeatedly referred to "intelligence design" (*Kitzmiller,* p. 122), which might not be a bad program of education in general. Superintendent Nilsen's "entire understanding of ID was that 'evolution has a design.'"

views, these ordinary people attempted to argue for the science of ID. They are not scientists, and they have little hope of articulating a scientific account of either standard evolutionary theory or ID.

Second, they may not even grasp the nature of their own religious views. They presumably do genuinely believe the first Genesis account of the origins of the universe and human life, and some of them might suppose that they know its truth from direct revelation. (One of the meanings of being born again is receiving a Christian revelation.) They were not challenged to show why their beliefs should be taken as true by anyone else, because religious beliefs were ruled out of court for the *Kitzmiller* and some prior cases. If seriously pressed on the origins of their religious views, they might refuse ever to give a *causal* answer other than revelation. Indeed, they would likely abhor the psychological implications of giving a causal explanation of their views, because such an explanation would cast doubt on the content of their beliefs. Had the trial been about religious beliefs, they might have been queried on the Genesis account, and the plaintiff's lawyers might have embarrassed them with the contradictions of that dual account, as noted earlier (again, for discussion of the two intertwined, contrary Genesis accounts, see J. Moore 2002, 30–38).

Third, the arguments for high-blown science are as much a mystery to them as is the account of "Genesis" or ID. As Dewey ([1927] 1954) notes, for most people, "save the scientific workers, science is a mystery in the hands of initiates, who have become adepts in virtue of following ritualistic ceremonies from which the profane herd is excluded." From the outside, this may sound like institutionalized religion—although from the inside it is very different. For most people, the evolutionary scientists' dismissal of creationism as just a mystery to cover for ignorance is no better than a contrary dismissal of the scientists' own claims; both must be accepted as mystery. After valiant efforts, Church fathers disagreed on which creation account is correct, and it was agreed that both must be accepted. Of the two accounts, the historian Andrew Dickson White wrote in 1898, to the natural mind these two views "seem absolutely contradictory; but by ingenious manipulation of texts, by dexterous play upon phrases, and by the abundant use of metaphysics to dissolve away facts, a reconciliation was effected, and men came at least to believe that they believed in a creation of the universe instantaneously and at the same time extended through six days" (quoted in J. Moore 2002, 37). When in doubt, try metaphysics to deal with messy facts.

If ID has a future, it must succeed as science rather than as a covert missionary of religion. In the latter role it is of little interest even to those who share its religious wellsprings, because it adds nothing to their religious views. And as science it is off to a very shaky start. The Templeton Foundation, a major supporter of projects seeking to reconcile science and religion, has offered grants for research on ID. Proposals "never came in," an official of the foundation says. "From the point of view of rigor and intellectual seriousness, the intelligent design people don't come out very well in our world of scientific review" (Goodstein 2005). This is a judgment by a very sympathetic agency. The loyalties and perhaps also the time of the proponents of ID are split between defending faith and doing science. They have not done well at either task.

The ruse of teaching the controversy is vacuous. There is no controversy, properly speaking. Calling the dispute a controversy is an instance of persuasive definition in an effort to give ID a scientific gloss. True, a controversy is a discussion marked by opposing views, and the proponents of ID oppose the proponents of evolutionary theory. But their opposition is to say little more than, "You're wrong." To controvert is to dispute or oppose by reasoning. Saying little more than "You're wrong" is not reasoning. If the proponents of ID actually go so far as to give explanations of aspects of life and species on Earth, then the proponents of evolutionary theory will be extremely quick to controvert their explanations, or to accept them. Much as in Hume's criticism of the argument from design, these proponents argue to a conclusion about causes from a bottom-line view of what the cause *must have been:* a mysterious being such as an all-powerful god.

There is an odd parallel between, on the one hand, the arguments that the possibility of ID discredits evolutionary theory and, on the other hand, the arguments of an earlier generation that the association between tobacco and lung cancer had not been demonstrated. One doctor standing against several thousand was cited as evidence of a controversy not yet resolved, so that tobacco could not be convicted. In 1969 an executive at Brown and Williamson (later owned by R. J. Reynolds) wrote that, "Doubt is our product since it is the best means of competing with the 'body of fact' that exists in the mind of the general public" (quoted in Michaels 2005, 96). Similarly, the arguments of two or three Michael Behes are supposed to show that there is deep, crippling doubt about evolutionary theory, even though this handful of scientists, creditable in their own realms, are confronted by thousands of professional biologists, geneticists, and geologists, and millions of hours of carefully reviewed research. For a hint of the massiveness of this effort, see the *Encyclopedia of Evolution* (Pagel 2002) with its thousand large pages and nearly 300 contributors. Indiana legislator Bruce A. Borders introduced legislation targeting evolution and its "lies" (Perkins 2006, 121). To impute lying to evolution theorists is a false and pointless claim bordering on stupidity. Thousands of scientists engaged in this research deeply believe what they find. It is inconceivable that they could all be participating in a conspiracy of falsehood with never a leak.

Most Americans do not understand or believe in evolution. Does teaching ID in schools and universities have consequences beyond possibly keeping a still larger fraction of Americans ignorant of the theory of evolution? Robert Schwartz (2005, 1438), a medical doctor writing in the *New England Journal of Medicine,* thinks it will have serious consequences, and he castigates Bill Frist (a graduate of Harvard Medical School) for supporting the teaching of ID in public schools. Schwartz asks,

> What would it mean to take intelligent design seriously at the medical school level? Its proponents tell us that gaps in our knowledge of how living organisms evolved vitiate the theory of evolution. Might we conclude, then, that the cancer cell and its evolution are so complex that a creative designer must be the cause of cancer?

A test of ID as a science would be that it has consequences for better medical treatment than can be had with treatment based on the supposedly false theory of evolution. There do not appear to be any such tests on the horizon at the moment, nor does the issue even get framed.

Incidentally, it is of interest to note a significant difference between justificatory argument in a court of law and argument in science. In the courts, one's associations may count as evidence, as though through guilt by association. For example, in *Edwards,* the Supreme Court took into account "the character of organizations advocating for creation science" (*Kitzmiller,* 22). The tax status, mentioned above, of FTE (religiously exempt despite publishing and selling the supposedly scientific textbook *Of Pandas and People*[29]) was taken by Judge Jones as showing that these backers of an alternative science were lying—their object was religious, not scientific. Also, the fact that virtually all of the organizations and individuals supporting ID and creationism are strongly religious has been taken by the courts to show the "true" motivations in pushing the adoption of ID, anti-evolution, and creation science in the schools.

In ordinary life, you and I are likely to adopt the courts' looser standard rather than the rigorous standards of science. Under those rigorous standards of argument, no scientists' values or religious commitments are relevant to the truth of their claims. For the ordinary person, those commitments of a scientist may be sufficient to dismiss the scientist's claims.[30] This fact is characteristic of the entire development of legal reasoning, which is the background of virtually all causal reasoning, presumably not

[29]Other textbook publishers might wish to seek advice from FTE's tax lawyers.

[30]The *New York Times* ran a series ("Politicized Scholars Put Darwin's Believers on Defensive in Debate," beginning 21 August 2005) on teaching ID, against Darwinism. The Times and many scientists saw evolution on the defensive. This was shortly after President Bush foolishly intervened in the controversy with the authoritatively assertive view that "both sides"—ID and evolution—"ought to be properly taught." After the rout of ID in

least because great values are often at stake in legal proceedings, so that great intellectual resources are brought to bear in grasping the principles of evidence for establishing causal effects. When "a seventeenth-century writer evaluates scientific evidence, or discusses conflicting claims in religion, he turns to the language of the law of evidence" (Franklin 2001, 12).

CONCLUDING REMARKS

Knowledge is a term with substantially different meanings within science than it has in ordinary life. Within science, a claim of knowledge typically means that there is carefully gathered evidence, other than testimony, to back up the claim. In ordinary life, knowledge is almost entirely grounded in testimony. Hence, in ordinary life, our principal task is very often the assessment of sources of knowledge, not the assessment of knowledge claims themselves. You might mishandle your present problem because your knowledge is defective, as, for example, when you crash your computer; and you might then have an incentive to go in quest of the knowledge that would keep you from making that mistake in the future. The same will often be true for medical knowledge, as when you suffer some pain or illness and go in quest of medical attention. But for the most part, the knowledge you apply to resolving a current problem will be the knowledge you have come to have for other reasons in earlier moments. It will not be knowledge that you deliberately go in quest of specifically for this occasion.

One could sensibly see the collision between Galileo's astronomy and that of the still somewhat medieval church as a collision between faith and the very idea of science. Scientific method is a field of knowledge that was discovered; one could date its discovery to the reasonings of Galileo (Margolis 2002, chap. 3). There were forerunners, but Galileo's science stuck, sparking further scientific inquiries. This field of knowledge is not easily learned, not least because it is not immediately evident to us in our daily lives that we should bother with such demanding rigor, or that we should be so strongly motivated by doubt.

Most of our knowledge fits much more nearly the standards of Samuel Johnson in his dyspeptic mood than those of Locke in his austere philos-

---

Kitzmiller, internal conflicts broke out in the ID movement, and it was the movement that went fully on the defensive. The Discovery Institute, the Dover Board, and the Thomas More Law Center disagreed over the battle that led to *Kitzmiller,* the Discovery Institute judging (in early November, weeks before the final decision) that the case would be harmful to the ID cause. The Discovery Institute issued a news bulletin accusing the Thomas More center of mishandling the case (URL: http://www.evolutionnews.org/2005/11/the_truth_about_discovery_inst.html).

ophy of science, or even the standards of current social epistemology. Meeting Locke's standards is impossible for the bulk of anyone's knowledge. I may attempt to follow his standards to some extent when I inquire into my own special academic concerns, as when I wish to ascertain how actual people handle choices in politics, morals, or ordinary pragmatic life, how the economic theory of knowledge works in the world. Even then, however, I rely on the opiniatretry that Locke reviles for much of what I know in my own specialized field of knowledge.

It is ironic that Locke wrote when the prospects for his vision had already failed for all practical purposes, even in science. By 1500 more books had been printed than had ever previously existed in manuscript form.[31] Many devices, some of them even mechanical readers, were invented in an attempt to reduce all of this vast collection of knowledge to something that a single pair of eyes could apprehend, as Locke would have wished, although he would further have wanted the owner of that one pair of eyes to investigate all this knowledge, not merely to read of the investigations of others. This movement to reduce all reading was transformed into an effort to have subgroups of readers assess printed works. The Royal Society of London made the idea of collective reading and assessment a standard part of its program (Johns 2001). This had happened two centuries before Locke wrote. Of course, practical knowledge in the lives of ordinary people must have been aggregated in similar but less formally organized ways from the beginnings of civilized life. Only thereby has civilization continued and progressed—because we do not generally demand that our knowledge meet Locke's or even contemporary scientists' standards. Ernst Mayr (1997) says that we should not expect to find truth in biology. All that biological science offers us is what is for now believable.

Finally, we might note an odd aspect of the division of science into cosmology and physics on the one hand and of biology and evolutionary theory on the other. It is partly because cosmology has no effect on our lives as we see them that we can make Albert Einstein into almost a pop icon, emblazoning his wonderfully wild hair and etched face on t-shirts, and on posters that compete for teenagers' wall space with posters of rock stars and athletes (see, further, Holton 1986, chap. 5: "Einstein and the Shaping of Our Imagination"). Medical science is fundamentally important to the health and lives of many of us, and yet many of us oppose the evolutionary theory that makes sense of medical interventions of many kinds. Evolutionary theory is leading to deeper understanding of many diseases and other health conditions, and that understanding may lead to a flood of vaccines against terrible diseases, and to antibiotic and possibly antiviral drugs.

[31]In 2003 there were 175,000 new titles published in the United States (L. Miller 2004).

CHAPTER 3

Democratic Participation

THE LIST of political matters that typical citizens do not know is daunt-ing. Explaining their ignorance and using it to explain various aspects of politics both pose serious tests of any theory of pragmatic or specifically political knowledge. Here are a few of the astonishing facts for the U.S. electorate. About 79 percent of Americans cannot name either of their state's senators, and 56 percent over the years cannot name any congres-sional candidate in their district, even at election time. Most Americans grossly overestimate how much foreign aid the United States gives. They know almost nothing about economic performance, and there are no sub-stantial "issue publics" who at least know about some major issue of the day.[1] Even very knowledgeable and sophisticated voters face grievous difficulties holding elected officials responsible for serving the voters' in-terests and, conversely, officials face similarly grievous difficulties repre-senting voters who are ignorant of policy and even their own interests (Hardin 2000, 2004a).

Let us expand on one of these issues: foreign aid. According to polls, a large majority of Americans think the United States spends far too much on foreign aid. Asked how much the United States spends, the average given in one poll is 18 percent of the total federal budget. Other polls give even higher numbers. The true figure is less than 1 percent. When asked to say how much it should be, the average proposal is about 8 percent, or more than eight times what it is (Kull and Destler 1999, chap. 5). Admit-tedly, correctly guessing such data goes well beyond normal abilities. But learning the truth about the actual level of aid makes most people think that current levels of foreign aid are not too high, and makes many think the level should be increased.

As it happens, then, voters who frame their votes for conservative, anti-internationalist candidates as partly in opposition to high levels of foreign aid are voting against their actual beliefs about how much aid the United States should offer. This sort of mismatch is in fact a much more general phenomenon. Many voters, sometimes called "conflicted conservatives,"

---

[1] The literature on this issue threatens to have more contributions than there are voters in U.S. national elections. Among many other items, see Converse 1975, 1990, 2000; Delli Carpini and Keeter 1996; Friedman 1998; Somin 1998; Bennett 2003; and many others. The most influential early statement is Converse 1964.

essentially assert their general conservatism even though the policies they favor are relatively liberal. For them, there is a misfit between their stances as voters and the actual values they hold (Stimson 2004, 87–95). It is plausible that the reason for this odd phenomenon is merely ignorance. A consequence is the persistence of relatively conservative government in the United States. These conflicted conservatives count about 22 percent of voters in the United States today, and they have been a substantial block for many decades.

As Michael Kinsley (1995, 5) says, the poll results on foreign aid show less about foreign aid than about American democracy:

It's not just that Americans are scandalously ignorant. It's that they seem to believe they have a democratic right to their ignorance. All over the country—at dinner tables, in focus groups, on call-in radio shows, and, no doubt, occasionally on the floor of Congress—citizens are expressing outrage about how much we spend on foreign aid, without having the faintest idea what that amount is. . . . People are forming passionate views about foreign aid on the basis of no information at all.

Kinsley finds these citizens somehow culpably ignorant. Yet they may be no more culpable than you would be if you did not know how to deal with someone who has collapsed before you with a possible heart attack or stroke. There are limits to what you can master intellectually, and you may be wise to invest your learning on ways to keep your family happy and healthy, or to invest your time in manifold pursuits such as outdoor activities, overtime work, reading magazines or novels, enjoying entertainment such as movies or concerts or poker night, and on and on, rather than in politics or mastering CPR (cardiopulmonary resuscitation).

Note that none of these conclusions is an indictment of citizens for their ignorance. They are likely to be ignorant because it is rational or sensible for them to be ignorant. Indeed, unless you have a professional or career interest in knowing much about politics, or you find it especially entertaining, you will sensibly invest in other activities instead. You might therefore be ignorant of foreign aid policy and rightly so. The only claim we might make against you in that regard is that you should not prate your opinion about foreign aid policy. But why should you know even enough to know that your opinions are ignorant and baseless? You have heard a lot of complaining about excessive foreign aid, and that may be the best knowledge you have for reaching an opinion.

It might even be nothing more than a social convention that foreign aid levels are high, a convention that is supported by repeated claims that it is true. Any politician or candidate who questions the convention is likely to be judged negatively for supporting the excessive programs. Everyone who knows better lets the convention go uncontested, and almost everyone else therefore believes it. The levels are high. How high? Well, that is less clear—and the level is not conventionally established. This vagueness may even help to enforce the conventional view that the level is high, letting each of us guess just what 'high' means. One wishes the pollsters would ask their respondents how they learned what the level of expenditure is. It seems likely that few have any idea, other than perhaps to say that everyone knows it—just as everyone knows most of what they know.

THE LOGIC OF COLLECTIVE ACTION

Suppose we all wish to accomplish some collective purpose, such as cleaning up our neighborhood or going on strike against our employer for higher wages. There are many popular comments on the likelihood of our success. For example, many of us might prefer to let George do it. Or if our group is small enough, we might nudge each other sufficiently to participate in providing our group the needed benefit. But if our group is very large, many of us might do nothing, in the implicit realization that the gain to ourselves from our own contribution to the effort will be far outweighed by the cost to us of making that contribution. Mancur Olson (1965; also see Hardin 1982) calls this the logic of collective action. Large groups typically require incentives outside the group provision to entice them to join the effort. For example, unions once offered health insurance and other benefits to their members, but only to their members. When in due course the unions helped to make government take over these and other provisions, they undercut their own future efforts at organization.

A particularly important case of this logic is voting in elections, which are analogous to the problem of union organizing. In the latter, if enough others take action and join a strike against their employer, they can expect to force a raise by getting the company unionized for collective bargaining on wages and other employee concerns. Suppose that what is needed initially is contributions to a strike fund over a year or so. And suppose the law requires that, if a union succeeds in negotiating a wage for its own members, that wage will also benefit nonmembers. You might rightly suppose that if ours is a very large firm, it is unlikely that your contribution will be what tips the proposed union into success. Now you can free ride on the efforts of others, and you will still be covered by any wage the union negotiates. If enough workers act on this logic, the collective effort might fall short, and there might be no union.

Now consider Anthony Downs's (1957) very similar logic of voting. Voting is typically the collective act of selecting a candidate (or policy) in the face of opposition. If the effort of voting carries any cost for you, you might wonder whether you should bother with it at all. In a large polity, such as a national election, the individual's effect on the outcome is truly negligible. This logic pervades academic discussions of voting, and it will be developed further below. Further references to the logic of collective action will assume large numbers of actors, each actor with negligible impact and therefore little incentive to act for the collective good.

Notice that, in the abstract, the union and voting problems are analytically similar. If enough contribute, we get a winning union or a winning candidate. If enough do not contribute, we do not get a winner, and, furthermore, those who expended resources or effort for our cooperative venture have also lost their investment. In both cases, all of our expenditures are sunk costs that either fail or succeed in gaining us our collective benefit. For example, at this writing, many losing candidates for their parties' nominations for the presidency in the United States face debts in the millions of dollars. These are painfully lost sunk costs.

THE ECONOMIC THEORY OF DEMOCRACY

In his economic theory of democracy, Anthony Downs (1957) presents two negative theoretical claims against the likelihood of making a broad participatory democracy work well. These negative claims are causally related, but are quite different from each other. First, he supposes that voters actually have little incentive to vote, because they cannot expect to have any impact on the outcome of any given election. Indeed, they have so little impact that any costs of voting, such as suffering through long queues or foul weather, trump any direct benefit from voting. This claim is a specific instance of the logic of collective action, as generalized later by Olson (1965). We will return to the implications of that logic.

The second major theoretical claim of Downs is that individual citizens have no incentive even to learn enough to be able to vote their own interests intelligently. This immediately follows from the first claim if we suppose that gaining relevant knowledge entails some costs. Because of voters' ignorance in political matters, Joseph Schumpeter ([1942] 1950, 262) argues that the "typical citizen drops down to a lower level of mental performance as soon as he enters the political field. He argues and analyzes in a way which he would readily recognize as infantile within the sphere of his real interests. He becomes a primitive again."[2] One might add that this citizen also builds opinions on cavalier "facts," as does the large current group of conflicted conservatives.

---

[2]A comparative study of the intellectual levels of discourses on politics and those on sports might be interesting. In both activities, IQ levels instantly fall.

Additionally, Downs gives us a model of how candidates must locate themselves in order to maximize their chances of being elected. This is the median-voter model, which says that to succeed a candidate must take a position at the median of a normal distribution of voters. A candidate who does not do this can be outflanked by another candidate who takes a position between the first candidate and the median voter. This model assumes that all policy issues aggregately reduce to a single left-right dimension. Hence, preferences over candidates cannot take all possible orderings, such as my preferring the candidate on the far left to the one on the far right *and* the candidate on the far right to the one in the middle. Note that the median-voter model seems to run against the second of Downs's theses—that citizens have no incentive to learn enough to vote sensibly—which seems to suggest that candidates should attempt to influence voters' knowledge.

Let us recast Downs's theory in the terms of the economic theory of the ordinary person's knowledge. Knowledge is prima facie central to the median-voter model, and to the issue of voters' incentive to learn enough to vote intelligently in their own interests if they do vote. One can also argue that Downs's first thesis, that the individual has no incentive to vote, poses a problem of knowledge of a somewhat different kind. The logic of collective action and Downs's narrower version of that logic are both relatively recent discoveries that are not well understood by many people. If ordinary citizens do not understand these difficult ideas, to which few of them have ever been exposed, we should not expect their behavior to fit Downs's variant of the logic of collective action. In general, the demands of these issues on individual-level knowledge are no different in kind from the individual-level knowledge demands for ordinary pragmatic choice in daily life and in planning future actions. In both cases, the costs of gaining information and the costs of mastering relevant quasi-theoretical understandings can be higher than the seeming payoff that would emerge from them. Moreover, most citizens have no reason even to realize that they lack some relevant insight into their incentives for voting.

Here I will generally focus on issues of voters' self interests, and will not attempt to take on such moral commitments as foreign aid, opposing abortion, punishing victimless crimes, or retributive views on punishment. These other issues sometimes override concern with interests for particular citizens, and they complicate any standardized assessments of voters' preferences. A full account of democratic theory would have to deal with these normative concerns, as well as with voters' interests. Unfortunately, knowledge issues around mere interests already call much of democratic theory into question.

It should be clear that an economic theory of democracy requires an economic theory of knowledge, especially of political knowledge. My object here is to recast the issues that voters face, by fitting them to the economic theory of ordinary knowledge.

VOTING AND ORDINARY KNOWLEDGE

In an economic theory of why the typical individual or even a particular individual comes to know various things, it makes sense to say you and I might both be rational even though you believe one thing and I believe a contrary thing, in some context. Hence, we might vote differently not because we have different interests, but because we have different beliefs about the candidates or the issues. I might eventually come to realize that my knowledge is mistaken and therefore correct it, especially after hearing your defense of your contrary knowledge. But there is no role for a super knower who can judge the truth of our positions. We are our own judges. If we wish to seek better knowledge, it is we who must decide from what agency or source to seek it.

Most of the knowledge of an ordinary person has a very messy structure, and cannot meet standard philosophical criteria for its justification. With characteristic force, David Hume ([1779] 1976), part 3, p. 180) spells out our problem: "Our thought is fluctuating, uncertain, fleeting, successive, and compounded; and were we to remove these circumstances, we absolutely annihilate its essence, and it would, in such a case, be an abuse of terms to apply to it the name of thought or reason." To understand political views and political participation, we need to unpack the mess of your thoughts and the likely very different mess of mine. We need a subjective account of knowledge, not a public account.

Much of the work on voting behavior and the apparent ignorance of many voters treats the issues as problems of psychological foibles in decision making (see, e.g., Popkin [1991] 1994; Baron [1988] 2000). Many—though not all—of these foibles can easily be seen as essentially economic constraints on learning how to judge complex issues, but I will generally not discuss the psychological approach to these problems here.[3] Much work also gives a fairly straightforward account of the problem of the status-based economics of knowledge. For example, Robert Dahl (1961, 1) notes that "knowledge, wealth, social position, access to officials, and other resources are unequally distributed" in American politics. I will also not take up this issue, but will discuss only the general problem of coming to know relevant things for intelligent political participation. Bringing

[3] Nor will I address the psychological problems of rationality more generally. See Plous 1993, Gilovich, Griffin, and Kahnemann 2002, and Baron [1988] 2000 among many other works on our psychological foibles in trying to make decisions in our own interest.

unequal positions into such an analysis would be valuable for a complete account of actual participation. Such a move could be carried out in ways fully consistent with the economic theory of knowledge.

The typical citizen can often judge politicians on their records only on testimony from others, testimony that might be ill-informed and biased in important ways. Hence, the political knowledge that you or I have is culled from a vast social system, not from anything we actually checked out. Much of it can only be generated by a social system. We depend on knowledge by authority because it is efficient and because, without division of labor in generating our knowledge, we would have no time for putting much of it to use. Since what we mainly want is to use it, we settle for taking it on authority rather than seeking to justify it. We have to rely on others or massively restrict or restructure our lives.

KNOWLEDGE OF HOW TO VOTE

The central problem of knowledge in representative democracy is what the typical citizen knows about the actions of public officials. If, in general, we make the effort to know something in large part *because it serves our interests to know it,* as in a pragmatic or economic theory of individual knowledge, then we cannot expect people to know very much about what their representatives do. In the argument of the economic theory of democracy (Downs 1957), a citizen typically does not have much interest in voting. The objective fact is that one vote has a minuscule chance of making a difference, so minuscule that, even when it is multiplied by the value of making a difference and getting one's preferred candidate or policy elected or enacted, the expected value of the vote remains negligible (see further below, "Understanding Whether to Vote"). Hence, if there is any real cost involved in casting a vote, that cost swamps the expected benefit to the voter of voting. Hence, by the pragmatic rule, there is little point in knowing enough actually to vote well.

The conclusion that we have no incentive to learn enough to vote well is part of Downs's (1957, chaps. 11 and 12) argument and, although his account is much less expansive, the conclusion is even more central to the earlier argument of Joseph Schumpeter. As Schumpeter ([1942] 1950), 262) writes, implicitly invoking his own pragmatic rule, "without the initiative that comes from immediate responsibility, ignorance will persist in the face of masses of information however complete and correct." I may have reason to acquire political knowledge because it gives me pleasure, or because I am a professional political scientist, but not because it will be useful in my causing beneficial effects through my role as citizen and voter.

Most of the subsequent research and debate on voting has focused primarily on the incentive to vote, rather than on the incentive to know enough to vote intelligently. The latter is at least logically derivative from the former, because it is the lack of incentive to vote that makes knowledge of how to vote well virtually useless, so that mastering that knowledge violates the pragmatic rule. Because my vote has negligible causal effect on democratically determined outcomes, there is no compelling reason for me to decide how to vote by assessing the causal effect of my vote on such outcomes. Or, to put this the other way around, the fact that I would benefit from some policy gives me no reason or incentive to know about that policy or to understand its implications, unless, by the pragmatic rule, I can somehow affect whether it is to be adopted.

If a citizen has no interest in voting, then the citizen has no interest in making the effort to learn enough to vote well. Something that is not worth doing at all is surely not worth doing well. If the problem of knowing enough to judge government officials is already hard, the lack of incentive to correct that problem is devastating. Indeed, the costs of knowing enough about government to be able to vote intelligently in one's own interest surely swamp the modest costs, for most people in the United States, of actually casting a vote, at least on commonplace issues of public policy outside moments of great crisis. The economic theory of individual-level knowledge therefore weighs against knowing enough to vote well, because the incentives cut heavily against investing to obtain the relevant knowledge. The typical voter will not be able to put the relevant knowledge to beneficial use.

In what follows, I will simply take for granted that typical citizens do not master the facts they need to know if they are to vote their interests (or their values) intelligently. There is extensive evidence on this claim, a very small part of which is cited in the opening paragraphs of this chapter. There is also, of course, great difference of opinion on the significance of this extensive voter ignorance on electoral choices. For example, Samuel Popkin ([1991]1994, 78) canvasses problems of voter ignorance in American presidential elections and then refers to "low-information rationality," which is rationality—voting one's interests or ideals—despite abysmal factual ignorance.[4] Critics of this thesis of Popkin and many others seem to see the thesis as the magical intelligent design of electoral choice. That design is unobserved and maybe unobservable, and that gives it at least half of its persuasive force.

---

[4] The literature arguing for the accidental rationality of collective voters' choices is large and growing. For early contributions that set the debate, see e.g., Converse 1990, Stimson 1990, Iyengar 1990, Page and Shapiro 1992, Grofman and Withers 1993, and Wittman 1996. Against the thesis, see Bartels 1996 and Somin 1998.

Popkin also argues for a Gresham's law of political information: bad facts drive out good facts. This law states that "a small amount of personal information [on a candidate] can dominate a large amount of historical information about a past record." The personal information might be some minor thing that comes up during a campaign. The trouble with the large amount of historical information that is, at least in principle, available is that voters do not typically know much of it, because it would be silly for them to invest the time needed to learn such information. Popkin's bad facts are often at least entertaining enough to make them memorable.

As evidence of how little voters even seek better information before voting, consider the difficulty candidates have in getting their message across to voters. Richard Fenno (1978) elegantly displays the burden that candidates for the U.S. House of Representatives face in merely finding people to talk to. They have to chase people down in various clubs or meetings, in stores and shopping malls, and at factory gates. They rely on their supporters to bring citizens and neighbors into their homes to meet them and listen to them. Being a door-to-door salesperson for some product or other is hard; selling oneself door to door must be still harder and more frustrating.

Even professional political scientists, who have a strong interest in knowing more about politics than their mere interest in the outcomes of elections would suggest, find it hard to keep up with much of what happens. Weekly tallies of votes in the U.S. House of Representatives and Senate, for example, are reported in some newspapers, but with such brevity that their larger meaning is often opaque to anyone who has not followed the relevant issues fairly closely, more closely than even most of those newspapers do. The *New York Times,* which bills itself as the "newspaper of record" for the United States has ceased publishing its regular reports of House and Senate votes in Washington.[5] Presumably, these votes no longer count as "part of the record."

Results of referendum votes on even relatively simple issues suggest astonishing levels of misunderstanding by voters. California voters displayed cavalier irresponsibility in a referendum on a so-called three-strikes sentencing law that mandates harsh minimum prison terms for repeat offenders (Estrich 1998).[6] In an early case to which the new law was applied, a one-slice pizza thief was sentenced to a term of 25 years to life, with no possibility of parole before serving at least twenty years, for his

[5]The "public editor" of the *New York Times* discusses the paper's failure to report even fairly important votes, such as the votes on cloture (ending debate) in the Senate and then on confirmation of judge Samuel Alito as justice of the Supreme Court (Byron Calame, "The Case of the Missing Role Call Votes, *New York Times,* op-ed, 12 February 2006, 4:14).

[6]This is California, so the law is actually a two-strikes law.

"felony petty theft" ("25 Years for a Slice of Pizza," *New York Times,* 5 March 1995: 1.21). Voters in California apparently also displayed complete misunderstanding of a referendum to require open primaries. (Technically, this was an initiative, not a referendum; an initiative is a popular vote on whether to ratify a legislative measure.) Adhering to this referendum could have disallowed California representation at the national party nominating conventions in the year 2000, but this is what the voters chose. After the electorate failed on this issue, administrative devices were proposed to enable the state to distinguish Democratic and Republican voters in primary elections, in presumable violation of the purpose of the referendum ("California Scrambles after Measure Fails," *New York Times,* 15 November 1998: 1.20). In this failure, democracy was a charade, and when it failed from ignorance we let a knowledgeable bureaucratic agency act against the democratic result. Very soon thereafter, the measure was overturned with finality in the courts (*California Democratic Party v. Jones* [2000]).

MEDIAN KNOWLEDGE

The argument of the median voter model of elections is demoralizing. It implies that a mere census of voters and their positions would define the median voter and therefore the outcome of any election. If so, then what would be the point of the elections and campaigns? Ostensibly, each candidate would use the electoral process to influence voters by convincing them that their real positions center on the positions of that candidate. To put this in a positive light, we could say that election campaigns are about giving voters the knowledge they need to vote intelligently in their interest. To put it in a negative light, we could say that they are about deceiving voters into thinking their interests are other than what they are, or that a candidate's position is other than it is.

Suppose now that voters are generally quite ignorant of the nature of even those issues that are of objective importance to them, and of the stances of candidates on those issues. In such an ignorant population, *the median of the distribution of voters is not well defined.* Hence, with ignorant voters the economic model does not imply that candidates must place themselves very near each other. A Newt Gingrich who takes a position significantly to the right of the presumed median voter nonetheless cannot be placed clearly by many voters, who may think he is close to them. The median voter theorem on candidate placement is therefore irrelevant in a world of even moderate ignorance.

Incidentally, the smeared median may help to explain the odd case of so-called conflicted conservatives (Stimson 2004, 87–95). Their preferred policies (to the left of center) and their preferred candidates (to the right of center) both fall into this broad smear. Accordingly, they need see no conflict in their views.

Moreover, the ill-defined median can be volatile. Because voters are ignorant, their positions may be relatively unstable and subject to sudden change in response to new information (Popkin [1991]1994, chap. 4). This means that a candidate's effort to inform voters can be risky. If voters were well informed, however, campaigns would have little effect unless candidates could generate new issues. The very fact of campaigns suggests the general ignorance of voters, and the quality of campaigns, perhaps especially in the United States, suggests that candidates believe that voters are abysmally ignorant.

In principle, if a candidate could do a sufficiently effective job of convincing voters where they—the voters—stand, that candidate might even shift enough people into some particular preference ordering as to make that new ordering the majority preference. One might suppose, however, that this would typically be a false achievement, because that candidate's success would in part be de facto a matter of deceiving voters about the voters' own interests.

UNDERSTANDING WHETHER TO VOTE

When I have taught the logic of collective action, it has often taken a great deal of persuasive effort to get the argument across, at even the general level, to many of the students. Even after I have seemingly managed to do that, some students have immediately argued against the logic in particular applications, such as voluntary payment of union dues in order to gain the collective benefits of union protection of workers. This is, in a sense, a surprisingly different result from the intellectual history of understanding the logic. Typically, the logic has been understood in a particular context, such as John Stuart Mill's discussion of the need for legal enforcement of a shorter work day in order to overcome the inherent incentive of individuals to get paid extra for overtime by free-riding on the voluntary agreement of everyone to work less (Mill [1848] 1965, 958; see, further, Hardin 1988b, 92–94).

Consider this logic in the context of voting in elections in substantial polities. The odds against a voter's ever making a difference are overwhelming. When there was a tie vote in a local election in New Jersey in 1994, this otherwise trivial outcome became national news because it was the exceedingly rare case of a tie in which one more vote could have made a difference. There have even been votes, in larger elections, that were de facto ties, in which the counting error was too great to know who really had won. In the New Hampshire election for the United States Senate in 1974, Louis Wyman and John Durkin were virtually tied at about 111,000 votes each, with relevant state agencies disagreeing over whether the Republican Wyman or the Democrat Durkin had won the vote. Eventually, the U.S. Senate declared the election undecidable and declined to seat either candidate. The vote was then retaken in a special election (which, remarkably enough, Durkin won by a substantial margin). This odd election shows that merely for practical reasons of difficulties in counting votes accurately, one more vote is extremely unlikely to make a difference in an election, even in as small a polity as New Hampshire, one of the smallest states in the United States. The individual voter essentially does not count. An editorial response to the chaotic presidential vote counting in Florida in 2000 was to lecture citizens with the claim that one's vote does count after all. The far more plausible inference from that debacle is that one's lone vote clearly could not have mattered, because it was swamped by the margin of error in counting and in cheating, not to mention the well-organized politicking to disrupt a more nearly accurate count.

This relatively commonsense claim about the near irrelevance of a single vote in Florida in 2000 may actually mislead us on just how little a single vote matters. The very best chance of my vote making a difference, in some hypothetical case, would come if, de facto, all other voters but one tossed a fair coin and voted for A when heads turned up and for B when tails turned up, while I voted definitively for A. With, say, a hundred million voters, my vote would have so little chance of breaking a tie even in this extraordinarily evenly matched election that, even if I were to value the election of A at $1,000, my vote would be worth less than ten cents (Hardin 1982, 60n).

Despite such numbers and such supposed logic, many citizens claim forcefully, and seem to believe, that it is in their interest to vote. Moreover, they demonstrate their commitment to this view by actually voting. The incentive problem is conspicuously overcome for about half the voters in U.S. presidential elections, and for even more of the voters in most other contemporary democracies. These voters overcome the slight costs of voting. One might give an account from a theory of knowledge of why people believe their individual votes matter. If such an account were successful, it would counter Downs's logic, and we might understand why there are substantially higher voting turnouts than that logic would allow, if only it were well understood.

In typical economic choices, it seems to make sense to suppose that people understand their own interests reasonably well. In collective action contexts, however, this supposition may not make sense. A standard quibble with rational-choice theories is that they require individuals to do what best serves their objective interests. If individuals act otherwise, then the theory is thought to fail. Unfortunately, this view short circuits the mental task of weighing one's objective interests in acting one way rather than another. If I conclude that my interest is other than what some objective analysis by a critic says it is, it does not follow *either* that I am right *or* that, if I am wrong, I act irrationally in acting according to what I believe to be my interest. *A fully adequate account of my rationality must account first for my beliefs and then for my action from these beliefs.*

At least in certain contexts, such as medical decisions, we generally have no difficulty with this two-stage requirement on judging someone's rationality. For example, it would be odd to say that George Washington acted irrationally in allowing the best medical people available to him to bleed him, possibly killing him or hastening his death, during his final, perhaps minor illness. He did the best one could do within reason, which is to say within the economic or rational constraints on what he could come to know about medical care. His doctor, Benjamin Rush, bled five pints in one day (Mitgang 1999).[7] When Washington died, Rush may have concluded that he had not bled the great man aggressively enough, and might therefore have determined to bleed people who suffered from, say, a cold and fever, more aggressively, lest he lose them, too. Given his sadly mistaken view of the efficacy of bleeding, he must have had doubts about what was the best treatment.

Our task here is to assess the rationality of individuals' beliefs about the rationality of acting for collective benefit, in the face of the logic of collective action. Many of those who vote do so for moral reasons of their duties, or the fairness of doing their part. But many seem genuinely to think it in their own interest to vote. They invoke a rational-choice version of the generalization principle in ethics (Singer 1961; Hardin 1988b, 65–68). That moral principle is a response to the query: What if everyone did that? For example, what if everyone took a shortcut through a lovely lawn or garden, as I wish to do in this moment because I am lazy or in a hurry? Well, if everyone did that, there might be an ugly path through the

[7]Rush was sued for malpractice in another case of supposedly aggressive bleeding. The later French physician and innovative medical statistician, Pierre-Charles-Alexandre Louis, did statistical tests of bleeding for cases of pneumonia. He found that early aggressive bleeding nearly doubled the fatality rate. Nonetheless, he concluded that this result was "startling and apparently absurd" and, against his own data, he recommended still more aggressive bleeding early (Louis [1835] 1836, 9 and 23; quoted in Morabia 2004). Giving up on a long-established medical practice was not easy, even in the face of clear statistical evidence against it. Washington and Rush can hardly be thought irrational in their belief in the practice.

splendor of the lawn or garden. But one could often answer such a query by noting that everyone does not, and evidently will not, do that.

Many voters seem to believe in a *pragmatic (nonmoral) version of the generalization argument*. They feel responsible if, after they fail to vote, their party loses. And if their party loses after they do vote, they console themselves with the realization that at least they tried. If they had merely a moral commitment to voting, they should feel guilty for not voting, independently of whether their party wins or loses. To feel regret about not voting because one's party loses makes no sense unless one supposes one might actually have made a difference.

I have tried to explain, to many people on many occasions, including many politically active and sophisticated people, the logic of collective action as it is played out in voting or union organizing. I was not trying to dissuade them from voting, but only to defend a casual comment on how voting is motivated, if at all, by moral commitments. Or I was trying to give an analysis of why the costs of voting dissuade many people. For example, it is much harder to vote in New York City today than it was to vote in Chicago or Philadelphia when I lived in those cities. In both of these cities, the polling places were in almost every block. One could vote on the way home without going out of one's way. Not so in New York. The result? Fewer voters in New York City. I have attempted to explain that this fact of differential costs of voting, and not some cultural claim about diverse, cynical, or uncaring New Yorkers, makes sense of the variance in behavior. That is not culture; it is politics. But very sophisticated people simply reject the entire argument of the irrelevance of their vote. And they commonly assert a pragmatic generalization argument in favor of voting, as being in their own and everyone else's interest. Utterly against the self-evident facts of low turnouts, they often even hold that everyone understands their principle and must reject my argument.

For some years, I thought that people would eventually come to understand the nature of this problem. I no longer believe that. I believe it is easier to understand the logic of collective action and to apply it to real problems of choice than it is to understand, say, the theory of relativity, quantum mechanics, or the workings of DNA. But for many people these are all equally incomprehensible—which is to say, not at all comprehensible. A major reason for their failure of understanding is that people typically suffer no grievous consequences from not understanding these things. As a result of their lack of understanding, some people may put a bit more effort into voting than they might under difficult circumstances, such as vile weather during a New Hampshire primary in early January. But that is not a great loss. It is, however, a striking fact that, although people seem not to understand their actual incentives in voting, they nevertheless do respond to those incentives to some extent, as the comparative behaviors of voters in New York City and Chicago suggest. Lower the hassle of voting and turnout will increase.

It would be a greater benefit to many people to understand the tax laws better than to understand the logic of collective action better. And they do not even master the tax laws very well. If the practices of many of my academic colleagues are indicative, they typically pay significantly more than they should under the law. Then why should they be bothered with the logic of collective action? It is a professional hobby of rational-choice theorists to understand it, and maybe that fact makes it easier for them to understand it. Or maybe rational-choice theorists are self-selected from people who find it relatively easy to follow such logical and economic reasoning more generally. They are then motivated by the interest they have in getting arguments right, in contexts in which getting them wrong leads to professional embarrassment. They are not motivated very much by the actual usefulness of putting the logic to work in their lives—although a few have become adamantly determined to live by its conclusions and not to vote.

Suppose we conclude that it is plausibly rational for a person not to master the argument of the logic of collective action, and that they therefore vote despite lack of objective interest in doing so. *Then why do they seem to follow the logic in not investing in the knowledge they would need to vote intelligently?* This is arguably the central theory-of-knowledge question in political participation. As a first answer to it, we can note that any kind of sustained investment in political knowledge might fail, because it gives too little positive feedback to fool people into believing their own action is benefiting them. But a relatively simple, single-shot action with a more or less immediate outcome might make understanding the interests at stake in the action much more difficult. The difference between your going a bit out of your way in order to vote and coming to know enough to vote your interests is partly a difference between a quick single-shot action and a sustained pattern of actions over a long period of time. The sustained pattern of investments in coming to know about political candidates may never be related to any sense that it made a difference, whether mistaken or correct.

Another difference between the two investments—in voting and in knowing enough to vote intelligently—is that there is a substantial public discussion of the first, but very little of the second. People come to have an active belief about the value of voting, but they may have no belief of any consequence about the value of knowing enough to vote intelligently. It is easy enough to understand that people learn wrong theories and then even apply them, especially when the consequences of their application are not substantially painful. With voting, however, it is not merely that people have failed to grasp the logic of collective action but that they have been actively proselytized their entire lifetimes for a contrary belief. Rather than investigate that logic for themselves, they take the view of the authoritative proselytizers.

Jean Shepherd, for 21 years a talk show host on WOR-AM New York, once gave his listeners an insightful lesson on ignorance in voting (best read with a nasal Indiana twang):

> They've been plugging all day long, on the air, that you should get out and vote. Well . . . this is one guy who says there's a lot of you who shouldn't. I've heard a lot of you discuss politics and I'm worried, when I think of you guys voting. I'm really serious. You know, they seem to think here in America that voting in itself is a positive virtue. In fact, I heard one spot by some friendly lady who does a program here on WOR that seemed to say in spite of the fact that you don't know anything about it, don't let that stop you, get out and vote, and thereby you will nullify the vote of someone who does know something about it. Well, all right, I'm just merely saying voting itself, friends, is not a virtue, and if you don't know anything about it, stay away. You're liable to get us all in trouble. (In "Word for Word—Kabuki Radio: 'Creeping Meatballism' and Other Peculiar Riffs on America," *New York Times,* 26 March 2000: 4.7)

For some of the scholars who contend that voters vote rationally despite voting in woeful ignorance, Shepherd's comments must be irrelevant and maybe even misguided, because these voters supposedly will follow cues that let them transcend their ignorance; or half of them will cancel the other half out, so that the smaller fraction of those who are well informed will decide the election. These possibilities sound like wishes, rather than arguments or demonstrations from data. Will all those campaigning be equally talented at giving cues, or at manipulating cues, or even outright lying to feign cues? Will the number of the well-informed on, say, the left and on the right correctly represent the fractions of those having each political interest? The problem of ignorance about how to vote seems likely to fit Schumpeter's views (cited above) better than the views of these scholars. If the typical voter resorts to primitive reasoning and relies on very poor data, what hope is there for representative democracy? (See, further, Hardin 2004b).

To change the focus of these observations, we can address the question from both the benefits side and the costs side. No significant objective personal benefits arise either from voting or from mastering the knowledge to vote intelligently in one's interest. That no benefits accrue from mastering the knowledge merely for the purpose of choosing how to vote follows, of course, from the claim that there are virtually no benefits from voting. For many people there seem to be, however, perceived benefits from voting—they evidently stop working through the issue before reaching the Downs-Schumpeter conclusion. This view may be a mistake, but it is not irrational, any more than it is irrational of me to get the arithmetic wrong in balancing my bank statement. Moreover, the Downs-Schumpeter conclusion was apparently not formally reached by anyone until very recently—it is genuinely hard to grasp.

If we are being proselytized to believe in the benefits of voting, then the costs of coming to perceive the logic against voting have been raised, perhaps very high for many people. It would be much harder to proselytize people for the view that massive study of current politics and politicians is in their interest, because the real costs of such study would be substantial and readily felt. To sum up, we can say that there are real differences in both the benefit and the cost functions of voting and of learning enough to vote intelligently. The differences in both of these voting issues suggest there is more reason to expect people to vote than to expect them to be well informed enough to vote intelligently in their interest. Hence, as in Shepherd's worry, there may be very many ignorant votes cast.

Finally, we may note that people often do understand the logic of collective action, perhaps especially in relatively local contexts in which the cooperative contributions would be costly and readily perceived. The slogan "Let George do it" is grounded in a recognition of the logic. It may have taken a very substantial level of proselytizing to get people not to see that logic in the case of voting, although the proselytizers may themselves have been led to believe in their own preachment.

Among those who have been best at understanding the logic of collective action are union leaders and members. This makes sense from the fact that theirs has been a problem of collective action from the beginning. They have long been forced to recognize that voluntarism does not work very well, and that coercive laws are necessary to induce contributions of dues and efforts. It was, as noted earlier, in the context of collective action for workers that Mill recognized the logic. Samuel Gompers (1905), an early leader of the American union movement, asserted the logic clearly a century ago. He had learned the logic through extensive, no doubt painful experience, at a level most of us will never even vaguely match.

Perhaps the first I ever heard of the logic of collective action was from a union neighbor, Sam Seely, when I was not yet a teenager, before Downs or Olson wrote. I asked him how he had voted on election day. He replied that he had not bothered to vote because his vote would not have mattered, and because it would have been a lot of trouble, since he would have had to knock off work early and lose an hour's pay or miss his pre-dinner beer on the patio. He lifted his beer to me and then took a dime from his pocket, flipped it to me, and said, "My vote is not worth this much." He was an adept not only of the logic of collective action, but of politics. I have long thought of his argument as the Sam Seely theory of politics. He had surely never read Gompers or Schumpeter, and this was before Downs and Olson, but he understood all of them at the most pro-found, action-guiding level. He would surely have fallen into the 2.5 per-cent of the public that Converse (1964), writing about that era, shows was elite enough in its political sophistication to understand the differ-ence between "liberals" and "conservatives." He knew how he should have voted if he had voted, and he predicted, rightly, that the candidate he opposed, Eisenhower, would easily defeat the one he favored, Steven-son, because, he supposed, people "liked Ike" and were not smart enough to see that Stevenson would serve the interests of most of them better.

Sam's logical sophistication was presumably grounded in his union ex-perience. For those who have not had such experience or a near equiva-lent, such thinking does not come as naturally. When the costs of volun-taristic collective action are substantial and clear, and perhaps especially when the significance of joint action is driven home repeatedly in some context, such as union or neighborhood organizing, people can grasp the logic of collective action clearly. Generalizing it, however, is quite another matter. Only with Olson's generalization in 1965 did the logic become generally clear to large numbers of social scientists with a strong profes-sional interest in understanding it. The best and the brightest of them had typically got it wrong before. Downs (1957, 266–71) himself famously seems to slip on his own argument when he discusses the value of voting per se as the value of making democracy work and survive, as if a reason for voting is to prevent the collapse of democracy. This bad argument—arguably orders of magnitude worse than the argument that it is in my in-terest to vote in order to affect the outcome of the present election—is commonly and perversely cited by critics as Downs's refutation of his own central argument. It is merely a casual error on his part.

In sum, many people do vote, despite the absence of a personal benefit from doing so. Hence, the Downsian instance of the logic of collective ac-tion is de facto resolved for a substantial fraction of the electorate. There-fore, the problem of investing in enough knowledge to vote intelligently may well be the more fundamentally serious issue in democratic theory, as Schumpeter seems to think. To assess whether it is, we would need even more extensive studies of the fit between votes and objective interests than we have had so far (see, further, the special issue of *Critical Review* 18 [2006]: (nos. 1–3).

MULTIDIMENSIONAL ISSUES

In many contexts, the Downs model of the distribution of voter preferences from left to right does not fit the reality. Kenneth Arrow ([1951] 1963) and, earlier, C. L. Dodgson (Lewis Carroll) supposed there may be a multiplicity of dimensions on which voters' preferences are arrayed. For example, we might have varied preferences on government expenditure in the economy that fit a left-right model. We might similarly have views ranging from more spending to less on military, health, education, and so forth, and these might not be related. Indeed, there could be as many dimensions as there are issues that are relevant to defining states of affairs. In some respects, Arrow's and Dodgson's vision of the nature of the issues over which a collective is choosing is a much better fit to European and North American national politics today than is Downs's. The left-right model of Downs's normal distribution arguably fit the politics of the 1950s better than it does today. I therefore wish to discuss the median voter model in the context of an electorate facing issues that are no longer simply arrayed along a single dimension. Because of this characteristic of contemporary issues, the knowledge demands for a voter today may be much severer than they were in the earlier era.

In a sense, the era in which the Downs model plausibly approximated reality was a golden age of simplicity, an age that may have lasted on and off for a couple of centuries in the Anglo-Saxon world, and for a century or more in other industrial states that became democratic later. But that era has now passed, perhaps only temporarily but perhaps permanently. Its passing may have significant consequences for the form that politics will take in the near future, because simple left-right conceptions of parties can no longer represent the key issues at stake.

One reason for contemporary multidimensionality is that there are many noneconomic issues today. I wish to focus, however, on issues that primarily concern interests, rather than those that are matters of moral commitment that is not based on interests and that might even run against interests. One might suppose that these issues must therefore really just be matters that can be arrayed on a left-right dimension, just as general economic policy once was thought to fit such a model. But where knowledge and understanding of the impact of various policies—for example, on environmental issues, military expenditures, basic research, education, health care, retirement policy, and on through the list of most major economic policies of contemporary industrial states—is at issue, we cannot simply put all these matters into an additive function that goes from, say, more government expenditure to less. I want more effort on the environment, you want less on the environment and more on health care, another wants to cut both of these, if necessary, to spend more on defense or education. If these were all marketable goods to be consumed at the individual level, then, subject to our resource constraints, I could buy what I want and you could buy what you want. But we typically decide collectively on the levels of provision of these things, and we all get from the process roughly the same levels, with some variation as especially in education and health care, which are partially bought on the market.

If we could believe that there is something like a basic welfare or utility function that we all share, as George Stigler and Gary Becker (Becker 1996, 24–49) have argued, we might be able to array these issues, at least in principle. But even then, the ordinary citizen cannot perform such a trick, and there will be remarkably strong disagreement on where to put our public money. Hence, although all these issues might be seen clearly as merely about interests, they define different dimensions, because individuals have such different evaluations of them. For private consumption goods in modern economics, this would merely mean that we would have reason to exchange with each other to improve our welfare. I prefer your bit of something to my bit of something else and you have the opposite preferences, so we trade. This is the great simplifying move of modern market economics: We can each trade off bits of some things for bits of others, all to increase our own welfares. After a round or two of such pairwise exchanges, we are all better off by our own lights.

But this simplifying move fails for many public allocations. For public provision of essentially collective goods we have to agree on single allocations of various things for everyone at once, and we cannot then trade with each other to come closer to our own preferred outcomes. We all get the same outcome. If we all were to start with the same set of private consumption goods, we could improve our lots by trading, but that is not the position we are in. I cannot trade part of my share of environmental protection for part of your share of health care coverage. We all start with the same set of collective goods, and there can be no trading. As a result, we each must view the collective allocations as occurring on de facto different dimensions, because I do not aggregate them in the same way you do. The aggregate of our collective allocations might seem splendid to you and miserable to me in comparison to plausible alternatives at the same total public and individual costs.

Even though they commonly cannot affect their own welfare through their private actions without interaction effects from the actions of others, most people other than possibly those who are politically well connected in the United States surely have more control in general over their own welfare through the private sphere than through the political sphere. They therefore have much greater incentive to understand their private concerns than to understand public concerns. This is an analog of the common claim in utilitarianism that we should typically focus our beneficent efforts on those close to us, because we can be surer of acting effectively for the good this way than if we try to act for the general welfare.[8] Ideally, we could overcome this problem of unequal incentives to a large extent if we could reduce collective goods to individual goods. This is not possible for collective bads, such as pollution, which are not deliberately produced but are, at best, external effects of desirable activities. And the reduction could not be efficient for many goods, like the U.S. Army, that are collectively provided by governments and other agencies.

It may also generally be harder to understand public concerns for such things as environmental protection than to understand at least the supposed implications of policies to enhance economic activity. For the short term of the present generation, workers might generally think it in their interest to increase wages even at cost to investment, while owners and the relatively wealthy might think it in their interest to increase investment even at cost to wages. But neither workers nor owners might have a clear sense of whether general environmental protections are in their interest, although they might readily conclude that protections that specifically burden their industry are not in their interest. Even workers exposed to carcinogens, such as benzene and the gases involved in the production of polyvinylchloride film (plastic wrap for food and other things), might think it in their interest to keep their jobs with such exposure rather than to escape the exposure by enclosing various processes and, coincidentally, eliminating workers.

CONCLUDING REMARKS

One might read recent elections in the United States, the United Kingdom, and Germany as responses to the fading of the traditional economic divide between left and right parties, between concern for wages and concern for profits, as leaders of both left and right parties begin to suppose that relatively free-market devices are best for running contemporary economies.[9] The focus in recent years has been on other issues, including the single-issue focus of many groups on such issues as abortion and gun control in the United States and the environment in Germany. Indeed, in Germany there is a specifically Green party, because environmental issues are not the natural concern of either the conservative Christian Democrats or the more liberal Socialists. These other issues are generally not

---

[8]This claim is a response to the supposed criticism of utilitarianism: that it violates our particularistic moral concern with our own families, and requires us instead to care only for the generalized other without special concern for any individuals merely on the ground of their closeness to us.

[9]The French have not joined the growing consensus.

conspicuously tied or related to the traditional divide over wages and profits. Hence, neither traditional party is able to capture them permanently for its agenda, and thus to help trump the opposing major party. Traditional parties and voters alike now face a world in which multiple issues de facto represent multiple dimensions.

The main left-right economic issue of massive government control of the economy defined the two chief parties in the United States and in many other democratic nations for much of the past century. Other issues were many and varied, but they commonly did not dominate the central economic issue—except during the two major wars. And as I write, terrorism and the war in Iraq appear to have become dominant issues.

It is the fact that various contemporary issues (which themselves seem like matters of mere interest) are collectively determined or provided that makes each an independent dimension for collective choice. Hence, so long as these diverse issues remain politically important, traditional left-right party alignments cannot fit actual political issues well. Therefore, the more of these issues we can remove from the collective agenda, the better our chances for making collective choice coherent. With many of these issues on the collective agenda, we may increasingly witness the break-up of any major party focus and, de facto, sharpen the relevance of the problem of a multiplicity of unrelated dimensions of major issues. The response of candidates to such a change cannot be that of Downsian candidates, which is to seek the position of the median voter. Instead, the response is likely to become unspecific and bland, the candidates not taking major policy positions other than those that can gain relatively general support. But of course, policies that gain general support cannot differentiate candidates.

In sum, the evidence says that the bulk of American and other nations' voters make the sensible choice to be relatively ignorant of politics (on France, for example, see Converse and Pierce 1986). The best theory we have says they are rationally right to be so ignorant. Hence, although we have democracy of a sort, it is wishful thinking to suppose that it is representative of people's actual interests. Ordinary knowledge trumps so-called rational voting. It also vitiates the median-voter theorem on candidate placement. That theorem, though a centerpiece of election studies over the past fifty years, should be set aside. And the account of ordinary knowledge may be the start of an explanation of the odd phenomenon of the persistently large block of conflicted conservative voters who vote against their own policy preferences.

Then why do so many people vote? (Editorial writers far more commonly wonder why so few vote. That is too easy to explain.) For many voters, the explanation is plausibly that, unlike Sam Seely, my neighbor long ago, they simply do not understand the logic of Schumpeter, Downs, and Olson. That failure to understand makes eminently good sense. Some people, however, vote for other reasons than merely to exercise the impact they will have. Consider one, possibly apocryphal, story.

Following the election of John Kennedy as president, there was a special election in Massachusetts to fill his seat in the Senate. There were two candidates for the Democratic nomination, and the winner of that special primary election was virtually guaranteed to be elected over any Republican candidate in the full special election. The two candidates were Ted Kennedy, the younger brother of John, and Edward McCormack, also from an important political family in Massachusetts (his uncle was Speaker of the U.S. House of Representatives). Generally reliable polls said Kennedy would win with about 60 percent of the vote. Election day was cold and possibly icy, making getting to the polls difficult. Edward Banfield and his wife were in their weekend home in Vermont, where they happened to be neighbors of one of Banfield's Harvard colleagues in the department of government. Shortly before the election, the two couples were together, and the subject of the election came up. Banfield's Harvard colleague was ill at the time, possibly terminally, but nonetheless he and his wife were planning to drive back to the Boston area to vote and then to return to Vermont.

Banfield tried to dissuade them with arguments that their votes did not matter, and that the trip on possibly icy roads would be dangerous and exhausting—and in any case it would be a waste of a precious day in their lives. The colleague's wife was aghast at the suggestion and said, roughly, "Ed Banfield, if you think like that, you ought not be teaching government at Harvard." Her clincher was to say, "Besides, he's voting for Ted and I'm voting for Ed." The Downs-Schumpeter logic of the costs and benefits of voting did not move them to reconsider the folly of their going to such trouble to vote. The tale may be apocryphal, but analogs of the story have surely played out many times.

CHAPTER 4

Liberalism

A COMPELLING FACT about liberalism is that it fits the economic theory of knowledge.[1] Indeed, that account of knowledge, if descriptively correct, virtually demands liberal organization of society to match the organization of knowledge. The core of liberalism is the decentralization of initiative. This distinction could be a normative principle, and it can clearly be defended normatively. But such decentralization is also compelling if knowledge and creativity are diffused through the population, and are not capable of aggregation in some central authority, as they might be in a relatively traditional, small, communal society. In a modern, complex society—even as of several centuries ago in northern Europe—central aggregation of the knowledge needed to oversee a great range of significant and far-reaching activities is impossible.

As Friedrich Hayek might say, liberalism fits the distributed knowledge of a creative social order. It does this because it gives autonomy to individuals and their own spontaneous, changing organizations. One might take such autonomy to be the central value of liberalism, or one might take the autonomy to be a means to other things, such as, especially, welfare. For Adam Smith, economic liberalism is justified as a way to enhance welfare through increased productivity. Blocking government intervention in the economy for capricious reasons makes almost all of us better off.[2] Decentralization of knowledge implies two fundamentally important facts: popular ignorance and government ignorance. Given government's ignorance of what it can actually accomplish in many realms, we must want it not to be empowered to act in those realms.

Hayek and the Austrian school of economics might better be seen as the Austrian school of social and political theory. The Austrian vision of distributed knowledge is consistent with John Stuart Mill's grounding for his principle of liberty, that individuals have the best knowledge of what

---

[1]For general views of liberalism, see Rosenblum 1989 and Kelly 2004. Rosenblum (1989, 5) defines liberalism as "a political theory of limited government, providing institutional guarantees for personal liberty." One cannot do better than this without adding a lot of extra words.

[2]It presumably would make someone with a monopoly grant from the king or queen worse off to eliminate such grants.

their interests are.[3] This claim can be qualified, of course, in ways that the individual would allow. For example, I would defer to judgment by medical professionals on some things that might be in my interest but that I could not understand adequately on my own. It is also consistent with James Madison's vision of a weak government that could enable people in their private activities but that could not readily interfere in those activities. Madison contrived a constitution for the United States that blocked government in many ways, most especially in protecting individual freedom from intrusions of government. As implicitly a theorist, Madison could well be seen as a forerunner of the Austrian school.

I wish to tie these three visions—Austrian distributed knowledge, Madisonian limited government, and Millian liberty—together with the economic theory of the ordinary person's knowledge, which is at the core of all these visions.[4] For the understanding of human behavior, whether normative or merely factual, we require a theory of the general, varied patterns of individuals' available knowledge—as in the economic theory of the ordinary person's knowledge proposed here.

Austrian Social Theory

We generally think of the Austrian school of economics, which includes F. A. Hayek (1960; 1980), Ludwig von Mises ([1922] 1981), and many others, as concerned centrally with economics. But in fact their vision is as richly pertinent to social as to economic theory, perhaps more so. Their concern is often framed as normative, but it is also descriptive and explanatory. In the Austrian view of economic relations, the knowledge of how to produce and market vast numbers of commodities cannot be centralized in any one person or agency. Knowledge is inherently distributed and local, and most of it is inaccessible to any one person or agency. This is an unchallengeable descriptive claim from which various theoretical implications seem to follow readily.

Rather than expounding on Austrian economic theory here, I wish to argue for an essentially Austrian theory of social relations more generally. But the argument for an Austrian social theory must be even more com-

---

[3]Mill says that, "with respect to his own feelings and circumstances, the most ordinary man or woman has means of knowledge immeasurably surpassing those that can be possessed by any one else" (Mill [1859] 1977, chap. 4, ¶4, p. 277).

[4]The Austrian, Madisonian, and Millian visions, coupled with the seeming fact that people place very high value on welfare, often especially own-welfare, yield a welfarist political theory that is essentially a mutual-advantage theory. Mutual advantage is not imposed or assumed, however, as it might be in an ordinal utilitarian theory (Hardin 1988b) or in contractarianism. Rather, it results from individual choices and the aggregation of individual values. I will not develop this thesis here. See, further, Hardin 2006a, and note 9, below.

pelling than that for an Austrian economic theory. The earliest understanding of liberalism is that individuals should be allowed to go their own way on many social issues. I will claim that that vision is equivalent to a social version of Austrian economics.

Again, much of the argument for Austrian economics is predictive and explanatory, although it is motivated by a central normative concern, which is productivity. That concern is imputed to or assumed for virtually everyone, so that the normative concern is itself factually determined and not theoretically imposed. Arguably, normative concerns are more important in an Austrian social theory, because it must often say simply that we should let people go their own way, merely for their own sake, and not for the sake of greater productivity in the larger society or anything else that would have such universal collective appeal. While virtually all might acknowledge the value of greater productivity, many might not grant the value of letting others lead their lives in certain ways. In many societies, however, it seems that the common view of politics is that it is to serve the welfare of citizens, so that its normative vision is the same as the normative vision of Austrian economics. The causal argument of Austrian economics is that, typically, individual welfare and aggregate productivity will be enhanced by decentralization of decisions that matches the actual decentralization of knowledge. The causal argument of an Austrian social theory is the same.

In a remarkable book, *Seeing Like a State,* James Scott (1998, 256) defends a thesis that is akin to the central vision of Hayek and the Austrian school of economics. The knowledge needed to run a society is widely distributed, and very much of it cannot become available to a central government. Hence, a central government should not attempt to manage society in detail, and it should not attempt massive redesign of society. Austrian economists generally worry about central control of the economy, but they could as well worry about central control of social relations more generally. Scott especially deplores what Hayek called cartesianism and what Scott calls the high modernism of arrogant redesign of major parts of society, as in the effort to design cities in supposedly more rational ways (chap. 4) or to reorganize peasants into collective farms in Soviet Russia or into Ujamaa villages in Tanzania (chaps. 6 and 7). The general thesis of the Austrian Scott is compelling, as are many of his particular arguments from it.

Scott also argues that the state imposes many things on us in order the better to monitor and control us. Among these things are standards of measurement, a uniform national language, definitive and legally recorded property lines and surnames, and centralized traffic patterns, as in railway routes that connect the periphery to the center, as in France with Paris at the hub of various spokes into the provinces (Scott 1998, chaps.

1 and 2). Some of these things are relatively recent in European society and even more recent in many other societies. Few of them were beneficial to those on whom they were first imposed. All of them enable the state to keep records on us or, in Scott's term, to make us legible. Our ready legibility allows the state to control us in various ways, such as to raise taxes and armies. In making us legible, the state typically simplifies the facts it reads from us.[5]

Many state activities transform the populace to make them fit such simplified facts, so that they can be observed and controlled (Scott 1998, 82). Scott supposes that the state's efforts to measure things through census and other devices commonly affect the things that are measured (22 and 82). Part of his argument is that this is deliberate policy, but sometimes he seems to imply that these things just happen. Hence, the state creates the kind of industry and farming it needs for legibility, as in the apparently decided preference for plantation over smallholder farming, even where the latter would be more productive (189–91). A second part of this thesis, that the state creates the kinds of people it needs for legibility, merits further argument and research.

There are at least two theoretical issues lurking here: the legibility of the populace (which gives Scott's book its title) and the value of local or distributed knowledge. The legibility of the populace is a sine qua non of very much public policy, whether good policy or bad (Scott 1998, 78). Government cannot carry out welfare programs without knowing who there is and who is in need. It cannot handle or provide farm subsidies, educational policy, health care, or services such as water and sewage without fairly specific knowledge of individuals. It also cannot collect taxes or regulate certain activities without such knowledge.

The value of local knowledge is brushed aside in high-modernist social design, as for example in Le Corbusier's urban designs, and in the totalitarian control of people for various purposes, such as remaking the Soviet economy and especially its agriculture. Le Corbusier's principles guided the architects Lucio Costa and Oscar Niemeyer in their design of Brasília, the new governmental capital of Brazil (Holston 1989). Brasília is a slight misfit for Scott's general thesis, shared with Jane Jacobs (1961), on the way urban planners bulldoze local communities and local life, because that city was built where there had been no local knowledge, where all the land was owned by the government and there was little or nothing to displace in building Brasília. But the consequent purity of the design accentuates the objection that it makes the city primarily a work of art rather than a place for comfortable and sociable living. It was designed

---

[5]These facts are interested (that is, utilitarian), documentary, static, aggregate, and standardized (Scott 1998, 80).

virtually against the creation of local street-level knowledge, through depriving people of the kind of street life that happens in naturally grown cities.

Liberalism essentially exalts local knowledge and values, insofar as these are the values of individuals, and of course it stands implacably against totalitarian control, which is often directed at redesigning not merely society and the economy but also the individual. When state capacity to make its populace legible is joined with high modernism in social design, totalitarian or immediately post-revolutionary government, and the absence of intermediary social structures, the state can take its population into disaster. The chain of argument is that "the legibility of a society provides the capacity for large-scale social engineering, high-modernist ideology provides the desire, the authoritarian state provides the determination to act on that desire, and an incapacitated civil society provides the leveled social terrain on which to build" (Scott 1998, 5, 89). One can add that this chain results in centralized designs that take little account of, and even thwart, local knowledge, and sometimes fail largely for that reason.

Scott is not particularly interested in the benign side of legibility, and most of his discussions are about state abuses of its knowledge of a legible populace and its controls over it. His perspective is usually that of the poor under the control of an autocratic state that massively manipulates them, ostensibly for their own good or the good of future generations. But in actual fact, as he notes, the devices for legibility can also be used for good purposes, such as monitoring and preventing diseases (Scott 1998, 77). Indeed, if a state is to have any policies that benefit the populace, it most likely can achieve its purposes better if it has knowledge about the populace—about who and where they are. The devices that produce legibility enable the state to make readier, better-targeted interventions, whatever the state's purpose. Thus the devices are neutral in the sense that they do not determine the direction of the interventions. A Nazi government can use the devices to track down those to be exterminated (78), and a welfare state can use them to distribute social security payments.

LEGIBILITY AND DEMOCRACY

For reasons of democracy and fairness, the U.S. constitution mandates a decennial census to allocate seats in the Congress according to population, and to make tax collections equitable (originally the taxes were to be head taxes levied by the states and turned over to the federal government). Without the facts from the U.S. decennial census, American democracy would be less representative, and the politics of redistricting or reallocating seats in legislative bodies would be far more capricious. Representative democracy and the census go hand in hand. If one values democracy, political fairness, mass education, and egalitarian policies, then one must accept the need for making a populace substantially legible to the state (Scott 1998, 339–40). Otherwise, the state cannot intervene to make sure that those who are qualified can vote, or to equalize opportunities and even welfares. For example, the census enabled the U.S. national government to enforce civil rights in southern states to a degree that would have been difficult or impossible if the population were not well known.

All of these—representative democracy, civil rights, fair taxation, but also conscription into the military—are part of the technological capacity to mobilize large populations, a capacity that developed over the past three centuries and has produced representative democracy, revolution, and nationalism, all of which are essentially modern phenomena (Hardin, forthcoming, chap. 1). Without the capacity for mass mobilization, the state could not control its "citizens" well (and the very idea of citizenship itself is essentially modern).

Before it had adequate measures of landholdings and other forms of wealth, the state was effectively blinded and could not levy taxes without sometimes grim caprice that would bankrupt some while leaving others untouched (Scott 1998, 2). Egalitarianism can be achieved by reducing all to abject poverty in an anarchic subsistence economy, or it can be approached by managing at least some of the distribution of the benefits of a highly productive economy. Without broad access to education, the idea of equal opportunity is a farce, as suggested by the ill-considered Supreme Court decision in *Wisconsin v. Yoder et al.,* which allows the Amish of Wisconsin to end their children's education at age 14 to protect them from the blandishments of the larger society (see, further, chap. 9). That decision also "protects" those children against opportunities to enter the larger economy.

A state controls many people other than the poor, and one might therefore think many people would want to block its efforts at control. For example, among recent politicians who have shared Scott's ambivalence toward state monitoring was Ronald Reagan, who put an end to data series that would be necessary for making policies in various areas.[6] In particu-

---

[6]This is a common move in many contexts. For example, supporters of the industry that produces "supplements" and alternative cures succeeded in getting a law passed in 1994 that deregulated their industry. The industry is now permitted essentially to lie about what its products do, and have been shown to do, so long as they do not claim to have a cure for a specific disease, such as cancer. They can say, without any evidence at all, that some extract of some plant "improves the function of a compromised immune system" (Specter 2004, 64).

lar, he ended the collection of divorce statistics in California and then the collection of various series of data on commercial activities at the national level. Knowledge of data in these and many other areas often politicizes them in the sense of provoking group politics to push for special treatment. A standing argument, for example, holds that accurate census data on ethnicity, religion, and language usage give potential political leaders the information they need to mobilize their groups behind demands to address their specific groups' concerns. Making not only the state but also such potential leaders ignorant therefore alters politics, in this instance possibly making it less conflictual. It would presumably require substantial study to decide whether the result of such enforced ignorance would be to enhance or to restrict democracy or welfare.

Making government democratic comes at the high cost of making the population well known to government. It also enables the government to set fairly detailed policy. Those who want a Hayekist liberalism would prefer to block such detailed policy. They would oppose representation of very specific issues and would want representation only of fairly abstract, general policies. As noted in chapter 3, this would mean that government would actually be more transparent, so that the ignorance of voters would not be as crippling as it is in our system of quasi-democratic policy making. Voters might then begin to understand their general position in the economy and polity, and might be able to vote more or less according to an implicitly ideological vision. They would not need highly detailed knowledge about policies or candidates. Perhaps oddly, therefore, liberalism and democracy would depoliticize much of our current political lives.

Seeing like Hayek

Many of the poor whose perspective Scott takes face massive economic transitions that supersede old ways of doing things and relieve the next generations of the grim life of relative rural poverty. Local knowledge does, of course, get destroyed in such transitions, but much of what is lost is local knowledge that has no value once economic progress sets in. Scott (1998, 301) extols the rich local knowledge that Andean potato farmers apply to small bits of poor mountain land to produce a substantial crop of varied strains of potatoes. In the face of poverty and necessity, as when most of the workforce is engaged in virtually subsistence agriculture, that knowledge is valuable.

But in a better economy, in which agriculture is the work of a small fraction of the civilian labor force (well under 3 percent in the United States), such knowledge—and possibly those bits of land—would be worthless, because the potatoes the knowledge produces cost far too much in human labor. It would be a good thing if prosperity were to save the next generation from needing and having this bit of local Andean knowledge. Scott (1998, 335) seems to agree with this general point in some contexts. For example, he notes that the knowledge of how to start a fire with tinder and flint stones is well lost once matches become available, as is much of the prior knowledge of peoples in many places and historical eras who have enjoyed great beneficial change. There may be sentimental losses even from wonderful innovations. For example, we might have had no *La Boheme* by Puccini if Mimi could have lit her candle with mere matches rather than by borrowing fire from Rodolfo.

Note now two ironic implications of seeing like Hayek. First, seeing this way ostensibly means, in theory, seeing from the bottom up, from local circumstances, although Austrian economic theorizing is as much from top down as any high-modernist theorizing is. Hayek and the Austrians have a very general theory about how knowledge works and where it resides. They may have come to this theory from particular instances that gave the theorists a deeper understanding. But they then go on to apply this theory to many new circumstances and even to the issues of national economic and social policy. Hayek's (1944) best-known book, *The Road to Serfdom,* was written as a general criticism of the effort to centralize the management of a socialist economy. His critique follows directly from his theory of distributed knowledge, and of the importance of entrepreneurial creativity. He did not need to know anything in particular about the Soviet economy to write that book.

Second, the Hayek vision says that there are many things, even whole classes of things, that the state cannot know. Therefore, any defense or expectations of the state must be built on what it can know, which is more or less the simplified facts that Scott notes. Hence, policies must be fairly general. But note that, somewhat metaphorically speaking, institutions, and therefore states, can know many things that individuals cannot know. For example, big institutions can amass hugely valuable aggregate data on a population and on their activities, as do, for example, the Centers for Disease Control in Atlanta (Scott's own example, 1998, 77). In the end, it is the institution that knows these things, although some of them might be put in an annual report or other document where, in summary form, the facts could be digested by individuals. For the most part, however, few individuals will come to know these data, despite their importance in policy design and implementation. Even those who do come to "know" them will at most take the data on faith.

Any Austrian economist supposes that we know some fairly general things about people, such as what motivations or kinds of motivation they are likely to have. It is partly their sense of the basically economic motivation of people who are involved in economic enterprises that leads them to deplore Sovietization of the economy and of agriculture. If we switch from individual farms to collective farms, we de facto make the production of the farm a collective provision, the rewards from which must then be allocated among the collective farmers. This makes my contribution to the general product virtually irrelevant to me, and I must now be motivated not by what I gain from my efforts but by what we all collectively gain from our collective effort.

To my knowledge, the Austrians did not fully articulate the logic of collective action, which runs against the hope of managing and even increasing production by making it a collective effort of millions of people—the grandest collective action in all history. Yet if one wishes to claim that local knowledge was the crucial problem with collective farms, one must explain why after nearly three generations the requisite local knowledge had still not arisen to run those farms collectively. What had happened, of course, was the rise of local knowledge about how to subvert the collective effort by capitalizing on standard individualistic economic incentives. The failure of collectivization was therefore a failure of incentives, not a failure to rely on local knowledge.

DISTRIBUTED KNOWLEDGE AND POLICY

The chief policy implication of the Austrian vision of the nature and distribution of knowledge in a society is that the central design and very extensive management of a modern economy are therefore unlikely to be as effective in creating great prosperity and innovation as is a relatively loosely run market economy. This claim could turn out to be false under certain circumstances, such as, for example, under conditions of extreme exigency when central management might, for all its inefficiencies and errors, get us through better than an unmanaged system could. For example, during wartime, when the value of immediate production overrides various economically future-oriented values, central managerial control of production might be far more successful for the short term than operating by standard market principles would be. It might be wasteful and inefficient in many ways, and might even slow some kinds of innovation, but it would be highly efficient in the one way that matters most at the time, as for example in producing vast numbers of jeeps or other military vehicles rather than in innovatively redesigning them.

Unfortunately, largely just because central control could be readily extended, the successful experience of mobilization in World War I may have contributed to the later centralization of the Soviet economy, and of many other irrelevant values, such as artistic taste and science. Scott (1998, 97–102) supposes that the efforts of Walter Rathenau to manage the production of materiel and other goods for the war effort of imperial Germany during World War I inspired Lenin ([1917] 1954, 195; quoted by Scott 1998, 100, emphasis added) to believe that the war "had accelerated the development of capitalism to such a tremendous degree, converting monopoly capitalism into *state*-monopoly capitalism." He then drew on Rathenau's model to design the Soviet economy. It was a drastic error to suppose, as Rathenau and Lenin did, that the management of a dynamic, innovative economy could be similar enough to the management of a highly and narrowly focused wartime economy to justify its central management by the state. Lenin should have taken a bit of the Austrian tonic and thereby spared three generations of Soviet citizens from the malaise of the planned economy. The German managerial successes in World War I carried the seeds of the ruin of the Soviet world.

One might respond to the claims of Austrian theory with the question: How can one show that no synoptic vision of the best social order is possible? The answer, of course, is that one cannot. The reasons for supposing that no synoptic vision will be credibly better than the best results of unplanned development of society are two. First, no such vision has ever informed a complex modern society. And second, it is, at least for a very modern society, profoundly hard to imagine spelling out a vision in sufficiently articulate ways to capture even a modest part of what is at stake in social order. Hence, the specter of unintended consequences weighs very heavily against synoptic design, although many societies have been redesigned as if that were a reasonable task.

These responses might seem still to leave the question: How can we be sure that we get the best result from unplanned development? Again, we cannot. But in many times and places, the best extant result has been remarkably good, and better than what might have been designed with the available technologies of the age. This claim would be true even of many anthropological societies. In more advanced societies, a bit of regulation, such as zoning land use, would be all that it takes to get fairly creative design. The great luck of the United States is that it had no centralized government before 1789. At its creation under Madison's constitution, the United States was a natural experiment in the national decentralization of initiative. Insofar as it puts Austrian social theory and Smithian economic theory to the test, those two theories pass reasonably well.

There is a lingering worry about what we can know synoptically about social organization. In a major work on induction (reasoning from individual cases or facts to a general principle), D. C. Williams (1947, 18; also see Franklin 2001, 371–72) notes that,

> In the political sphere, the haphazard echoes of inductive skepticism which reach the liberal's ear deprive him of any rational right to cham-

pion liberalism, and account already for the flabbiness of liberal resistance to dogmatic encroachments from the left or the right. The skeptic encourages atavistic rebellion with, "Who are we to say?" and puts in theory the forms and methods of democracy on a level with the grossest tyranny.

Liberals cannot be certain, and they admit it, while ideologues of the extreme left or the extreme right are certain. The most a liberal can say in response is that these ideologues are almost certainly wrong. With their belief in their own certainty, such ideologues have led many societies to disaster in the twentieth century. A response by supporters of one or another general program is that Stalin or Mao or Nehru personally wrecked the theory and did not apply it correctly. But there is no way to put theorists in control to guarantee that all will go well. The ideologues with their certainties can only make excuses for their programmatic failures. They cannot prevent them.

CIVIL LIBERTIES

We can amplify some of the discussion above through consideration of a particular set of goods that are collectively secured through government: political and personal liberties. The liberties I have are almost entirely in the context of my private life, not in the context of my public or political life. I may have the political liberty to vote and even to run for office. But most citizens do not typically have the liberty actually to make any difference to their own welfare through politics. I may indeed come to have substantially enhanced welfare from my political activities, and I might even vote with the majority to achieve benefits for us. But if my vote is worthless, then the liberty to cast it is of little value either. Having the liberty to cast it is roughly as valuable as having the liberty to cast a vote on whether the sun will rise tomorrow.

In general, the ratio of liberty to restraint is greatest for those in a frontier context, in which they need not be bound by any cooperative or coordinative arrangements. But that is not a very desirable state of affairs, because the frontier context is likely to be impoverished, and liberty with poverty does not enable one to do much or to prosper well. The anarchist's liberty comes at a dreadfully high price. To be much better off, one must submit to substantial restraints of social order for mutual benefit. This is an instance of Brian Barry's (1980) argument that, in democratic politics, it is better to be lucky than to be powerful. It is better to just happen to be with the majority than to have a little bit of influence over public policy. One does not then cause one's preferred policies to be adopted, but one benefits from their adoption. Most of us who have liberty are merely lucky to have it; we did not bring it upon ourselves.

The liberty we gain from democratic politics is, usually, the liberty we get from constitutional government and its protections. When democracy fails in the sense of producing an anti-constitutional regime, as it did in Germany in the 1930s, liberty may fail with it. An anti-constitutional regime can be democratic in the strongest sense of the term in the sense that it can be wildly popular, as such regimes have been in many fascist and other nations historically. The popular election of an anti-constitutional regime is itself a failure of democracy; a polity democratically votes to end democracy.[7] That failure may lead to the loss of liberty, but it is not itself a failure of liberty.

The fact that we can readily recognize the infraction of a personal liberty gives reason to defend liberties through individual actions—that is, of necessity, through courts rather than through majoritarian devices. It is not merely that we need to fear a tyranny of the majority, but also that we should doubt the capacity of a majority to act on its own behalf in general defense of liberties. The generalized logic of liberties might seldom impress itself upon citizens. The specific violation of my liberty, however, will immediately impress itself upon me. Hence, although we have a genuinely collective interest in various liberties, we should want to have them enforced on behalf of individuals.

In this respect, liberties can be handled to some extent the way we might want other collective allocations to be handled: individually. That is to say that, ideally, we could reduce collectively provided goods to individually provided goods. This move is not possible for collective bads, and it might be inefficient for many collective goods. As long as there is great demand for such goods and for the regulation of such bads, therefore, we can expect politics to be multidimensional, and we can expect voters to be rationally ignorant of their own interests and of candidates' positions on all the dimensions they face. Finally, we can also expect that voters can no longer simply rely on traditional left-right parties to represent their interests on all these dimensions.

One can actually go further, to say that there are collective implications of individual liberty, and that these may actually entail benefits to others from your own private liberty. In brief, the argument is this. If, for example, your rights of free speech are abridged, typically by some local authority, you can take that authority to court to seek to have your rights protected and honored. When you do that, you automatically help to secure the rights of others in your society. Hence, although you ostensibly

---

[7]This is a much more general problem in the conflict of democracy (majority rule) and liberties (in a sense, individuals rule). See, further, Narveson 2002.

seek an individual benefit, you effectively help to provide a collective good. One might speak of this, in Mancur Olson's (1965) terminology, as an instance of a group that is privileged in the provision of its collective good. One person values the good highly enough to provide it essentially for all. Collective action on behalf of a whole society is typically hard to motivate. Action that has benefits to an enormous collection of people but that is justified already for a single individual is a rare category. Yet, through a bit of legal magic, the defense of individual rights has this extraordinary collective quality. One often hears of the logic of rights. This bit of magic in securing collective interests through individual actions is the grand logic of rights.

One might raise two objections to this argument. First, some might not actually value the right to free speech, and might prefer to be able to block many kinds of speech rather than to protect it. Of course, that can be true and often is; and it probably is true of most of the individual rights protected in any constitution that some people would rather they not be protected. It is still the case, however, that in defending my right to free speech I am simultaneously defending your right, independently of whether you want to exercise that right or you want me not to.

Second, one might argue that, case by case, there will commonly be losers in any decision to protect someone's right. The reason to take one's case to court would be that someone else has blocked one's exercise of a right, and presumably that someone loses if the courts protect the right. Moreover, a claim of right for one party often entails a claim that some other party has a duty. Again, the issue here is not that each individual defense of a right is itself not without losers, but rather that protecting the right generally is desirable for certain citizens or even virtually all citizens. The design of rights comes prior to actions, and it generally would not make sense to argue for a right exclusively in an individual context or case by case. In court, you may defend your right to act in a certain way, but you do so in defense of a right that was created in the law before your action. Your successful defense helps secure that right for others thereafter.

Incidentally, although Thomas Jefferson and others characterized certain rights as natural, the defense of the original Bill of Rights of the U.S. constitution seems clearly to have been animated by the view that protection of these rights would serve the mutual advantage. Many of those rights were directed at abusive practices of the British Crown. There was possibly little chance that the new U.S. government would ever have commandeered private homes of citizens to house soldiers, but the English practice of doing so still rankled; and the U.S. Congress strongly supported the adoption of an explicit constitutional prohibition of any such actions by the U.S. government. Today, it is probably far more common to defend rights in terms that were not those of the generation of James

Madison by claiming that they contribute to Kantian or Millian autonomy. Madison's welfarist defense did not depend on such later views.[8]

In this respect, political theory is similar to legal theory. The best way
to protect me legally against, say, theft is to have prohibitions on everyone, including me. I cannot expect any support for solipsistic law that
prohibits all others but allows license to me alone. As Hobbes ([1651]
1994, chap. 16, ¶8) notes, law was arguably brought into existence to
limit the "natural liberty" of particular men. It does that by limiting all,
but some of us, perhaps even the overwhelming majority of us, might
not require the constraints of law to keep us from major offenses against
others.

Ironically, both the form of liberties and the strategy for defending
them fit the Austrian theory. They are both individualized. True, my going
to court to enforce my right in some context contributes to the collective's
interest in maintaining the same right. But my action is wholly motivated
by my interests, except to the degree that others, such as the American
Civil Liberties Union, join my case in court. I want the individual protection but it is available only collectively.

LIBERTY AND WELFARE

If individuals give heavy weight to welfare values, the Austrian vision is
essentially utilitarian.[9] But even if individuals do not focus on welfare values, one could still think that a kind of Austrian laissez faire is correct for
social relations. Some society might not give heavy weight to welfare values, and therefore need not be particularly utilitarian, but that would be
because its citizens, as individuals, did not give heavy weight to welfare
values. In the Austrian vision each citizen in such a society should be left
free of constraint, with the result that welfare would not be collectively
very important, even though it might be important to some individuals—
all subject to some variant of Mill's harm principle that says an individual is free to do anything so long as the action does not harm anyone
else.[10] The welfare of those to whom welfare is important might suffer
substantially from the low level of overall productivity because, for ex-

[8]These later views make rights-protections a moral rather than a constitutional issue.
They are largely irrelevant to extant constitutional provisions in the United States.

[9]It is ordinal utilitarian, because there is no theory of how to add welfare or utility across
individuals to get a sum of utility. In ordinal utilitarianism, we can say that one state of affairs is better than another if everyone is better off in it. Hence, the theory is one of mutual
advantage. See, further, Hardin 1988b, chap. 3.

[10]Mill calls this a simple principle ([1859] 1977, chap. 1, ¶9, p. 223). The massiveness of
the literature commenting on it suggests that it is not all that simple.

ample, my welfare is arguably more the result of the overall welfare of my own society than it is of my personal efforts. And in any case, my welfare is heavily influenced by the range of opportunities provided by my society.

In our actual world, with the virtually inescapable interaction between states and peoples, it might be very difficult for any society to become autarkic in its social values, and to give little weight to welfare values. It is difficult because, in any society that is left very far behind in economic development, large sections of the populace are likely to want greater prosperity, and to want the consumptions that are available in prosperous societies. Hence, we may experience what the critics of globalization bemoan, which is the seeming westernization of every society. A distressing aspect of such "forces" is that, although many people might wish to live in a non-westernized society, they can generally do so only at the price of suppressing the desires of their many compatriots who share many of the supposedly western values. It is not practically possible to create genuinely autarkic societies that can survive without at least some of their citizenry succumbing to the blandishments of greater material prosperity.

It is perhaps in this Austrian vision of social order that we can see most clearly why economic and political theories were joined in the work of Hume and others in the rational choice school. They were joined not because they had the same value theory, even though they generally assumed welfare values. The central, fundamental feature was, rather, that they were grounded in *individual* values, whatever those might be. Political philosophy need have no value theory at base. It can merely posit the structure of institutions that enable people to seek their own individual values.

It would be wrong, in the shibboleth of our time, to say that the institutions could be neutral, that is, that they would have no effect on what values people sought. A massively coercive religious state could have great impact on individual values, as seems to be shown by the cases of Iran under the Ayatollahs, and of Afghanistan under the Taliban. But liberal economic and political institutions likely would substantially undercut such values, as the Taliban and Ayatollahs clearly realize. An individual immersed in a licentious society can find it difficult to sustain personal adherence to a rigidly religious or moralistic value system. Some value systems therefore seem likely to require specific institutional supports, and it is prima facie false to suppose that any institution can be neutral with respect to all values or value systems.

What seems to be evident, however, is that individuals left to their own values commonly have strong welfarist preferences, although the occasional Blaise Pascal might prefer asceticism. Market economic and liberal political institutions allow them to pursue those values. In both cases, the central theoretical move is to create institutions that let individuals seek their own values, which in experienced fact generally means to seek their own welfare to a substantial extent. The institutions of market economics and of liberal politics are mutual-advantage and in both economics and politics the underlying individual value theory is own-welfare. These two—own-welfare and mutual advantage—work well together, the first at the individual level and the second at the aggregate level.

Critics of consumerism and welfarism (can one genuinely object to welfare?) often suppose that people are manipulated into having the strong welfarist urges that we witness. Barry Schwartz (1986), for example, frames his criticism of contemporary welfarism as "the battle for human nature." The battle that he sees is carried out by academics with variant visions of human nature. That would be merely an academic debate, perhaps even in the derogatory sense of that phrase. Sometimes, however, Schwartz's claim seems to be that economic theory has itself reformed the values of masses of people. This seems implausible, without a lot of argument to demonstrate the intervening causal connections between academic visions and popular visions. What seems far more likely is that individuals put in the way of various material and nonmaterial pleasures find them to be very appealing, and they seek them, work for them, and give over much of their lives for them.

The drive for many of these pleasures must be programmed into us biologically, and all the blandishments of advertising and commercial exposure can at most only heighten them or make them more urgent. Even under the most rigorous institutions, determined to block such drives, they will out. Some of our pleasures, such as opera and high-style food, seem so artful and so far removed from most human existence that one might even think them contrived. But many people seem genuinely and deeply motivated by such pleasures, and one could as well say that their beauty is among the great achievements of civilization as say that their appeal is somehow false or unnatural. It is not economic or social theory that has produced preferences for such consumptions, but experience itself. Indeed, such consumptions do not much appeal to some of the academic theorists whom Schwartz and others think to be misguided.

Ironically, at least one of those critics, Allan Bloom (1987), was among the most sybaritic of academics, and among the most dependent on the larger framework of the commercial society, that he seemingly deplored. It seems likely that he fully understood his relationship to that commercial society and that he thought it reasonable to value that society for what it did for him, even while holding it to be a corrupting influence on others.[11] In such a view, he would be, like Edmund Burke, a conservative

---

[11]Saul Bellow's character Ravelstein is modeled on Bloom, and represents him as having such views. See Bellow, *Ravelstein* (2000).

elitist whose criticisms were more of other people than of the society itself, because no society could be built on an elite class by itself.

Concluding Remarks

Madison essentially proposed a government of decentralization of enterprise to individuals. This was before the rise of the modern corporation, and before corporations put enormous pressure on the maintenance of an Austrian state as nonintrusive (Berle and Means 1932; also see Hardin 2004b). Ironically, the first modern American corporation rose while Madison was president of the United States.[12] The nearest equivalent to Madisonian theory in the twentieth century has been Austrian economics, as represented by Hayek and others. Theirs is ostensibly an economic theory, but in fact, as noted earlier, its most cogent insights lie essentially in broad social theory.

An especially odd aspect of the current hegemony of Austrian and Madisonian views, even if without those labels attached, is that the Austrian and Madisonian views as articulated by Hayek and Madison are almost purely theoretical. In their times there was no way to test their visions on the ground. But now the decentralist vision has been and is being tested, and it seems to be doing very well. Madison himself was not willing to practice his theory once he got in office, and perhaps Hayek and others would not have been either had they gained political office. But the comparison of the Soviet world, admittedly a bad version of socialist statism, and the sometimes severely trammeled markets of the more prosperous West give us a chance to see a crude, perhaps second-best test of the Austrian-Madisonian views played out. The economic theory of knowledge implies that we can have clumsy, intrusive government or we can have liberal, limited government.

The overwhelming difficulties of an epistemology that is not grounded in decentralization wreck the prospects of a deliberate instantiation of any egalitarian or Rawlsian system of distributive justice. John Rawls's enterprise in practice would require a relatively thorough political-sociological theory of what form of society would produce the best—or any—achievement of distributive justice. But this would require a theory of what form of society would be most creative and productive. It is inconceivable that we can even vaguely approach such a theory. We cannot even assess which of two serious contenders among extant orders or potential orders comes closer to egalitarian distributive justice.

[12]The first corporation with a significant number of stockholders, all of them minority stockholders, was the first of the large New England textile mills, organized in Waltham, Massachusetts, in 1813 (Berle and Means 1932, 10–11).

What is more important for the large part of the world that now faces liberalization of politics and economics is that this program cannot handle the radical problem of economic development: equality now or greater prosperity for all later. There can be no natural experiment in limited government as there was in 1789 and thereafter in the United States. Politics today cannot develop more or less in silence and out of sight—we know too much for it to catch us entirely by surprise.

The focus on knowledge elements of social order suggests concern with intellectual and economic development. One might argue against such development, as the Taliban, the Ayatollahs, and many other fundamentalist religious sects do. But no one can sensibly argue against it per se, because to do so would be to favor the most primitive level of development. One could only argue against further development beyond some point. What point? Where we are now, presumably? Even then, how can we recommend rigorous ignorance of anything new or different? Ending development is incoherent with liberalism, with the decentralization of creativity and initiative, and with autonomy, however defended. Such a liberalism cannot centrally direct the end of technical and economic progress, because it cannot control individuals so extensively.

In closing, note that, arguably, the twentieth-century U.S. president who best approximated to the Madisonian ideal was William Howard Taft (1909–1913), who lost re-election in a three-way contest against two ardent centralizing statists: Theodore Roosevelt and Woodrow Wilson (Chace 2004). Wilson's victory in that election put an end to substantially limited government in the modern Untied States. As if to mimic the idea of limited government, Taft was a relatively weak president. Weakness has been characteristic of many one-term presidents—perhaps the electorate misunderstands its own interests and prefers strong presidents who might then intrude into their lives in unwonted and unwanted ways. If knowledge is distributed, any claim to grasp it fully at the center is false. As in D.C. Williams's characterization of the inherent weakness of the liberal position of skepticism, as quoted a few pages above, the electorate takes the claims of near certainty too seriously and votes for self-assertively strong candidates, who will become misguided officeholders.

CHAPTER 5

Moral Knowledge

WHY DO PEOPLE have the moral views they have? This question suggests many issues. I wish to address only the general structure of the ordinary person's learning of morals. I will not address the moral theorist's program of justifying morality or a particular moral theory. Rather, I will focus on the plausible nature of common reasoning about morality. In rough outline, reasoning about morality must be quite similar to practical reasoning in dealing with other matters on which we must act, and must therefore decide or reason through what to do. Reasoning about morality will turn on the moral knowledge available to the reasoner. That knowledge would have been gained in ways similar to the learning of any other knowledge. An immediately obvious fact of ordinary morality is that the ordinary person does not specialize in moral theory. Those who do specialize in it often create arcane theories that are far beyond the ken of ordinary people. Such theory is essentially irrelevant to our understanding of ordinary persons' morality.[1]

A common move in much of contemporary moral theory and criticism is to test the theory under consideration against "our" moral beliefs. If the theory does not match those beliefs, intuitions, or so-called common sense, the theory is presumed to fail. If this device makes sense, then we should shelve all our moral theories and simply act from our intuitions. In *The Methods of Ethics* Henry Sidgwick, the great Victorian moral philosopher, makes a nearly opposite move in his account of the method of utilitarianism. He supposes that commonsense morality has a utilitarian basis (Sidgwick 1907, 423–59). Sidgwick's is a complicated sociological and psychological claim that neither he nor many others who have made it have backed with much compelling argument. I wish to defend this claim from the perspective of the economic theory of ordinary knowledge. Our knowledge about anything, including morals, should fit this theory, as will follow from an analysis of the commonsense foundations of practical reasoning about morality, which is to say, the foundations of ordinary persons' reasoning.

Immediately one may object that there are grievous difficulties in supposing there are foundations for such reasoning. An obvious major

---

[1]Richard Posner, a federal judge on the seventh circuit, supposes that what he calls academic moralism is also far beyond what can be expected of judges (Posner 1999, chap. 1).

difficulty in the commonsense foundations of morality is the inherent nature of practical reasoning in general, especially with respect to acquiring relevant knowledge. Another, which especially bothers philosophers, is skepticism about the objectivity of morality. Yet another, which may be related to problems of objectivity at the level of theory but need not depend on it, is what Sidgwick (1907, 507–9) calls the dualism of practical reason and motivation. In this dualism, practical reasoning may give me a reason for acting in some way. If there are practical reasons for acting morally, as Sidgwick seems to believe there are, these may conflict with reasons for acting in one's self-interest. This duality is a problem that affects ethics in its practical application. But it may also affect the content of our moral knowledge, though it seems unlikely to affect many other kinds of practical knowledge.

For Sidgwick, reason seems to provide us good grounds for making universal claims in moral theory, and also provides good grounds for first or even exclusive concern with self. If we suppose that that motivation is not innately determined by our recognition of the rightness of a moral theory, these considerations of practical reason leave us with a potential conflict of motivations. We can characterize Sidgwick's "dualism of practical reason as a conflict between a utilitarian account of duty and an egoistic or prudential account of rationality" (Brink 1988. 303). Unfortunately for universalizing moral theory, motivation seems for most people to fit reasoned concern with the self much more forcefully than it fits concern with universal well-being.

Again, I will focus on the nature of practical reasoning about morals. To the extent it affects such reasoning, I will take up Sidgwick's dualism of reason. There is, of course, an enormous contemporary literature on what constitutes a reason for acting, a literature that goes well beyond the relatively simple formulation of this issue by Sidgwick. I will not attempt to bring that large philosophical literature to bear on the problem of the dualism of practical reasoning, but will address the dualism as only an aspect of the ordinary person's reasoning about morality.[2] An economic account of reasoning about morality that did not consider this dualism would be flawed, simply because the dualism is essentially a problem of motivation, which is the core of an economic account.

Throughout the discussion, note that in any views on commonsense moral knowledge the focus must be on our collective knowledge, not my knowledge or your knowledge or the knowledge of any other lone person. Despite this emphasis on the social origins of our moral knowledge,

---

[2]That literature is at once too complex and too simplistic for understanding the ordinary person's reasoning. It is philosophically too artful; and it often far too trivially focuses on nonstrategic actions, such as turning on a light (Hardin 1988b, 68–70).

such knowledge is not different from other practical knowledge. With moral knowledge, however, it is extremely difficult to imagine that it could have any other than a social origin. Socially constructed knowledge and morals may be incoherent in various ways that may turn on the aggregation or blending of individual motivations. We might attempt to treat what Sidgwick calls the common man's views as merely a problem of the internal structure of an individual's views, but such an attempt is likely to involve a fallacy; much of the content of the individual's views, perhaps virtually all of it, will come from collective understandings and views. If most of my knowledge is socially received, an internal analysis of my personal body of knowledge cannot get at the issues that bother Sidgwick. What we need is an external, social account, but one that is grounded in the nature of individual action and knowledge.

INDIVIDUAL MORAL KNOWLEDGE

When you face a moral (or any other practical) decision, you have available to you a lot of knowledge obtained in various ways about many things, few of them relevant to the choice you face. You may also be able to find more knowledge that is specifically relevant to the choice at hand. If you are motivated by a particular, explicit morality, your actual choice will be a function of the bits of knowledge you have. Some of that knowledge might count as moral beliefs, some of it as beliefs about objective states of the world. But you might not know enough to keep these categories straight.

As a user of your knowledge, your pragmatic problem is not so much how confident you are of the correctness of your knowledge, but merely of the confidence you have in that knowledge relative to other bits of alternative knowledge. You might hesitate to make strong claims for the rightness of your knowledge, but you might not have the luxury of hesitating very long in acting on it. When we later judge your action—whether its rationality or its morality—we should judge according to the pragmatic considerations that drove *you*. The answer to the question, "Was it moral (or rational) of you to do what you did in some particular situation?," depends on whether your action was morally (or rationally) consistent with your knowledge at the time. The answer does not depend on whether your action was in some more general sense the best thing one could have done in that situation. Rather, the answer depends on your life history.

Why does the economics of knowledge or belief matter for a utilitarian or any other consequentialist moral theory? A theory of practical knowledge is necessary for reaching normative judgments about normative claims. If I wish to say you were morally at fault for choosing one action rather than another, I will have to assume that you understood your actions well enough, or that you were culpably ignorant for any failure to understand your actions. Some of your beliefs might be wrong but not culpably so. For example, most people a couple of centuries ago did not know the microbe theory of contagious diseases. The massive growth and articulation of science since then means that not even a scientist can understand the findings of the specialists in other fields. Indeed, the methodology for your knowing many things in your own field is different from that for knowing virtually anything in other fields. The methodology of trusting the practitioners is a compromise. As of right now you cannot know as well as they can. But this is a perhaps complex variant of the "ought implies can" problem. You cannot know those things better; therefore it cannot be true that you ought to. Perhaps you could have come to know them better, but probably only by forgoing the stronger knowledge you have in your own field. But again, as of right now you cannot know them.

This view of the role of knowledge in a claim of moral responsibility calls into question the standard utilitarian move to look to the actual consequences of actions for summary judgment of their morality. This move requires that the judge has a superior methodology for reaching the correct judgment of what to do. Perhaps a particular judge does have. But this cannot be a claim for a transparent trump. The trump cannot be seen for what it is from its simply being laid on the table. Typically, it must be argued and defended against the actor's own judgment. Moreover, the actor being criticized for moral failure did not have the trump argument when it was needed. But it would be foolish to say that those faced with decisions should not act until they have perfect understanding—they will never have perfect understanding. In a utilitarian account, actors can only be judged by what they know or reasonably believe, and by how their actions fit with their knowledge. What we need, therefore, for making moral assessments of actions is a plausible theory of the actor's knowledge. The economic theory of knowledge is a compelling account of the actor's knowledge, and of the meaning of its being called "reasonable."

On the economic theory of morally relevant knowledge, the demands of morality might seem stricter for you than for me. You may know much more about relevant causal relations than I, and you may also be more accustomed to and, therefore, more adept at figuring out what action is right in some context. Indeed, it may typically be true that a moral theorist faces sterner demands than the average person faces. The moral theorist is specialized—just as the auto mechanic or the dentist is—and should be expected to perform better at her specialty than those who are not specialized.

TESTING MORAL THEORIES AGAINST COMMON SENSE

Before turning to the general thesis on moral knowledge, let us consider first what is the nature of the contemporary claim that theories may be tested by their fit with commonsense morality. Perhaps the claim is based on an assumption that we have encoded within our minds some kind of true morality, as in the view of Thomas Reid ([1764] 1970; [1788] 1969). This morality might be limited to a handful of rules, or it might be quite extensive. That this inherited set of principles could be a complete moral theory was once a common view. For some, this view followed from the supposition that morality has a content analogous to that of mathematics or logic, about which our rational inquiry can lead us to correct results. Among the most extreme variants of this view is that of H. A. Prichard ([1912] 1968), 17), who supposes that we have a moral faculty that allows us simply to see the rightness or wrongness of various actions. He says that those who are properly brought up need only let their "moral capacities of thinking do their work." Apparently, Prichard's faculty cannot be taught to anyone past schoolboy age. This is an interesting ethological constraint, analogous to the ethological constraints on the development of the brain that prevent a person who has never encountered language from acquiring it after about age twelve, or that prevents a bird from learning to chirp in the song of its species if it does not hear the relevant chirping before some age.[3]

It seems unlikely that any of these positions can yield objections to any moral theory on the ground that it violates "our" intuitions about whether some action is right or wrong. We are not endowed with any such faculty as Prichard needs for his moral theory. Of course, intuitions of various kinds are clearly necessary for virtually all moral theories. Indeed, intuitions of some kind are necessary for mathematics, for the sciences, for common sense. But intuitions in such fields are typically held subject to testing, or to weighing against alternatives, or for logical and conceptual fit. Even once rock-solid intuitions about the geometry of space have been chiseled down by Einstein's theory of relativity and later advances in physics. To suppose that one could have a correct intuition about the rightness of always telling the truth seems utterly preposterous. One might have systematic intuitions, such as about fairness or welfare or of the scaffolding of Kant's complex moral theory, from which a relatively focused substantive conclusion could be deduced. But *a direct substantive intuition* about lying or any other ordinary action cannot be compelling.

[3]Ethologists can cruelly rear a bird in isolation to test this claim. For humans, they must rely on accidental cases of children who have grown up in the wild, such as the wild boy of Aveyron (Lane 1976).

In any field but ethics, holding such intuitions with deep commitment, despite lack of theoretical or empirical warrant, would be seen as an intellectual disqualification. As Brandt (1979: 21) cogently says, "it is puzzling why an intuition—a normative conviction—should be supposed to be a test of anything."

For others, the supposition that we are imbued with moral views followed from the—usually theological—supposition that humans were created with whatever faculties they have already in place. Sidgwick (1876b, esp. 55) argues that the theory and broad understanding of evolution, which implies a long historical derivation of our instincts and capacities, undercuts the theological view. Without some remarkably inventive argument, such a view is not tenable for anyone who does not believe that a deity created us with such rules or principles in place and ready for use.

A much more limited version of the view could follow from sociobiological claims about the development of action-guiding principles that might be genetically selected because they contribute to the survival of groups of humans. But such a set of moral principles cannot be sufficiently articulate to give us useful tests of much more general and complete moral theories than what might have been selected (Hardin 2006c). Moreover, it seems plausible that inconsistent rules would have been selected. For example, a strong instinct for self-interest must surely have been selected. In practice, this instinct might then conflict with any instinct for altruism or benevolence that might also have been selected. Even apart from their likely inconsistency with one another, the fact that action-guiding principles are selected by evolution does not make them right on any but a purely naturalistic theory—as Sidgwick (1876b) concludes in his criticism of Herbert Spencer. The morals of tyrannosaurus rex must have differed significantly from those of trilobites and those of humans. It is obviously not such a sociobiological view that motivates the commonsense critics of moral theories.

Finally, a perhaps less limited version of the view could follow from social selection of principles—not genetic selection. These principles may survive through being passed on to others by learning, or through the creation of institutions that survive their original justifications.[4] This form of establishing the "truth" of moral principles, however, shades into something similar to the cognitive processes of working out a moral theory. And it has an air of relativism if it is conceivable that we could have developed different, contrary principles that would survive. It also does not work in general (see further discussion below).

[4]G. E. Moore (1903, esp. chap. 5) argues for such a view; F. A. Hayek makes similar arguments, apparently without recognizing that they are utilitarian, in various works (e.g. Hayek 1960, 67). For a brief discussion, see Hardin 1988b, 14–18.

It seems unlikely that any of these positions can yield objections to any moral theory on the ground that it violates "our" intuitions about whether some action is right or wrong. There is another way to put contemporary commonsense objections to moral theories, however, that may be more defensible in principle. That way is suggested by the sometime phrasing of the critics that a result of some theory runs counter to "our best-considered judgments." The chief difficulty with this phrasing is that most theorists might readily claim themselves to have come to their own best-considered judgments. If the critics mean this, they are merely conceited solipsists who claim, "*My* best considered judgment differs from yours and that proves you wrong." If the critics are making a claim that is worthy of attention, they must mean something more explicit with their invocation of "our."

What might be a compelling content for the commonsense criticism? One possibility is that the critics are saying something analogous to Sidgwick's view of the limits of reason in ascertaining what is moral:

> On any theory, our view of what ought to be must be largely derived, in details, from our apprehension of what is; the means of realising our ideal can only be thoroughly learnt by a careful study of actual phenomena; and to any individual asking himself "What ought I to do or aim at?" it is important to examine the answers which his fellowmen have actually given to similar questions. (Sidgwick 1907, 2)

Commonsense morality, and the apparent intuitions we have about rightness and goodness, may grow out of our moral debate, theorizing, and practice. We might start by supposing, with Sidgwick (1907, xxi), that evolution might have given us moral views or sentiments. Or we might merely choose to treat others with respect for their views, at least tentatively, while we work out a clear position. But we might still follow a utilitarian (or other) moral principle whenever it seems clear and compelling, either in the more or less abstract or from past experience.

John Rawls ([1971] 1999: [20–21] 18) calls his own such reasoning about morality the "method of reflective equilibrium." That method involves little more than giving serious attention to the weight of prior collective wisdom on our subject, while also attempting to bring theoretical order to it, letting neither theory nor collective wisdom always trump the other, but going back and forth between the two and letting each correct the other. This is the method of much of the greatest moral philosophy over the past few millennia. It is clearly outlined by Sidgwick in manuscript notes for a lecture on the development of his own thought (Sidgwick 1907, xv–xxi) and is raised in context throughout his *Methods of Ethics,* although he does not call it a method (also see Sidgwick 1876a). The collective wisdom at issue is not merely that of past philosophers and writers on these subjects but that of social practices and norms that have arisen in various ways. Again, Sidgwick thinks the study of commonsense morality is attractive because our underlying morality is in fact utilitarian. If he is right, it is ironic that, in contemporary writings, commonsense morality is commonly invoked to prove utilitarianism false.

A striking feature of this view of the role of collective wisdom in moral thinking is that it is similar to the role of collective wisdom in practical reasoning more generally. Almost all of what I might claim to know rests on my accepting authoritative assertions by others. Some of these others know some of the same things I do, but more nearly directly, at least in part. In the lives of many people, moral knowledge may have essentially the same character as any other practical knowledge.

Remarkably, such sloppiness in our practical reasoning and in our ground for belief may not get much in our way. Often the best reason for believing something is to know that almost everyone else believes it (Margolis 1987, 135). Many causal and other relationships we know only from experience. But a causal account of most of the things we "know" would demand far more theory than we can master. If we try radically to manipulate variables, we change the problem to one far beyond our present pragmatic understanding, and we may lose all mooring (Sidgwick 1907, 467–74; see, further, Hardin 1988b, 22–29). Accepting what others believe is often smarter than attempting to bore deeper on our own.

Practical knowledge for most of us most of the time is inherently without foundations—or at least without anything that would count as foundations in a philosophical theory of knowledge (see, further, Brink 1989, 100–122). If we are willing to accept certain things, then certain other things follow. At first consideration we might not, on this framing, wish to conclude that we then know those other things. We might suppose we know them only if the things we might be willing to accept are themselves known. But these things are in the consequent clauses of other, similar if-then statements. There is no place to begin with any of our knowledge of the world. We merely do accept many things, and therefore we can get started on mastering other things. As Sidgwick ([1895]1905: 427) writes: "It is as true of the intellectual as of the physical life that living somehow is prior to living ideally well: and if we are to live at all, we must accept some beliefs that cannot claim Reason for their source."[5] Skepticism about knowledge that cannot be "better" grounded than such acceptance virtually on faith is an artifact of theorizing. All of our knowledge is finally based on mere acceptance of some of its bases.

[5]As quoted in chapter 1, Wittgenstein (1969: §344), speaking pragmatically rather than morally, says essentially the same thing: "My life consists in my being content to accept many things."

Our beliefs do not come to us one by one. Neither can an individual come by all beliefs one by one in any order. They come more or less in packages. We make sense of them only by their fit with other beliefs, and even by the ways they help make sense of our other beliefs. This is, however, not necessarily a demand for complete consistency or coherence, which are likely impossible for any important beliefs (see Davidson [1970] 1980, 221).

The general issue here may just sound like an ordinary person's problem. That it is not is suggested by the development of economics over the past century or so. Economics became an articulate, relatively successful enterprise when it became antifoundationalist. Marginal-utility analysis takes place against a background of what we might call gross or absolute utility (the numerically added sum of the utility of everyone), except that it is not at all clear what gross utility could be. Given an acceptance of this background, however, marginal analysis makes very good sense and can be very powerful. It was in the long intellectual struggle to make sense of gross utility that the idea of the marginal theory was developed, but the marginal theory is itself the starting point for neoclassical economics, in which additive or gross utility is rejected.

If our practical knowledge cannot be traced back to clearly understandable foundations, then seemingly we must enter it laterally as much as hierarchically. Practical knowledge grows by sideways augmentation, the accretions overlapping extant knowledge. Moreover, we might be unable to take an overview of all of it to test it for coherence. We might quickly recognize that incoherence and inconsistency are problems when they become evident, but we might often miss inconsistencies merely for want of effort, logical capacity, or sufficient completeness to make various connections. This rough view is part of the economic theory of ordinary knowledge, and it may be Sidgwick's (1907, 509) own view. In general, we cannot require of people that they master logic or probabilistic thinking in order to count as rational, although it is often said that people have a duty to know more or better (Montmarquet 1993; Hall and Johnson 1998). On the criterion of even barely mastering probabilistic reasoning, evidently almost no one was rational until about four centuries ago.

For anyone concerned with practical uses of knowledge rather than with knowledge per se or its justification, the question of why we know what we know may be more important than that of how we know or ought to know it. Why do I know the things I know, whereas you know other things? Principal reasons are that, in street language, the things I know came cheaper to me than many other things and they pay me better. In quick summary, the answer to the question why we know what we know is that the content of what we know is largely adventitious.

Before proceeding, note that, on the economic account of practical reasoning, I face constraints, I do not choose them. If I could escape them, I would. One of the constraints on my actions this moment is the limit of my past investments in learning that could be applied to my choice of actions now. In some sense, I—or some past version of myself—did choose these constraints, but I did so in response to constraints that limited what investments I could make overall.[6]

Suppose you grew up among the Azande in central Africa before the intrusion of anthropologists, and you have a collection of beliefs many of which anyone who has grown up in an advanced industrial state would consider incontrovertibly wrong (Evans-Pritchard 1937). Indeed, if you'd grown up in a modern state and held such beliefs, we would hold you crazy. Yet it would be odd to call Azande beliefs crazy for the Azande. Why? Essentially because of the economics of belief. For an individual Zande the costs of knowing better might be egregious. More generally, we must suppose that individuals' intellectual histories matter for explanations of their views, knowledge, and theories. In various respects, the nature of such facts also matters for philosophical discussion.

The typical user's knowledge of morals must be similar in many respects to my knowledge of machines for producing my written documents. Such similarity is especially clear for the Azande, for whom moral and other practical considerations may be all cut from the same cloth. For us as children, they may also have been heavily interwoven. Much of the guidance that adults give to children is expressed in moral terms but is about the children's interests, and vice versa. For example, children are told that lying or breaking promises is wrong and, in virtually the same breath, they may be told that being untrustworthy harms their longer-run interests. Both claims are arguably true for truth telling and promise keeping. This is fortuitous for morality, because these cases usually bridge the dualism of practical reason that bothers Sidgwick by simply making morality consistent with self-interest (Sidgwick 1907, 508). As Hume says, whoever makes a promise "is immediately bound by his interest to execute his engagements, and must never expect to be trusted any more, if he refuse to perform what he promis'd" (Hume [1739–40] 2000, book 3, pt. 2.5, secs. 10–11). Promise-keeping is a convention, a social construction, not an a priori notion of the right, despite the massive literature that treats it otherwise. Under that convention, interest in maintaining a

[6]It is therefore wrong to think of constrained optimization here on analogy with David Gauthier's constrained maximization. Gauthier's (1986, esp. pp. 157–89) constraint is a deliberate choice of the agent to cooperate rather than defect in prisoner's dilemma interactions. On the economic account of knowledge, common sense does not constrain my optimization. Rather, common sense is constrained in its striving to optimize.

relationship or a reputation is the first obligation or reason for the performance of promises.

Perhaps we should conclude that it was a sly bit of persuasive definition that put truth telling and promise keeping in the category of the moral. The overwhelming bulk of cases of truth telling and promise keeping may be sufficiently motivated by self-interest, especially as enlightened by consideration of longer-run effects on one's reputation and relationships (Hardin 1988b, 59–65). If such commonplace problems of enlightened self-interest are given a moral gloss, morality may seem very attractive. Acting morally may even seem typically to fit the Socratic program of being shown to be identical with acting from self-interest. Then, in cases in which morality comes at a price, it may also come as a habit or an attitude that helps it override self-interest.

The great problem in morality is to justify to you that your very slight interest should not override a passing stranger's overwhelming interest. Simple reciprocity in ongoing relationships is not difficult to motivate, either from morality or from self-interest (Sidgwick 1907, 508). But self-interest would permit vicious disregard of the interests of another, especially a stranger, whereas morality would not. Law that is enforced can overcome vicious disregard in some contexts, such as, for example, in outlawing murder. But morality might work to override self-interest in contexts in which law alone cannot align self-interest with the interests of others, because using law for daily interactions would be prohibitively costly and unworkable. And one may wonder whether we do not live in more or less constant vicious disregard of some large number of people, such as those suffering starvation in the Sahel, or brutal rape and murder in Darfur.

THE STRATEGY OF KNOWING

Practical knowledge may be viewed as a whole or piecemeal. Many of our judgments of actions, perhaps especially the actions of others, are made piecemeal. My old car is slow to start and I flood it, ruining any chance of starting it for a while. You may say this is an irrational response to the problem, which could have been resolved easily without creating a new, harder problem. In an important sense, you may be right, of course. The analytically correct response to my car's slowness may be as you say it is. But in a larger, holistic sense, your criticism may be wrong. Yes, it would be better for me to do what you say, if only I knew it. But it might not be rational for me to know that in the first place. To know it requires happenstance experience with balky cars, from which I might finally have learned how to diagnose and handle them. Or it requires deliberate effort to learn more about the way they work, effort that might not pay off for my limited needs. It may also involve the grievous difficulty of remembering what I've learned if it is not somehow readily deducible once I begin to understand the workings of car engines. If it is merely a rule or a list of procedures, I may remember it only if it has to be invoked very often.

In sum, we may suppose that repeated experience and the expectation of more to come might justify my taking some trouble to learn more about things such as the workings of my car and might help me to remember what I've once learned. Our knowledge is a bit like government classification of knowledge; we bother to know some things only on a need-to-know basis. Once we take into consideration the costs of knowing certain things, we may readily conclude that knowing them is not worthwhile. For example, we let doctors handle some of our problems, although we may begin to second-guess doctors for a problem that we suffer over a long time, and that gets different treatments from different doctors. And most of us know very little about how the cars or other machines in our lives work. If it makes strategic sense not to invest in acquiring specialized knowledge because the investment will not pay, then, when I flood my car out of ignorance, it is perverse to say that my action is irrational per se.

Many of the subjects of vast numbers of experiments on rationality that seem to show people are irrational might better be seen as evidence that good reasoning is costly and not always worth mastering. Good reasoning with respect to a particular class of problems, such as dealing with cars that do not perform perfectly, may be harder to master for some than for others. It may be that some of those who perform badly in many experiments are more rational than those who perform well. They are more rational in a holistic sense that includes the costs of investing in specialized abilities. It is a standard line that to consider every case on its merits is not to consider the merits of the case. I may generally be rational to have some overview on how much one should be concerned with the details of the problem needing instant decision. This is not to say that we should have general theories of how to decide. Even habits will help greatly in lowering our overall costs of decision.

That a formal decision theorist performs better than typical experimental subjects follows in large part for the simple reason that she has invested heavily in understanding the relevant class of problems. Her motivations for such investment are that it presumably pays, not in improving her capacity for rational decision, but for its own sake in her career. It may be that she chose or happened into her career in part because she found the problems of decision theory especially interesting, and because she had natural talents for dealing with them. Still, it is unlikely that much of her mastery of the issues was directly pragmatic in the sense that she learned what she needed for making better decisions in her own life. Most of us could not plausibly justify even a small part of her investment for ourselves.

The background or holistic consideration of whether it is worthwhile to learn something is in many respects a more important issue in our grasp of practical reason than is the large question of foundations and their justification. This is not to say that people actually reason through the costs and benefits of investing in knowledge about, say, how their cars work or what is morally right. We may more often merely happen into our particular range of knowledge when we are pushed by needs to know in various moments, when we are accidentally put in the way of knowledge of some things, or when we have more interest in consuming a particular kind of knowledge as an end in itself than in using it as a means to other ends. For example, hobbyists and sports fans often consume the facts of their subjects because the consumption itself is pleasing or interesting.

A general theory of justified belief might ground the strength of belief in X in the effort taken to justify believing X. But this is wrongheaded. What I implicitly must first decide, case by case rather than a priori for every case, is how much it is worth to me to invest in testing my belief in X. Because every belief is inherently grounded in efforts that are more or less costly, and that must therefore trade off against efforts to ground other beliefs, it is perverse to construct a general theory of just any belief. It may be true that I would have less confidence in belief X just because I have not done much to test it, whereas I have much greater confidence in belief Y because I have done a lot to test it. But belief Y may be only loosely related to other strongly held beliefs, whereas X may be very tightly bound up with other beliefs.

The Economics of Moral Motivation

Sidgwick (1907, 506) concludes *The Methods of Ethics* on a note of grievous doubt. He notes that if we could assume a god of a kind that would punish wrongdoing and reward goodness, a utilitarian might reasonably suppose that the individual would then have motives of self-interest "to promote universal happiness to the best of his knowledge." We may come by our moral knowledge as we come by any other knowledge. But acting on my knowledge of how to start a car without flooding it may immediately benefit me, whereas acting on my moral knowledge may often more likely cost me.

The critical feature of the social evolution of practical knowledge that can serve the self-interest of those who learn it is that the knowledge can be tested in various ways. For example, I can use various software programs and discover which of them is best for my purposes. Although much of my knowledge is merely accepted from those around me or from the larger society, I am still the one who puts it to use on my own behalf. The collective wisdom may be influenced by all of us who use bits of that wisdom to serve our separate interests. If what serves my interests is relatively similar to what serves others' interests, the result will be fairly systematic testing of our wisdom to improve it with use.

The economic incentives for gaining knowledge may be biased in favor of nonmoral practical knowledge, in part because we may have far more occasion to need nonmoral knowledge. This initial bias in favor of gaining nonmoral knowledge may lead to increasing bias as further knowledge builds on extant knowledge. The general reason for much of morality is that individual interests conflict in ways that recommend that some individuals yield their interests to others. But, if from nothing more than greater experience or practice in obtaining our own interest, we may tend to see and seek to resolve issues in our own favor to the neglect of others' interests.

If social selection of moral rules and institutions is affected in these biased ways by the dualism of practical reason, we may have less reason to trust it than we have to trust social selection of machinery for writing or of other matters that serve our interest. The drive for acquisition of knowledge about matters of mere self-interest is more nearly univalent than is the drive for acquisition of knowledge about moral matters. We might therefore expect the former kind of knowledge to be less likely to fall into confusion.

Even institutions established to serve merely the self-interests of individuals fall prey to compositional problems in aggregating the effects of all our motivations. The actual structures of institutions that arise from individually motivated actions may be not only unintended but also perverse. There can be individually rational failures of collective action to generate collectively beneficial results. There can be individually rational failures of coordination that leave us repeatedly trapped in an inferior outcome. And there can be sensible resolutions of piecemeal problems that are not sensible resolutions of the overall collection of problems. All of these failings can result from strictly self-interested choices by all concerned.

Social Evolution of Collective Moral Knowledge

Suppose our moral rules take the form of norms that have evolved socially, as proposed largely without argument or compelling examples by G. E. Moore (1903, esp. chap. 5), Hayek (1960, 67), and many others. In the social evolution of pragmatic norms, which might often be seen as merely efficient and effective habits, the role of testing is clear in many prudential matters. Lack of such testing is a fundamental problem in the spontaneous discovery of good moral norms, especially if these are primarily for collective benefit. An issue is the sheer difficulty of carrying out tests of large numbers of trial norms. What the market or even a partial market can do for selection of what serves individual interests cannot be put to use for collective interests, especially for collective interests at or near the whole-society level. Selecting norms for dyadic and very small-number interactions may be relatively easy, because such norms may be very nearly congruent with enlightened self interest, as in the cases of promise-keeping and truth-telling. This will often not be true for larger-number interactions, unless these are norms for mere coordination on actions or outcomes that all prefer if all are coordinated (Hardin 1995, chaps. 4 and 5).

If there is a motivational problem, as in Sidgwick's dualism of practical reason, we may never succeed in testing a collective-action norm, because we may never have enough people following it to know whether it is generally beneficial. There are often great personal incentives to our trying to discover and to make use of scientific or useful truths, but typically there are no comparable direct personal incentives for discovering or making use of moral principles.

The worst problem for an argument that social norms must be generally beneficial, however, is that we can easily find examples of socially evolved norms that are not at all beneficial. Consider a woefully sad case. St. Kilda, an island lying west of Scotland, was once inhabited by a people with little outside contact, whose population and society collapsed over the course of the nineteenth century. Apparently, a chief reason for the collapse was an odd norm for infant care. It is believed that a mixture of fulmar oil and dung was spread on the wound where the umbilical cord was cut loose. The infants commonly died of tetanus soon afterwards. The first known tetanus death was in 1758, the last in 1891. Around the middle of the nineteenth century, eight of every ten children died of tetanus. By the time this perverse pragmatic norm was understood and antiseptic practices were introduced, the population could not recover from the loss of its children (Maclean 1980: 121–24). St. Kildans had followed this awful norm for more than a century. The last remnant of about three dozen people left the island in 1930 (142). (For other similarly destructive social practices, see Diamond 2005.)

One might suppose that a disastrous social norm cannot survive because the people, as in the case of the St. Kildans, finally cannot survive it. But a society with many norms is unlikely to depend for its survival on the beneficial consequences of every one of these. Hence, many could be not beneficial in even the most hopeful evolutionary vision. Social evolution is no guarantor of beneficial arrangements.

If we now add motivations of universalistic concern of unequal strength across individuals, the impact of those motivations will depend not only on their average strength relative to self-interest, and on the misfit between individually rational and collectively beneficial outcomes, but also on the distribution of those motivations. If stronger universalistic motivations tend to be associated with the leadership of institutions, they may be very effective. If they are randomly distributed, their effect may still be significant but less so.

To gain some purchase on understanding these issues, note that we may view the object of universalistic motivations in utilitarianism as a collective benefit that somehow aggregates individual interests. That is to say, collective and individual benefits or interests are not different in kind.

Suppose we are in a group that would benefit from universalistic actions by all of us. But we are afflicted by the dualism of practical reason, because each of us individually would be better off acting from individualistic rather than universalistic concerns. The position of each of us is analogous to that of someone involved in a collective-action problem of the provision of a collective benefit.

Suppose some of us have a greater relative concern for the collective benefit than do others who share an interest in its provision. This could happen either because we in fact directly benefit more or because we are more strongly motivated by universalistic considerations. The effect of either of these reasons will be the same, but our concern here is with the latter reason, the stronger universalistic motivation. That some of us have a stronger universalistic motivation means that it will often typically take fewer of us to act successfully for the collective interest, so that we are more likely to achieve the utilitarian result or at least to tend toward it. This is analogous to the provision of a straight collective good for which some of us have much more intense demand than others have. The group of intense demanders may face a less grievous problem of collective action than the overall group faces simply because the demanders are a smaller group.[7]

This result may seem perverse: at the same average level, an unequal distribution of universalistic motivations may produce better results than an equal distribution. Having a few Sidgwicks may do more to improve the world than having a slight addition to the average person's utilitarian commitments.

On this brief account, the collective result is achieved by voluntaristic action by all of us. Often, however, we will have institutions to produce

---

[7]For more extensive argument, framed for cases in which variation of direct individual benefits is the reason for differential actions, see Hardin 1982, 67–75.

collective results and to organize individual contributions to them. For our governance, Hume supposes we require a small number of people who, "being indifferent persons to the greatest part of the state, have no interest, or but a remote one, in any act of injustice; and being satisfy'd with their present condition, and with their part in society, have an immediate interest in every execution of justice, which is so necessary to the upholding of society." He further supposes that these few persons will be our governors, and that most people would be too self-interested to serve us well as governors (Hume [1739–40] 2000, book 3, pt. 2, sec. 7, ¶ 6).

Hume gives no account of why just those persons would come to be our governors. How might the distribution of universalistic motivations in governing institutions be causally related to their strength relative to self-interest? In a quasi-democratic institution, those who display universalistic motivations may be trusted more than others, and may therefore tend to be selected for leadership. But those who are more strongly motivated by self-interest may invest more in gaining leadership positions that are potentially rewarding. We might be better served by Pericles or Nicias, but Alcibiades or Cleon might successfully compete with them for leadership. There is no analytical answer to how the balance will tip in general.

In some ways, Hume is optimistic: he expects the occasional Pericles to be available. In other ways he is pessimistic: he thinks we cannot manage without a Pericles. Contrary to his apparent view, there may be good reasons for expecting even basically self-interested officials to act reasonably universalistically with respect to some aspects of larger public interests (Hardin 1988a).

Even when motivations are more nearly universalistic than individual, they may still fall far short of universality. Reinhold Niebuhr (1932, 91) remarks on the "ethical paradox" of patriotism, which "transmutes individual unselfishness into national egoism." It may be that patriotism generally has beneficial effects on the whole, as Mandeville ([1705, 1714] 1988; see also Holmes 1990) argues of individual egoism that "private vices beget public virtue."[8] Indeed, the so-called realist tradition that dominated Western theorizing in international relations during most of the twentieth century arose in reaction to what the realists thought were destructive moral claims. In particular, the realists reacted against Woodrow Wilson's plans for remaking the world, which they thought moralistic and destructive.

To justify his claim about the tendency of our socially selected norms and our institutions to be utilitarian, Sidgwick must suppose that the differential effects of the motivations behind these are ultimately utilitarian. Alternatively, one might argue for social selection of institutions and

[8]Patriotism has few advocates among moral theorists, but see MacIntyre 1984 and Rorty 1998.

norms that are more beneficial. Such an argument would have to be made at an aggregate level. In those groups or societies or nations that develop utilitarian norms and institutions, individuals thrive better than they do in those that do not. As a result, the group also thrives better. That is a complex argument that is likely to face insurmountable problems of factual accounting. It seems plausible that other forces for selection would swamp utilitarian forces, especially if selection involves survival in a contest between societies, and not merely selection within an isolated society (Sidgwick 1907, 470–74).

AUTHORITY AND MORAL KNOWLEDGE

Suppose we accept the account of the similarity between moral knowledge and other forms of knowledge. Nonmoral knowledge about how the world works is gained at costs that recommend economizing on how much we gain and, especially, relying on experts. As noted in chapter 1, virtually all that any person knows may rest on accepting authoritative assertions by others. In a society in which moral knowledge is typically enunciated by a single body or organization, such as the medieval Catholic church, one might expect relatively wide deference to authority on moral matters. In a society in which moral authority is in great dispute, as it is in many contemporary secular and multi-religious communities, authoritative assertions may be less trusted as guarantors of correct views. It may then be only the most commonly held views that one may readily accept on "authority." For example, almost all of us may accept the rightness of truth telling, but only most of the time (Nagel 1998; Nyberg 1993; Campbell 2001).

Suppose that an institutional authority, such as the earlier Catholic church, is widely accepted. Will its views tend to be utilitarian over time, as Sidgwick supposes? Unfortunately, its individual officials will face their own personal dualism of practical reason. They are apt in many contexts to tend to push views that benefit themselves and their associates in preference to pushing strictly universalistic views. This may be true even though there may be a tendency to select these officials for reasons of their greater universalistic commitments. For example, the demand or even supposedly divine command that people tithe a tenth of their annual produce or income to support the church must surely involve a dualism of motivation on the part of church officials, who enjoy the luxury that the tithe affords them.

Other kinds of institutions, such as those that seek material gains, may often be constructed in such ways as to match official incentives with the interests of those whom the institutions are to serve. Such institutions need have little conflict of motivations other than the usual conflicts over whether to cheat under threat of penalty, either from the law or from loss of reputation. We who wish to economize on our knowledge may readily follow the lead of such institutions and let them be our authorities for certain kinds of knowledge.

Those who concede moral authority to various institutional leaders might, on the contrary, recognize the betrayal they suffer. For example, many alternatives to the Roman church were groups, including such orders as the Jesuits and such renegades as the Lutherans, who objected to the apparent luxury of the lives of many priests and, especially, of the papal regime in Rome. Some part of the intensity of feelings among East Germans toward Erich Honecker and his fellow governors and among Romanians toward the Ceausescus in 1989 must have come from the sense that these leaders of an egalitarian ideology had benefited far, far more than equally.

This is a much too cursory account of the likelihood that institutionalized moral authorities may be as trustworthy and as trusted as institutionalized authorities over other realms of knowledge. But it seems implausible that Sidgwick's claims that our commonsense moral principles are driven by utilitarian concerns could be grounded in the special quality of institutionalized moral authority.

CONCLUDING REMARKS

The foundations of the typical person's knowledge are in sand; there is no bedrock. For many people the claims of moral knowledge may be as compelling and valid as those of any other kind of knowledge. There is no more reason to put the theorist's scare quotes around "knowledge" when it is preceded by "moral" than when it stands alone, at least when we are speaking of the knowledge of ordinary people. Moral knowledge generally gives reasons for acting morally; other kinds of knowledge give reasons for acting both morally and self-interestedly.

This dualism in our reasons for action may be seen as a conflict between self-interest and morality in our motivations. The dualism may finally contribute to skepticism for ordinary people. If part of our tradition of moral knowledge picks out certain people or role holders as moral, but our experience suggests they are morally deficient, our whole tradition may be cast into doubt. Contemporary scandals in the Catholic church might end by undercutting beliefs and membership. Moral commitments that are socially derived are at risk when social cues are mixed, as they must be if they come from individuals who are motivated by dual commitments.

Sidgwick (1907, 2) recommends that we attend to the evidence of what is moral that may be derived from "a careful study of actual phenomena."[9] But, because such evidence is fraught with problems of the foundations of ordinary practical knowledge and of the dualism of practical reason, we cannot place great confidence in it. Even though it may inform our theorizing, we certainly cannot suppose that commonsense knowledge trumps our theoretical reasoning in any but the very general sense that we must frame our theorizing against the background of our commonsense knowledge.

It is instructive that Sidgwick reaches a result analogous to that which economists also conceded toward the end of Sidgwick's own life:

I hold that the utilitarian, in the existing state of our knowledge, cannot possibly construct a morality *de novo* either for man as he is (abstracting his morality), or for man as he ought to be and will be. He must start, speaking broadly, with the existing social order, and the existing morality as part of that order: and in deciding the question whether any divergence from this code is to be recommended, must consider chiefly the immediate consequences of such divergence, upon a society in which such a code is conceived generally to subsist. (Sidgwick 1907, 473–74)

The moral theorist or the moral chooser must be only a marginalist, taking the gross value of things as they are as a base on which to build outward.[10]

[9]Passage quoted in full above.

[10]Jack Smart suggests that the days of marginalist moral theory may be past in this era, in which disasters can happen suddenly as the result of seemingly minor actions (in seminar, Australian National University, August 1990). Actions in the distant past that introduced devastating diseases to unwary peoples may have posed similar problems. Many of the disasters we potentially face may partially be the result of poor causal understandings.

CHAPTER 6

Institutional Knowledge

Two important knowledge issues arise in the context of institutions, especially institutions that are organizations. Such institutions have physical locations with mailing addresses, although this characteristic is being transformed in the contemporary world of the internet and pervasive globalization. A generation ago, one might also have said they have telephones, but these have since been replaced by answering machines. The first knowledge issue, of course, is merely the complications of ordinary knowledge in institutional settings. The second is the change in moral perspectives that institutions introduce. Let us address the first of these issues before turning to the second issue, whose analysis depends substantially on understanding the nature of institutional knowledge, both its weaknesses and its strengths, which often turns on the weaknesses.

One might object to the use of the term 'institutional knowledge' on the ground that institutions are not sentient, cognitive agents and therefore cannot have knowledge. This difference can be seen as merely part of the claim that individuals and institutions have different ways of knowing. It is reasonable to say that institutions do know, in the simple sense that they store knowledge in various ways. For example, they can have files, procedures, and norms that no individual could overview, and they can access masses of data in their files. You can ask an institution a question about its knowledge and it can answer, accurately and often very quickly, as if the information were at the metaphorical tip of its tongue. To take a very simple example, the U.S. Bureau of the Census has vast reams of data that no individual can overview. Those data can be manipulated by individuals, especially with the use of computers, and any small part of the data may be well known to a particular individual. But there are data in the Bureau's files that would swamp the capacities of any individual actually to know them in any but a summary fashion.

The knowledge of the Bureau is different from an individual's knowledge in other ways as well. In particular, the Bureau obtains its knowledge very deliberately, through the efforts of thousands of data collectors and millions of individual contributors of the data. The Bureau is a generator and organizer of knowledge. An occasional individual, such as an empirical social scientist, might similarly generate and organize some array of knowledge, but the scale of an individual's efforts is trivially smaller than that of the Bureau.

As an analog of the institutional vs. individual choice problem, consider the so-called Enormous Theorem in mathematics. This theorem gives an exhaustive classification of all finite simple groups. The full proof is in about 500 separate publications by more than 100 mathematicians. It constitutes 15,000 pages in various publications plus some unpublished results. Some of its pieces were directly worked out by particular mathematicians who could be said to have an overview of at least those pieces; others were accomplished by computer, and some of these calculations are plausibly so complex or massive that no particular mathematician can claim to have an overview of them.[1] Naturally, no single mathematician might be thought to have a confident grasp of the whole theorem—all must rely on the reputed expertise of the individual contributors to the theorem, including computer programmers and chip designers.[2]

The knowledge that big organized institutions have is partially analogous to this proof. No one has a full overview of the knowledge of such an institution or organization. (One might make an analogous claim of the nature of individual knowledge; it is compartmentalized in the brain and cannot be overseen by any one part of the brain, although some writers on rationality implicitly assume that it can.) And yet it seems meaningful in some perhaps odd sense to say that the institution or organization has a vast body of knowledge at its useful disposal.

In part, the distinction between individual and institutional knowledge is merely a matter of degree or scale. At some point in the spectrum of the aggregation of knowledge by one person to the aggregation of knowledge by a huge organization, such as the body of mathematical group theorists or the Bureau of the Census, it might not be clear whether we should call the resulting knowledge 'individual' or 'institutional.' But at the extremes, the differences are clear, so that we can sensibly speak of modal differences in the knowledge capacities of institutions and individuals. Typically, we will expect some kinds of knowledge to be more in the capacity of individuals, and other kinds to be more in the capacity of institutions. For example, your personal knowledge of a friend's foibles, desires, successes, and failings is not likely to be in the purview of any institution. But the knowledge that the Bureau of the Census has far transcends anything of like kind that you could have. Indeed, one might suppose that its ca-

---

[1] For a brief but perhaps dated discussion of the theorem, and of efforts to simplify it to a perhaps more manageable 3,000 pages, see *Scientific American* (April 1996): p. 29.

[2] Computer proofs are an increasingly frequent problem for mathematicians. In 1611, Johannes Kepler speculated that the densest way to stack spheres is the way greengrocers stack oranges: in a pyramid. This sounds like a simple enough problem, but only recently did Thomas Hales of the University of Pittsburgh and his student Sam Ferguson, aided by computer, prove the conjecture. A dozen mathematicians reviewed the proof for four years and concluded that it is 99 percent certain to be correct. "Random Samples," *Science* 299 (7 March 2003): 1513.

pacity for knowledge of certain kinds on a vast scale is a defining characteristic of an institution.

As a result of its special capacities, an institution can make some kinds of decision far better than typical individuals can. Indeed, many of our purposes cannot be achieved without the use of large institutions. Not only is the achievement of such purposes not within the purview of a single person, it is not even subject to the overview of a single person. Hence, there are things that institutions can do that individuals acting spontaneously could not do as well, if at all. We must therefore want institutions to help us accomplish some goals.

This conclusion raises issues of both the capacity for gaining knowledge and the capacity for dealing with normative issues, and of the differences between individual and institutional capacities. Obviously, if we as individuals cannot even have an overview of an institution's knowledge and how it puts it to use, it would be absurd to say we know that the institution performs as well as it possibly could with respect to its mandate. Indeed, it might be impossible even to know whether one institution performs as well as an alternative might.

Normatively, institutions must typically act in ways that result in trade-offs between individuals. Creating an institution or even adopting a particular policy may be expected to benefit all in general, but it will commonly lead to net costs for some in any given action of the institution or application of the policy. A welfarist argument for institutions seems compelling, but it has strong implications for the necessity of making such trade-offs between individuals.

STRATEGIC INTERACTION AND INSTITUTIONS

An apparent disanalogy between institutional knowledge and the proof of the Enormous Theorem is that the latter can be broken down piecemeal and each piece can plausibly be worked on independently of the other pieces. An attempt to alter or redo a small piece of some institution, however, is often likely to ramify through the institution and affect other aspects of it. The parts of an institutional organization do not simply add their effects to those of the other parts. Rather, they interact. This means that we often cannot improve an institution except by trial and error, comparing each variant institution, as a whole, to the others. But this will commonly be impossible.

If the effects of the parts of an institution cannot be decoupled from the effects of other parts, institutional design is inherently strategic. In this respect, institutional structure is similar to human interaction more generally: one of my actions typically cannot be grounded in a simple assessment of its direct consequences, but must rather be based on the expected result of what not only I but others do, including what others might be expected to do in reaction to my action (Hardin 2003).

The far more complex and arguably more interesting problem for institutions is the consequences of strategic interactions that are *internal* to the institution. Because the relations between parts of a complex institution or organization cannot be fully grasped by anyone, it is implausible to say that such an institution is designed in the straightforward sense in which one might say that a person designed a particular artifact, such as William Paley's pocket watch of chapter 2. Rather, institutions are inherently, as Adam Ferguson ([1767] 1980, 122) noted, of human making but not of human design. To a large extent, institutions simply happen.

Yet, it is still true that we actively want to have certain kinds of institutions make certain decisions and to implement them. Principal reasons for wanting them are that they have capacities individuals acting spontaneously lack. They can resolve problems that would pose insuperable obstacles of collective action or even mere coordination for individuals. They can have the power to bring about extraordinary results and even to override what many individuals might attempt to do to block such results. For the present discussion, however, the most interesting capacities they have are capacities for mastering knowledge that go beyond individual capacities. These capacities are, as are their organization and their power, enabling; and they can be enabling for us in the pursuit of our personal projects.

But the ways institutions gain knowledge can also be disabling, in the sense that they can make themselves incapable of addressing finer, variant, or atypical effects on the welfare of specific individuals. This is an important fact, and it will turn out to be, oddly enough, a positive fact in the account that follows. The virtual impossibility of having large-scale social institutions take interpersonal comparisons of welfare into account in many contexts will yield an argument in favor of taking such comparisons seriously in social policy.

INSTITUTIONS AND MORAL KNOWLEDGE

The knowledge requirements of utilitarianism are different in kind from those of certain other moral theories. For example, a rigorous Kantian theory requires action according to specific rules or norms that declare some kinds of action wrong and other kinds right, or even required. Such theory depends on our being able to derive relevant rules from abstract principles independently of specific knowledge of the practical world. Intuitionism and those parts of any moral theory that depend on direct, substantive intuitions that certain kinds of action are right or wrong, evidently require an unusual intellectual faculty that no one has yet spelled out with care—although some philosophers have been morally certain that they had command of a relevant faculty. Recall the claim of H. A. Prichard ([1912] 1968, 17) in chapter 5 that we merely look at the problem and know what we morally ought to do.

Utilitarianism depends on having access to knowledge that is, in principle, similar to the knowledge for general practical choice and judgment, as does any other morality to the extent that it is about consequences and their causes (as Dewey ([1929] 1984, 218–19) argues). Whether we make good choices, either morally or self-interestedly, turns heavily on whether the happenstance knowledge available to us while we are choosing is relevant and good.

But an individual can have some kinds and bits of knowledge that an organization cannot sensibly be designed to have. For example, I can know you and your tastes and the effects on your welfare of various policies. An organization for implementing national policy might not conceivably come to have such knowledge of anyone. And if it did have it of some individuals, it could not have it of all—and for procedural reasons that can have a moral or practical justification, it might therefore be excluded from using the information even on behalf of the individuals for whom it does have the knowledge. (Institutions may commonly be expected to work better if they follow standard procedures to assure that they not be careless or capricious.) On the other hand, a policy organization can have command over massive data on the general population that few if any individuals could ever be expected to have, and it might therefore be able to make better judgments of the comparative overall impact of variant policies than individuals could.

An institution can also have command over distinctively institutional devices for reaching decisions. It can break tasks into parts that are addressed by different specialists, and can pool specialized knowledge in hierarchical and group decision making. An institution is typically focused on a fairly limited range of kinds of problem to resolve. It can therefore invest much more in resolving those kinds of problem than any individual could justify investing. It can effectively use division of labor and specialization to heighten both the efficiency and the quality of its resolution. And an institution may have a regularized system for collecting the information it needs for its decisions, a system that might be able to collect information that no individual could hope to collect.

As a result of its special capacities, a highly organized institution can make some kinds of decision far better than typical individuals can. Hence, there are things that an institution can do that no individual and no spontaneously interacting group of individuals would be capable of doing, because only a relevant institution can know what it takes to do those things. If specialization is likely beneficial, then organizational pooling of specialists is likely also to be beneficial. Institutions have several advantages over merely aggregated individual actions. They can coordinate large numbers of actors and they can counter perverse incentives. An especially important reason for both of these is that they can collect information that most individuals could not collect, or that individuals acting spontaneously could not collect as efficiently. Without such information, it might be virtually impossible for a population to achieve some collective benefits. This means, of course, that the institution has both practical and moral capacities that individuals cannot have. Hence, the institution ought to do some things that individuals cannot do and that individuals therefore cannot be said to have a moral obligation to do. There are some things we can say institutions ought to do when we cannot sensibly say individuals ought to do them.

Unfortunately, whereas institutions have capacities that give them advantages over individuals, their capacities may also give them disadvantages. I can come to know you in a way that no organization could. Among the ways that I can know you and a particular organization cannot know you may be many that are centrally important in determining your welfare or the welfare effects on you of various actions or rules. Hence, there may be real trade-offs in opting for organizational resolutions of many problems. It is only somehow "on the whole" that an organization may be superior to aggregated individuals in handling certain problems. For other problems, individuals may be better left to their own spontaneous devices.

INSTITUTIONS AS MELIORATIVE

Commonly, not only do we need institutions to accomplish particular purposes, but we could claim that having an institution of a particular kind rather than not having one would benefit everyone. Hence, we could offer a mutual-advantage argument for the existence of some institution. For example, we might readily say of the general framework of government that it serves mutual advantage in comparison to having no government. This is Hobbes's justification of government (Hobbes, [1651] 1994, chap. 18, ¶20; see Hardin 1991, 156–80, and 1999, chaps. 1 and 3). Yet we cannot generally claim of the details of government and of policy that these serve mutual advantage better than certain alternative details or policies would. Even for such details, however, an institution has available some kinds of knowledge that an individual could not be expected to command.

For reasons of differences in their knowledge, institutions and individuals can do different things, because they can only expect to do what they have knowledge for, or can gain the needed knowledge. (They may also have significantly different causal capacities, but our concern here is primarily with knowledge. Their causal capacities are, of course, entangled with their capacities for gaining knowledge.) Again, this difference entails a normative difference in what can be done, and therefore what ought to be done, by either individuals or institutions. In the jargon of moral philosophy, "ought implies can," that is, one cannot be held responsible for failing to do what one could not do. Because what individuals can do and institutions can do differ in some respects, what they ought to do differs in those respects.

When we choose to use an institution to help accomplish some purpose, we inherently make what I will call a meliorative, not a mutual advantage, move for the reason that we then base our choice on average or aggregative principles that may run net losses for some together with net benefits for others. Melioration can be taken as strictly pragmatic or as a moral idea equivalent to utilitarian value theory.[3] In essence, *recourse to government or other complex institutions to accomplish our specific ends is in general a meliorative but not mutual-advantage move.* This claim is generally true despite the caveat, discussed in the next section below, that a choice of institution or policy might be grounded in such limited knowledge that it could appear to be mutually advantageous even if its specific actions are not.

Consider an example of this general conclusion. It is a commonplace claim that the most important values in the common law are to achieve definitive resolutions of cases at hand, and to establish rules to guide future actions so to reduce the need for repeated recourse to the law. We need resolutions of conflicts in order to go on with our lives. And we need rules that allow us to act in the confident expectation that our actions will stand against legal attack, so that we may sensibly and confidently invest in our projects and our lives. What the judge actually does in the common law, when a case arises in a new context, is to establish a rule to guide *future* actors while treating the present litigants *as if the rule had been in place when they acted.* The new rule may not serve your advantage, but having the Common Law capacity to make and apply the rule serves the advantage of all of us in general. This accomplishes both of the values of the common law: it resolves the case at hand and it guides *future actions of everyone* cognizant of the law. In criminal law, retroactive laws are not valid. Such laws would hold someone accountable for an action that was not criminal at the time (ex post delicto). In civil law, retroactivity is often

---

[3]Melioration is essentially Dewey's value theory.

almost necessary. In the criminal law we do define new crimes and prescribe new punishments in response to new offenses, but we do this without imposing punishments on those who gave us reason to revise the law.
The miscreant moves on without the new punishment, which will apply
only to future cases.

In the civil law, one or the other party to a complaint will be left in the
lurch until a new rule is adopted and applied to their case. Clearly, one of
the litigants is likely to be a net loser from the decision in a case that establishes a new rule. Yet, we may generally conclude that it is better to establish that rule than not to do so, and that, whatever rule we establish,
we must resolve the dispute at hand. If the parties to the litigation in the
present case are similarly situated, so that both might be expected to gain
more in the long run from one rule than from an alternative rule, we
might easily suppose that resolving the case by adopting this preferred
rule is mutually advantageous with respect to future interactions.[4] But
commonly, we would have to conclude that the actual decision makes one
of the litigants in the present case a net loser in comparison to how that
litigant would have fared under an alternative rule.

The usual defense of the common law therefore is meliorative rather
than mutual-advantage. It is grounded, perhaps only implicitly, in the view
that some parties' losses are outweighed by other parties' gains. Analo-
gously with Hobbes's defense of having government, one might reasonably claim that having definitive resolutions of cases makes all of us expect to be better off than if there were no such resolutions. Hence, in
advance of any interactions, we all want a system that gives definitive resolutions in any cases that might arise later. But, again, one commonly
cannot claim that the details of the resolution in a particular case make
everyone better off.

A general problem of institutional decision making is that institutions
must commonly make stochastic or probabilistic decisions about what is
most likely to be true of typical individuals. Sometimes the decision can
be classed as one of mutual advantage, sometimes not. For example, we
might choose to vaccinate all children against some dreadful disease, such
as smallpox in the years before it was eradicated in most of the world, or
polio still today. Yet we may know that the vaccination itself will likely
give the disease to some of those vaccinated, even while it protects the
vast majority against contracting the disease (Hardin 1989). In this case,

---

[4]In commercial law, this assumption might often be valid. In tort law, it is likely less commonly valid, because some people are unlikely ever to be the inflictors of a certain kind of
harm, but only the sufferers of it. For example, those who seldom or never drive but who
are often at risk from cars as pedestrians are not in the same situation with respect to certain liability rules for vehicular traffic as those who often drive. See, further, Hardin 1996,
2010–11.

we might readily conclude that adopting the general policy of vaccination is mutually advantageous, because all children are similarly situated and face, so far as we know, similar risks of contracting the disease from the vaccination or of being subjected to an epidemic if there is no vaccination. The odds are that every child who is vaccinated will face far less risk of getting the disease.

But we might actually be able to reduce the total number of infections by vaccinating only some large fraction of all children. The live Sabin polio vaccine yields some herd immunity, that is, protection of those not vaccinated. The incidentally protected herd might be at less risk of contracting the disease from vaccination than are those children whose vaccination protects the herd. And in any case, a particular disease may not be capable of spreading even if only some fraction of the population is vaccinated. Now we could say, again in advance of adopting a policy, that it would be mutually advantageous to all children to vaccinate only, say, 70 percent of them. If we could get the percentage exactly right, it would then be a matter of indifference to each child whether she was or was not vaccinated, at least insofar as risk of disease is concerned. If, however, we are unsure of the right percentage, and we wish to play safe and vaccinate more rather than fewer, those who are vaccinated might be put at greater risk than those who are not. The actual choosing of which children to vaccinate is then not a matter of mutual advantage, even though selecting the percentage to vaccinate could be. (Of course, those children who do eventually contract polio do not join in the mutual advantage of the vaccination program. They face mutual advantage only ex ante.)

Choosing which children to vaccinate has more the character of the choices made in a typical cost-benefit analysis, in which the costs to all are weighed against the benefits to all, although some may be net beneficiaries while others are net losers. It is hard even to imagine a workable alternative to cost-benefit analysis in many contexts, such as the siting of roads, although there can be compensations of the net losers to, in legalese, make them whole. But for obvious reasons of the problem of strategic misrepresentation of preferences in order to gain advantage, the assessment of costs and benefits must typically be somewhat stylized rather than personalized. Hence, standard compensations may not satisfy all the losers. As in Hobbes's argument for government, having a system of eminent domain and stylized assessments of costs for public projects might be mutually advantageous in principle or before it is applied to a case, but its actual working in any particular instance is unlikely to be.

Note that the problems discussed immediately above need not be unique to institutional settings. An individual might also face choices that benefit some at the cost of others, and might make calculations similar to those of an institution. But this is the constant daily fare of institutional decision making and of public policy, where as it may be a relatively small part of the lives of many of us as individuals. And this task of cost-benefit analysis far more clearly defines the purpose of an institution than that of an individual.

APPARENT MUTUAL ADVANTAGE

Some argue that we should not make the interpersonal comparisons required for melioration, but there are contexts in which that argument seems implausible. For example, an intervention to stop a disastrous conflict might seem almost surely to entail net losses to some in order to bring general benefits to all. Almost everyone might agree that the end of conflict, even at such individually specific costs, would be a better state of affairs than the continuation of the conflict. Some might, of course, argue, from a libertarian or other theory, that no one should intervene, even if such intervention would produce a better state of affairs. More generally, however, it seems plausible that all major social institutions and policies are likely to entail melioration that implicitly involves interpersonal comparisons or weighings that are not mutually advantageous, despite the appearance of the general policy in advance of any applications of it.

At the level of knowledge that many institutions can actually accommodate or claim to have, they typically act to the mutual advantage of those whose interests they address. They act from knowledge of typical or even statistical or average cases. More particular knowledge might show that there is wide variation around the average case, and that a policy directed at the average case imposes net losses on some. But commonly, an institution cannot know enough in detail about each of us even to know that it is trading off your welfare for mine. It therefore makes its decision as a matter of expected mutual advantage, not of interpersonal comparison.

Many institutions similarly act from knowledge of typical cases, but still make comparisons of welfare across different classes of such cases. These institutions may then act to meliorate rather than to serve mutual advantage. For example, hospitals are far more attentive to some problems than to others on the simple, and generally agreed, ground that those problems more seriously affect health and, therefore, welfare. Your rampant infection merits more immediate attention than my sprained wrist. Similarly, an institutional body devising a tax scheme might make the scheme progressively more burdensome for those with higher incomes, on the widely agreed view that the welfare effects of progressivity are generally good. One who has special familiarity with a few particular persons might argue that the welfare effects of these policies on those persons are perverse, in the sense that they cost some people far more than they benefit others. But the institutions that set and implement the policies might not command the special knowledge needed to reach this conclusion.

In general, we face two quite separate problems of choice about collective matters. First, we create institutions and organizations to handle certain issues. In our expectations and our intentions, the creation of a particular institution may be genuinely mutually advantageous (although the choice between alternative institutions might not be). Second, we—or our institutions—adopt specific policies and implement them. The choice and implementation of many actual policies will not be mutually advantageous. Our two choices, of institutions and of policies, are analogous to a limited extent. Even though an institution might be expected by each person to be beneficial to him or herself, it may nevertheless be true that it would also be expected by everyone that it would bring net losses to some. My expectations of net benefit in such a case would be statistical. I might expect a range of possible effects on me, from net losses to net benefits, but with the expected value overall of net benefits.

Adopting an actual policy will be similar, in the sense that it will be based on statistical expectations of the costs and benefits of the policy. Those expectations might, again, come from a range of possible outcomes for particular individuals, with some of them losing overall while others benefit. The difference between the two—adopting a policy and creating a policy institution—would often be that actual individuals might be surer of where they are likely to come out from the policy. For example, a new policy of progressive taxation would affect many people in ways they could confidently predict.

INTERPERSONAL COMPARISONS OF WELFARE

One might wish to say that melioration approximates to mutual advantage in policy contexts. But this does not relieve the fact that it is not actually equivalent to mutual advantage, and that it requires de facto trade-offs across individuals. Hence, a rigorous opponent of interpersonal comparisons must oppose almost all public policy. The only such genuinely rigorous opponents in print are hard-nosed libertarians, some of whom think we would manage to be as prosperous without institutions as we are with them. They therefore disagree fundamentally with Hobbes, whom they should see as their most threatening intellectual opponent. I think Hobbes has far the better case to make, even though he may exaggerate the extent to which efforts at reform threaten massive destruction from civil war and anarchy (Hobbes, [1651] 1994, chap. 30, ¶ 7).

The most articulate early voice against interpersonal comparisons is the Italian economist Vilfredo Pareto ([1927] 1971). He proposed that our policy decisions must make no one worse off and must make at least one person better off. Virtually no significant policy action can meet this standard. The general run of economists who claim to have inherited Pareto's value theory, and who sometimes assert the impossibility of making interpersonal comparisons of welfare, are not Paretian in actual practice. They regularly prescribe both institutions and policies, and they are the authors of countless cost-benefit analyses. The ardor with which economists have defended the impossibility of interpersonal comparisons is more than matched by the energy with which they have urged policies requiring trade-offs that could only be grounded on the assumption of such comparisons.[5] Still, their inconsistency is no proof of the correctness of making such trade-offs. But if Hobbes is even roughly right, the impossibility of escaping the stasis of failure in adopting institutions for collective purposes is a powerful argument *for* the correctness of such trade-offs, and of the de facto interpersonal comparisons they imply.

This conclusion suggests a slightly tricked up justification of such comparisons. In the abstract in general, we all would want a better-regulated world, one in which life would be much better for most of us and, in our expectations, even for each of us. Once we have the institutions needed for such regulation, we cannot practically escape making trade-offs between individuals—perhaps often unidentified and even unidentifiable individuals, but trade-offs among them nevertheless. *We cannot have the institutions that are in principle justifiable unless we also take the eventual trade-offs. By mutual-advantage argument, in principle we ought to have those institutions. But if we cannot have them without their eventual trade-offs, then we ought also to have the trade-offs.* One of two contrary conclusions follows. The first is that the rectitude of interpersonal trade-offs follows from an argument grounded only in mutual advantage. The second is that we should not have institutions at all, because we cannot make interpersonal comparisons.

The second of these conclusions could be taken as an implication of the doctrine that ought implies can, as stated earlier. If we metaphysically cannot make interpersonal comparisons, then we ought not. Hence, we also ought not justify a system that depends on making such comparisons, and we should junk institutions. The first and contrary conclusion could be taken as an injunction to condone trade-offs or, even more strongly, to take interpersonal comparisons seriously. I concur with the

---

[5]Presumably, their fees for the latter vastly exceed anything they have earned for the former.

stronger version of this conclusion. I think we should (and do) take interpersonal comparisons seriously. I do not have a metaphysical argument to establish how such comparisons can be given meaning in principle, or an argument to show how we can know another's welfare in order to compare it to our own.

But the weaker version of the conclusion seems incontrovertible: we ought to condone interpersonal trade-offs. The alternative—to suppose that we ought not have institutions to enhance welfare—is preposterous. Faced with the comparative difficulties of supposing we ought to have such institutions and of supposing we ought to condone the requisite interpersonal trade-offs, one who is motivated by the pragmatics of living well—for oneself and for others—must find the latter difficulty less implausible than the former.

Concluding Remarks

Institutions, unlike individuals, are generally forced to make meliorative moves that are not mutually advantageous. You and I can agree to act in ways that serve our mutual advantage without making any claims of interpersonal trade-offs. Indeed, that is the nature of ordinary exchange. It serves our mutual advantage. I trade what I have for what you have, and we are both better off. Perhaps one could reasonably say that you are made much better off while I am made only slightly better off. And perhaps one could even argue that we should not exchange, but that you should merely give me what you have because your gift would make us jointly better off than our trade would make us. But the trade is still merely mutually advantageous, and therefore utilitarian with respect to the status quo before the trade, without any judgment of how much better off it makes the two of us together. Variance among the individuals that institutions address virtually guarantees that their actions will not have this character in actual fact, even though an institution might be incapable of judging that its actions do impose net costs on any particular persons.

The role of courts of equity at their height in England was to handle the variant cases that were decided properly according to the law, but that imposed supposedly unreasonable penalties on parties who were in some important respect unlike the standard parties before the law. One can imagine a similar device to accommodate claims that specialized knowledge outside the normal purview of an institution would justify special treatment of someone. But one cannot coherently expect that an institution be able to treat every case as special in this way, and still do a good job of accomplishing its purpose of serving our interests. Moreover, if an institution adopts a policy of allowing special appeals to "equity," it must likely do so only for extreme cases, not for relatively close calls. Their capacity for streamlining and standardizing decision making is a very important part of what makes institutions useful to us. We cannot simultaneously wreck their standard procedures and expect them to continue to be as useful. Again, it is plausibly mutually advantageous that we create such institutions, even though, in specific instances of their acting, they may inflict net costs on some, and we know ex ante that it is extremely likely that they will do so.

CHAPTER 7

Religious Belief and Practice

ONE MIGHT SUPPOSE that, whatever form it takes, a theory of knowledge must be generally applicable to all knowledge. Hence, the explanation of religious belief is merely a part of the explanation of beliefs more generally, although it might exhibit special characteristics, in part because of differing incentives on offer from the larger society of the believer. But even for religion, an ordinary person's knowledge must depend in general on the costs and benefits of discovering bits of it and of putting them to use. Once discovered, however, a bit of knowledge will be counted as true to the extent that it comes from a credible authority, that it fits coherently with other beliefs, that it corresponds with the world, or that it once seemed to meet one of these conditions.[1] One's belief in the truth of that bit of knowledge might also depend on the rewards of counting it as true, on its usefulness to oneself in some sense. In what follows, I wish especially to address this last possibility as applied to religious beliefs.

One possible response to the claim that religious belief is well grounded is that there is a causal connection between the truth of believers' beliefs and the fact that they believe what they do. They suppose that something about the content of the belief compels them to believe. This supposition, the main issue in justifying religious beliefs, runs against two difficult facts. A standard causal analysis would start from correlation of the phenomenon to be explained with various plausible causes. In the case of religious beliefs there are two striking correlations. First, there are numerous mutually contradictory sets of religious beliefs, so that the content of religious belief does not generally correlate with the fact of belief. The explanation of belief and the explanation of the content of belief therefore require separate arguments.

Second, the content of individuals' religious beliefs correlates very strongly with the beliefs of their particular communities. In sum, the fact of belief does not correlate with the content of belief, but does correlate with accidental factors in the believers' social context. Moreover, *this correlation is radically stronger than the bulk of all correlations taken seriously in the social sciences.* Such extremely high correlations would

---

[1]It is also plausible that we count something as knowledge by a mistake of cataloging. For example, I overhear a claim made by a stranger on the subway, and I then forget the source and merely count the claim as true by authoritative assertion.

commonly be considered knock-down proof of a causal relation. You believe what you do *because* your community believes it. In a standard quip, religious belief is inherited (Boyer 2001, 317).

This fact of inheritance even explains most of the apparent growth in conservative evangelical church membership in the United States, contrary to a common supposition that the growth comes from conversions of nonconservatives or even nonprotestants. For the past many decades, women from conservative protestant denominations have had one more child than women from other protestant denominations, who are not even reproducing themselves, giving birth to less than two children each. This demographic fact explains about 70 percent of the denominational growth in membership. The other 30 percent comes largely from the conservatives' greater success in holding on to their own members (Hout, Greeley, and Wilde 2001). Although many of the evangelical churches constantly proselytize, their growth is almost entirely internal, not from attracting new converts. The de facto function of proselytizing is not to find new members but to help lock in extant members.

Oddly, these correlations are common knowledge even among religious believers, who often consider them to be a problem. Thomas Hobbes ([1651] 1994, chap. 43, ¶ 8) forcefully asserted this relationship three and a half centuries ago: "For what other cause can there be assigned why, in Christian commonwealths, all men (either) believe (or at least profess) the Scripture to be the word of God, and in other commonwealths scarce any, but that in Christian commonwealths they are taught it from their infancy, and in other places they are taught otherwise?"[2] Religious belief is very much a matter of happenstance knowledge (as is almost everything we know at any given moment, and necessarily so). Moreover, we can probably presume "that four or five of the world's six billion people are dug in, entrenched, at ease with their commitments, unmovable, not shopping for change" (Marty 2005, 149), even though they know there is a divergent plurality of views.

Chapter 2 addresses religious moves directed at blocking the teaching of evolution in the schools, or at least to impose an alternative scientific

[2]This chapter is entitled: "Of What Is Necessary for Reception into Heaven?" The beginning of this paragraph is also interesting: "It is manifest, therefore, that Christian men do not know, but only believe the Scripture to be the word of God; and that the means of making them believe which God is pleased to afford men ordinarily is according to the way of nature [that is, not mysterious], that is to say, from their teachers. It is the doctrine of S. Paul, concerning Christian faith in general (*Rom.* 10:17): 'Faith cometh by hearing,' that is by hearing our lawful pastors. He saith also (vss. 14, 15): 'How shall they believe in him of whom they have not heard? and how shall they hear without a preacher? and how shall they preach, except they be sent?' Whereby it is evident that the ordinary cause of believing that the Scriptures are the word of God is the same with the cause of the believing of all other articles of our faith: namely, the hearing of those that are by the law allowed and appointed to teach us, as our parents in their houses, and our pastors in the churches."

view of creation to compete with evolutionary theory. There the purpose was not to understand religious belief per se, but to put it to the test of its being a science in its guise of intelligent design, or ID, and especially to analyze the popular understanding of what counts as scientific in a realm of great popular interest: human origins. Many serious theologians object to the move of claiming that ID is science. They think it demeans god and undercuts the core of religious belief, because it reduces the status of god to just another creature to be analyzed in more or less physical terms (see, for example, Gilkey 1985, 101–2, 114; 1988, 486; Coyne 2005). This move destroys much of the mystery of religion and the idea of god. In *Kitzmiller,* Federal Judge Jones declared that members of the Dover school board who claimed to advocate teaching ID as a scientific theory were duplicitous, that their true objective was to teach religion, contrary to the Establishment clause of the U.S. constitution and to the ruling of the Supreme Court in *Edwards v. Aguillard* that creationism cannot be taught in the public schools. In Jones's view, the Dover board members were acting on their religious beliefs, which were constitutionally barred from consideration.

At issue in this chapter is to understand religious belief itself, including the content of the belief as itself just so much knowledge (or belief, if one prefers the philosopher's vocabulary to that of the people who say and think they know). For that, we will need an adequate theory of belief, a theory of knowledge. Many people think religious belief is an especially difficult problem: how do people come to have such beliefs? The problem is of the theorists, not of the people. Such beliefs, while not universal, are extremely common; they are and have been held by apparently billions of people.

Recall that the philosophical theory of knowledge applies to *the objects of belief,* not to the believers. It is typically about the criteria for counting something as knowledge. These criteria can be about the objects themselves, or about the procedures followed in assessing the objects. On this kind of theory, religious belief or knowledge is highly problematic. One could not give the criteria that justify counting such belief as knowledge. Or, if one did propose such criteria, they would almost surely be different from the criteria for other knowledge. As the defendants in *Kitzmiller* found, they could not construct criteria according to which ID would pass as science and, hence, as intersubjective knowledge.

Leaders of the contemporary religious movement against evolutionary theory attempt to establish an additional criterion for calling some claim true: mystery. If we do not understand the world, invoke god. Unfortunately, this rule must apply to absurdly many things, including trivially unimportant things. But today it no longer applies to some things to which it would have applied a few centuries ago. On this criterion, the field of play for god is shrinking.

RELIGIOUS KNOWLEDGE BY AUTHORITY

Because of the high costs of acquiring all knowledge on our own, as noted in chapter 1, we typically rely on authority for most of the knowledge we actually have. Notoriously, most of us rely on the authoritative knowledge of professionals, such as doctors, lawyers, and many others. But we all rely essentially on the authority of various historians for the bulk of what we claim to know about the world's past history, and we rely on the authority of numerous writers and people in the media for the knowledge we claim to have about our own contemporary world. In all substantial areas of our lives, we necessarily accept much of what we know from authorities of various kinds, some of them quite reliable, some of them not. This is not a criticism of anyone; we all have to do this if we are to make time to live.

The nature of religious belief for most people is that the beliefs were taken on authority at a very young age. Suppose I have grown up as a believer in some religion. I may now simply never question the early authorities, not least because I may never even suppose my belief was grounded in authority, may not even know or intuit why I have my belief, but may only suppose I have it on the unquestionable authority of its truth.

Of course, I might question the belief or aspects of it under some circumstances. For example, suppose I have a fundamentalist Christian belief that those who believe go to heaven and that those who do not are damned to eternal suffering in hell. Now a friend asks me about my beloved and wonderfully generous aunt, who regularly asserts the silliness of this belief and who slyly comments on the hypocrisy of most of those who profess it. That aunt, my friend notes quizzically, must be doomed to burn in hell. Suppose I simply find such brutal and incomprehensible "punishment" for mere lack of belief to be utterly incongruous, indeed, misfit with the loving god of my religious belief.

I now look again at my pastor's favorite biblical passage, John 3:16 and the following verses. It seems to say my aunt is condemned merely from lack of belief, while such scoundrels as Tom Delay, Torquemada, and so on appear bound for heaven. Now I wonder where hell fits in all this, especially because, to listen to my pastor, hell seems to be the most important element in our system of belief. But for me, hell and its grotesque misery are not there. My belief may have begun to unravel, because now I am trying to understand it, and am not accepting it without question. I put my beliefs to the test of a commonsense version of a coherentist theory of knowledge. Because the whole package of beliefs is supposed to be about something good and decent, part of the coherentist test must be about the inherent decency of the implications of the beliefs. But I may not be able to see how the golden rule could be part of a coherent system that includes sending my wonderfully generous and sweet aunt to roast in hell for all eternity, for the simple reason that she does not believe what we all recognize to be profoundly mysterious. J. L. Mackie (1955) argues that the only way to bring such patently incoherent beliefs into a single theological position is to reject reason entirely.

Now, even if I revise my core beliefs, I may have great trouble revising all of the bits of understanding in my mind that were influenced by my prior beliefs and my upbringing in them. I may, that is, still have strong ties to my earlier beliefs. For example, I may continue to have a strong commitment to the golden rule of doing unto others what I would have them do unto me. But I may never again accept on dead authority the core of my previous beliefs. Indeed, I may even come to view many of the commitments I still have as deeply contrary to those that I now question.

The anthropologist Anthony F. C. Wallace (1966: 264–65) speculates that religion must inevitably die in the face of superior knowledge from the sciences, because the scientific spirit of questioning knowledge will finally undercut religious beliefs that are founded essentially in authority. It is possible that this argument is correct, but only at the level of a particular individual. For example, a leading youthful advocate of creationism in the Netherlands chose, with financial support from his coreligionists, to get an education in geology in order to be able to match wits with scientists, to show that creationism is correct, and that Charles Darwin's evolution and Charles Lyell's ([1830–33] 1990) arguments about the age of the Earth as inferred from geological formations are false. In four years at Princeton he received his doctorate and became apostate (*Science* 258 [16 October 1992]: 487). One doubts that his less educated coreligionists back home became apostate.

In its fullest implication, Wallace's speculation assumes that the lessons of the sciences must spread to cover the entire society. This may be a fallacy of composition, applying an individual-level argument to the collective or societal level, where science is unlikely to be mastered. Or it might be merely too optimistic about the spread of scientific understanding. Deep knowledge of the sciences is relatively restricted to a small part of the population, and even for those few it is restricted to certain areas of inquiry.

One might suppose Wallace had physical and life scientists in mind. But if so, a 1969 survey of 60,000 U.S. professors defies Wallace's expectations. A majority of physical and life scientists claim to be religious (Stark et al. 1996, 436; Stark 2003, 192–97; also see Larson and Witham 1998, 1999). One might suppose they have no special qualification to treat religion scientifically, with the potentially skeptical stance they take in their own fields of expertise. The great physicist Wolfgang Pauli is supposed to have responded to a very artful bit of mathematics of quantum mechanics with the dismissive comment, "That's not even wrong." Wallace expects science to reach roughly this view of religion, for religion is a theory that cannot be given even a testable sense, and it is neither true nor false.

The scientists who are most likely to find difficulties with any specific religious belief are those who, because of the nature of their own science, are qualified to study relationships between specific beliefs and specific societies. Perhaps it should be no surprise that anthropologists might be especially inclined to wonder what religious knowledge is and how it can be credited, and psychologists might follow soon after them in disbelief. Students of religion in these disciplines actually come to be in the position of the standard philosophy of knowledge: they wonder what the criteria are for a specific *belief* to be counted as true. And the majority of them are not religious—they cannot believe the content of any religion. The central claims of many religions test credulity.

These specialists in religion are apt to know about, and even to have studied, the Egyptian gods that mingle body parts from different animal species, the elephant-headed Hindu Ganesh (the god of harmony), the Cherokee buzzard that dug out the valleys and piled up the mountains, the panoply of rapaciously joyful Greek and Roman gods, and a list that goes on into the hundreds, maybe thousands (see, e.g., Bonnefoy and Doniger 1991). They also question certain "survivor" religions, based on communal principles of formerly desert nomadic tribes, that are brutally applied to our contemporary world.[3] For example, when the Israeli Phinehas zealously drove his spear through Zimri and his Midianitish woman in their tent (Numbers 25:6–8), he was plausibly acting on behalf of a tribal group whose life-or-death fate depended on strong internal loyalty. To follow Phinehas's example today would be criminal.

A very different, rather too artful explanation for these results in surveys of academics has been proposed by several social scientists. They suppose that "the social sciences lean toward irreligion precisely because they are 'the *least scientific* disciplines'" (Stark et al. 1996, 436; also see Wuthnow 1985, 197). Their "semireligious reliance on nontestable claims puts them in direct competition with traditional religions." Even if one insists that theirs are the least scientific disciplines in the sciences, many social scientists—but not physical scientists—focus their research on trying to understand religious belief. More generally, those who adopt the scientific spirit most assiduously might eventually come to contest authority in all

[3]It is interesting that superstitious beliefs are also strongly held by academics in humanistic disciplines, but rejected by scientists and social scientists (Vyse 1997, 37–41). Scientists who believe in god do not believe in magic numbers and signs. Social scientists more often reject both bodies of belief; and humanists and artists more often accept both bodies. But the data are often unclear and inconsistent.

contexts, and might then come to wonder how they could possibly believe the content of any religion for which the only source of evidence is the claims of worldly authorities.

The anthropologist might also take note of religious practices that seem more like fads than defensible beliefs. For example, the practices—quaking and shaking in religious ecstasy—that gave Quakers and Shakers their popular names were merely a fad. And we now witness a contemporary fad, one only recently developed, of belief in the rapture: any day now most of us will be left behind when the true believers are suddenly snatched from our midst, leaving us to face our ends in airplanes whose pilots have been snatched away, or in cars that face careening driverless cars on all sides. People in the Middle East, China, and India might scarcely notice the loss of the few true-believing Christians among their populations, and they might be startled at the sudden collapse of American civilization— although not more startled than America's most determined nonbelievers. Quaking in ecstasy, belief in the rapture, and, more generally, various forms of mysticism are all time, place, and community specific. Although any given mystic is apt to think his or her revelations and feelings are strictly individual, mystics are collectively produced.

Against the general thesis that religion must fail in the age of science, many contemporary sociologists and economists argue that as one denomination liberalizes, new, more rigorous sects may arise (Stark and Bainbridge 1985; Montgomery 1996a). In these accounts, liberalization results from the increasing prosperity and education of the original church's members, who chafe under its originally strict regime and increasingly doubtful tenets. A new, fundamentalist sect arises not from the exclusion of its members from the former church but by cloning or separation as they seek to maintain strictness. This motor (or driving force) is plausibly in keeping with Wallace's claim about the spread of scientific understanding, although it is more specific, it is argued at the individual level, and it is not subject to a fallacy of composition. James Montgomery's (1996a) full model of this movement is based on Albert Hirschman's (1970) scheme of exit, voice, and loyalty. Prosperous members of a fundamentalist church exercise voice to reduce its rigor while less prosperous members exit to form a new sect. The eventually prosperous children of fundamentalists may act from loyalty to remain in the church of their parents long after their own personal views have become less strict.

In Montgomery's account, exit is from the bottom of the hierarchy of prosperity, although there must commonly be exit from the top of that hierarchy as well. For example, politically liberal religious believers left Southern Baptist congregations during the virulently racist days of the Civil Rights Movement when many southern church leaders seemed more concerned with segregation than with salvation. Montgomery's story is built from the histories of such churches as the Congregationalist, Unitarian, northern Baptist, and Quaker churches, all of which moved from being fundamentalist to being very liberal—in some cases virtually to the point of dispensing with belief in a god engaged in human affairs. The histories of these churches fit Montgomery's general model very well. There may not be a substantial parallel development in Islam except, perhaps, in immigrant communities in the West (as discussed in chapter 9).

INCENTIVE TO BELIEVE, OR COUNT AS TRUE

Suppose that expressing some view is rewarded with approval and, hence, brings pleasure. Children experience this constantly as they learn mastery of their world. They are rewarded even for getting arithmetic right. Knowledge is commonly reinforced or tested by consequences. If being rewarded is a consequence of expressing some view, which is easier if I believe that view, might I therefore come actually to believe it? Prima facie, this seems to be an odd question. The question is not about the incentive to discover the truth of the view but actually to believe it is true. We do not generally decide to believe that something is true. Belief or recognition of truth happens to us through the persuasiveness of the content or source. I might dearly wish to believe I lived in Bellagio several months every year, or that everyone's life were idyllic, but it is impossible for me to believe those things. In some sense, I even have incentive to believe that everyone's life is idyllic, because that belief would spare me various moral and political burdens. But, again, I cannot possibly believe such a thing.

Yet, anthropologists have long argued that beliefs are caused by their effects. Their argument is functional. A belief or pattern of behavior is explained by its *function* for a group or society if and only if the function is an effect of the behavior; it is commonly supposed that a shared religion is a cohesive force and is therefore beneficial for a society; and this cohesiveness maintains the religious belief by causal feedback from the populace. This result need not be intended and, indeed, it would often not even be perceived or understood by the members of the society. Perhaps the best known such functional explanation is that of seemingly implausible religious beliefs—the odd ritual of the rain dance works to build solidarity in the community, thereby giving it greater capacity for survival and flourishing, thereby intensifying belief in the community's religion and the benefits of their rain dance.

This structure of explanation works for many behaviors or beliefs (Hardin 1980; 1995, chap. 4; but see Elster 1979, pp. 28–35; also see chap. 8 on culture). For example, one might be convinced that performing some ritual before working would bring luck that would lead to much greater productivity and success in one's efforts. This might give one great confidence in setting out to work, or might simply get one quickly past the moment of starting up every day, so that one would actually be more productive, and this result might reinforce one's belief in the ritual of bringing good luck.

Let us focus on the functional account of religion. The seemingly difficult step in the account is the claim that religion is good for the members of the religious society. Some argue that religion is generally *good for a society* because it motivates a spirit of cooperation and can underlie social order. This is likely not easy to demonstrate empirically, and it cannot be supported by a casual, subjective assessment of differences between societies with and without religion. Some of the most brutal societies in history have been driven in service of religions to levels of violence and intolerance that are hardly believable. During the Crusades and the Inquisition, life for many was brutalized in the name of Christ. Today, much of the Islamic world is being brutalized in the name of Allah.

We might suppose that the function of religion is to provide comfort, and we have no difficulty agreeing that comfort is commonly good for people. Although we cannot choose to believe in order to have comfort, many writers suppose that comfort is a big issue for religion (Shermer 2000, e.g., p. 47). One might ask, can the causal connection between comfort and beliefs be demonstrated empirically? On a casual, subjective assessment, it appears that religious belief can bring comfort to many people, by giving them some hope for a future that is less harsh than their life in the present. A prevailing image of Catholicism in Italy is of elderly widows dressed in black who, in their loneliness, dominate attendance at mass. For some religions, such as Orthodox Judaism, one might suppose that communal succor is very important, possibly even the mainstay of Orthodox loyalty.

ADAPTIVE KNOWLEDGE REVISION

Although religious beliefs may indeed be reinforced in this indirect functional way, through their more or less beneficial effects on the believer, including the effects of producing pleasurable camaraderie or solace, they can also be produced in a somewhat more direct way that might even be consciously intended. The argument is a causal one, turning on the economics of knowledge and the longer-run coherence of a dynamic system of ideas or knowledge—all, again, at the level of the individual rather than at the level of the philosopher's quasi-public knowledge. This can happen through adaptive knowledge or belief revision, which can be reinforced by an individual's reliance on the division of labor that passes the task of assessing some knowledge to supposed specialists.

Consider some well rehearsed claims about the apparent benefits of religious belief. It is commonly, but cavalierly, said that someone believes in a particular religion *because* she gets comfort from her church or synagogue or mosque. One might even go so far as to say that she believes because she gets comfort from her beliefs, such as the belief that her dull, perhaps painful life will be followed by a glorious afterlife. This might be an implication of Marx's remark that religion is the opiate of the masses, who, sedated by belief in the afterlife, fail to overthrow those who exploit them on Earth. Though this might be an antifunctional or dysfunctional explanation, it might be as powerful as most functional explanations: a minor quotidian interest trumps a major life interest through its functional reinforcement.

If we unpack such claims, however, we come up against a problematic core. True, one might join a religious group for the social comforts it offers its members. But one can gain such comforts even without believing. If I have incentive to appear to believe, I may readily be able to feign belief along with the hypocrites my aunt scorns. But if my incentive is actually to believe, as in Marx's remark, I may still not be able to believe. In the anthropologists' functional explanations, the subjects need not face a problem of virtually choosing to believe in order to benefit. Nor might they face a problem of the incoherence and prima facie implausibility of their beliefs (although the anthropologist might wonder how belief survives contrary data on the causal effectiveness of, say, rain dancing).

Madama Butterfly says to B. F. Pinkerton, "I want to adopt a new religion. . . . I'll pray to the same god as yours" (Puccini [1904] 1992, 52, two-thirds of the way through Act 1). What will Butterfly do if she gets to go with Pinkerton? Against her plan, Hobbes ([1651] 1994, chap. 26, ¶41; chap. 27, ¶¶1–2) says that our beliefs are not subject to command. (Because we do not choose or control our beliefs, he concludes that only actions should be regulated or punished, not beliefs.) Belief in Pinkerton's religion includes belief in an afterlife. The latter belief could be very persuasive.

In an initial psychological account of believing what one has incentive to believe—believing for benefit—we might suppose that such a result is analogous to adaptive preference formation. Just what the psychological mechanism or motor of such adaptation could be is unclear, although one might simply assert that there must, on the evidence, be such a motor. In some other cases, the form of the adaptation could be roughly analogous to that of sour grapes. In Aesop's fable, the fox, who cannot reach the grapes he desires, comforts himself by supposing that the grapes are sour after all. In this fable, it is preferences that adapt to the range of possibility. Of course, the reaction of sour grapes is merely one possibility for anyone in the position of the fox. One might crave something unobtainable to such an extent as to pine over it, or to resent its unavailability, or even commit suicide over it (as Butterfly does when her preferences are not fulfilled). Indeed, such reactions might be more common for major preferences than is the disgruntled reaction of declaring sour grapes. For example, it seems likely that there are more people who ardently and even resentfully wish they had more wealth than there are people who have adjusted to their poverty through revaluing wealth as really sour rather than sweet, as an obstacle to good life rather than an enabler of it.

Our problem, however, is not revision of *preferences* in response to some kind of incentive but change of *beliefs*. Can there be adaptive knowledge revision? Plausibly there can. I will propose one way in which such revision might make sense, even without a special psychological motor such as, say, reduction of cognitive dissonance. Suppose I am in a community of people who believe X and who generally support those who seem to believe X and to shun those who do not. I might see it as in my interest now to profess belief in X even though I do not actually believe it. I thereby enjoy the camaraderie of my group.

Now, as a result of my participation in the life of the group, I hear many things that actually support the belief that I merely pretend to have. After some—perhaps long—time, I may begin to have difficulty separating various other things I seemingly know from belief X, which begins to be reinforced by this growing body of related knowledge. Eventually, it may even happen that the best way to make sense of a wide array of related things is actually to believe X, and I may therefore come to believe it as an almost necessary or deductively entailed part of this larger, coherent body of beliefs. It follows then that I am led to my belief in X by the incentive for having it, or at least for credibly professing it and living among those who have it. I do not directly believe merely because it is in my interest to do so, but I do other things that are in my interest and in doing these things I come to believe. The belief is an unintended consequence.

Indeed, my change in belief might even happen as an intended consequence, as in Pascal's wager. Pascal supposed that one might be quite unconvinced of the truth of Christian doctrine, but that one might think it at least possibly true. That doctrine is that one goes to heaven if one is a true believer and practitioner, and to hell if not. If the doctrine is false, the greatest loss that one would suffer from leading a religious life is the loss of a few decades of perhaps greater pleasure. If the doctrine is true, the greatest loss one would suffer from not leading that life would be eternal suffering. Even the slightest chance that the doctrine is true therefore makes one's preferred choice the religious life, at the relatively minor risk of briefly missing a bit of pleasure. Of course, that calculation need not convince one of the truth of the doctrine. But outwardly living the religious life might be sufficient in the long run to lead one to believe the doctrine. Critics of Pascal's wager argue that it is contrary to logic to suppose I could consciously trick myself into believing what I do not believe. But Pascal's device is not one of logical trickery. It is one of dynamic psychological change, as entailed in the brief account above. Indeed, Pascal seems to have held a theory of knowledge roughly like that presented here.

The evolutionary theorist George Price found himself believing in a fundamentalist Christianity. He saw his change of belief as logically necessary, because he could find no explanation for a certain series of events other than divine intervention.[4] He wrote his co-worker, William D. Hamilton, the great evolutionary theorist, about his beliefs and Hamilton responded that he could not accept Price's logic. Hamilton likened his own resistance to Christianity to "the Irishman who was asked whether he liked oysters and he replied, no, he didn't like oysters and he was glad he didn't like them because if he did he'd be eating them all the time when he hated the damned things." He also attempted to argue against Price's beliefs: "Why should we respect Moses if he was just a puppet carrying out maneuvers to foreshadow the crucifixion, and why respect Jesus for following a canon that he was bound to follow anyway? A plot so elaborate would make life meaningless if one believed in it—and ugly too." Price responded with his far better grasp of the nature of knowledge and belief: "The question is not whether you like it but whether it is true. What difference does it make whether you approve of it or not? Do you think that is something that I wanted to believe in?" (Schwartz 2000, 56–57).

Finally, note that beliefs may readily be grounded in the rewards of holding them in the case of children, who may naturally associate their own pleasure or benefit with the good. Praising a child's prayers, joining in her enjoyment of religious ceremonies that occasionally single her out for caring attention or praise, and otherwise rewarding her for her assertions of belief and for the consistency of her actions with her asserted belief may all directly reinforce her belief. For the child, there need be no feigning, because reward to self and belief seem united. Even the child, however, may feign belief when there is pressure to assert a belief that is not credible. For example, in *Le livre du mon ami*, Anatole France's (1892, chap. 8) autobiographical ten-year-old hero is pressured to own up to his sins in the confessional, although in all innocence he cannot claim to have sinned. But one must go to confession every Saturday and, without sin, there can be no confession. Eventually, he finds that a bit of

---

[4]This illogical conclusion is weirdly similar to the ID movement's argument from design.

creative lying about a pattern of sin of which he was not guilty saves him from the constant embarrassment of being without sin to confess.

COMMUNAL SOURCES OF BELIEF

For religious beliefs, we might imagine that most people are even less energetic than Samuel Johnson. They need not even hold out their hands, because the knowledge they get floods over them in a communal downpour. They hardly ever have occasion to doubt anything so massively supported by those around them. The English philosopher G.E.M. Anscombe ([1974] 1981), a convert to Catholicism, says that children must be taught some of the more incredible articles of Catholic faith at a very early age, or they will have a hard time ever coming to believe them. For example, only someone gifted with a child's magical thinking can accept the story of transubstantiation (Anscombe's own example) that turns a wafer into the flesh of Christ and wine into the blood of Christ, which decent Catholics then consume. Once taught at an early enough age, however, a person might survive adult reasoning without loss of the implausible belief. Indeed, even after the loss of central religious beliefs, someone intimidated by the invocation of the cross throughout childhood might still be motivated by its image in later life.

As in the earlier discussion of whose experts one should believe, we might suppose that one's community's religious views are a good source of information on the validity of one's own beliefs. It is a perverse source if we wish to claim that our religious beliefs are true in some ordinarily objective sense of "true," as many devoutly religious people insist their beliefs are. If I believe both that my religious beliefs are true and that there is a very high correlation between an individual's religious beliefs and the beliefs of that individual's community, I face a difficult logical problem. For religious beliefs, this may be a particularly fraught issue. Many with strong religious beliefs would be undeterred by mere logic or well-informed arguments and might assert that, despite all the logic of the facts, they simply cannot doubt their beliefs. As the American historian Edmund Morgan (2000, 47) writes of the American fundamentalists, "The conflicts that outsiders observe between factual statements in the Bible and the facts of history, human experience, and scientific observation are not as troubling to Fundamentalists as we may think they ought to be."

Ken Driggs, a Mormon historian and lawyer in Atlanta, puts the case for communal sources of religious belief and commitment clearly:

The starting point is that I am a committed Mormon. I can't imagine anything else. Once you make that decision, nothing knocks you awry.

I am aware of the conflicts; I know the Book of Mormon does not stand up to historical examination. But for me to decide that the problems are insurmountable would mean walking away from five generations of people before me. What really clicks, what really keeps us there, is the culture. (Wright 2002, 57)

COMMUNAL ENFORCEMENT OF BELIEF

It is a striking fact of religious commitment that people tend to share the commitments of their community, family, and friends, as Hobbes notes. Moreover, people in a community in which some are religious, may present themselves as religious, or as committed to the local religious code on certain matters, even though they do not genuinely share the local commitments. Why? Suppose I am a committed Muslim, Catholic, or fundamentalist Protestant, as are most of my community, and suppose you conspicuously doubt our beliefs. According to many religions, it matters for afterlife or other rewards whether one has the beliefs or exhibits the behavior prescribed by the religion; indeed, some Islamists suppose that nonbelievers and especially apostates should be killed. But since the truth of the beliefs is not readily demonstrable to one who does not share them, it may also be doubted by one's children or even, in a difficult moment, by oneself. Having people around who question the beliefs is therefore a risky matter if their views might persuade others. The community of believers will therefore have strong incentive to shun unbelievers and those who act against the tenets of their religion. Many religious groups have, in essence, a norm of exclusion against those who do not live up to the group's beliefs (Hardin 1995, chap. 4). Hence, they gain no information from those who are excluded.

Suppose that such a group dominates my community, and that there is a strong norm of exclusion. I now must, in my own interest, either share their beliefs or act as if I do. Or suppose that such a group did dominate my community, say, a generation ago but that its adherents are now a diminishing number. Because we have so long practiced our norm of exclusion, it may not be clear to anyone who are now the predominant types in our community: the formerly dominant believers or the increasingly numerous nonbelievers. Hence, we may all continue to abide by and to enforce the norm of exclusion against miscreants. To cite a pernicious example, we may be like the whites in the southern United States during the last days of Jim Crow laws that segregated blacks from whites. That is, we may go along with the norms of racial exclusion even though many of us do not share the racist beliefs. It is only when the occasion arises for us to act, and to discover how many of us there are who would stand against racism, that we finally escape the self-control that our now misplaced norm of exclusion exercises over us (Griffin [1961] 1976, p. 153).

Why would I live up to a norm of exclusion that I did not actually approve? Life in the community is more comfortable when one is accepted rather than excluded from its various activities. If I were really the only person who disapproved the local racism, I might not have any choice but to go along with it or virtually to leave the white society. This fact might mean that, over time, the racist norm would tend to get reinforced by the departure of those who disapprove it, leaving behind those who are most comfortable where that norm prevails. The result is a communal norm that comes into being and is maintained partly by indoctrination, partly by selection, and perhaps partly by feigning.

Under some circumstances, however, maintenance of the racist norm, for whatever reason, would tend to affect the beliefs of everyone in the community, making them more likely actually to share the racist beliefs. This would be especially true if there were an out-group in the society, as there typically is in the case of racism, which is directed at a racial out-group. It is the opportunity to express and act on the norm of exclusion that inculcates it, and that gives opportunity for shunning that enforces it and makes it more salient. A religious norm is similarly more likely to be enforced and to have strength in a context of contrary possibilities than in a context of general acceptance that tends to provoke no enforcement. Hence, it is fundamentalist movements within relatively more liberal milieus that have very strong norms.

Causally, it is not the fact that fundamentalist religious views are more forceful than liberal religious views that matters for their intensity, but rather the fact that they are embattled against the liberal tendencies that give the context for their intensity and force. It is virtually in the nature of more liberal views that they cannot generate norms of exclusion. There is a commonplace presumption that intensity of belief merits some consideration from others, especially in political contexts, for the supposed reason that such belief is more deeply held. The presumption is false. It is merely the strategic generation of the norms of exclusion that perversely makes commitment to such belief so intense. The belief is intense, because violation or neglect of it has severe personal consequences—not merely because it is inherently intense in its nature.

A common political claim for intense belief is that the state or the larger society of those who do not share the belief should give deference to it and to those who hold it. For example, the state should make special provisions to allow holders of the intense belief to reinforce the belief among their members. For example, the Israeli state protects fundamentalist sects of Judaism by outlawing traffic through their neighborhoods on the Sabbath. The claim here might be perverse. Nonbelievers might deserve greater protections from the state than do the artificially energized believers.

SINCERITY OF BELIEF AND KNOWLEDGE

Because religious (and moral) norms may be socially enforced with quasimoral judgments and sanctions, so that practice and belief may diverge, there is a striking difference between religious (and moral) belief and nonreligious pragmatic knowledge. One may often wonder about the sincerity of those who claim to hold religious beliefs, whereas one would typically not even think to wonder about my sincerity when I claim to know, say, how harsh the winter was, how to make my car start, or whether Caesar was a Roman (see, further, Foley 1994, 53; Coady 1994, 81). In this era of increasing fraud in science, perhaps sincerity in the form of honesty is a major issue even in science. To some degree, however, it is not only its normative quality, but also—and perhaps more so—its problem with sincerity that distinguishes religious from nonreligious pragmatic knowledge, and that leads us to speak of belief rather than of religious knowledge.

The problem of sincerity of religious beliefs can run very deep. For example, the eventual President George W. Bush and I grew up in a society in which many people touted religiosity but did not act according to their asserted religious beliefs. Social conformity in expression was pushed by the fact that many of these people would have been uncomfortable in the presence of those who did not profess strong religious beliefs. Indeed, they would have been more uncomfortable among doubters than among people whose beliefs were professedly strong, but substantially different from, even contrary to their own. Yet they would also have been uncomfortable among those who professed the same beliefs but professed them sincerely. Their own professions were like those of Stendahl's ([1831] 1953) young Mathilde in *Scarlet and Black*, who adopts airs of devotion that are motivated by the response they will bring from her small society, not by actual belief, or like those of the contemptible preacher in William Gass's (1966) *Omensetter's Luck*, who seems more concerned to have people think him good than actually to be good.

Against the importance of the problem of sincerity in distinguishing religious from nonreligious knowledge, one might assert that the deeper problem here is a lack of experimental testing for religious belief. But this scientific vision is a very late historical development—one could plausibly characterize it as the invention of Galileo, who is often called the first physicist. Admittedly, the separation of religious and nonreligious pragmatic knowledge is also a late development. But the separation was well understood long before Galileo. For example, Pythagoras reputedly asked someone to stop beating a dog because he recognized in the dog's yelp the voice of a deceased friend. The notoriety of this story has presumably turned in large part on the incredibility and, hence, supposed insincerity of Pythagoras's claim.

Even those who seem most deeply committed to their religious beliefs and who seem unfailingly to act according to them often express doubt about their own sincerity. The tradition of such self-doubt in Augustine, Pascal, Kierkegaard, and others is immanent in the religious life.[5] The tradition of skepticism about pragmatic knowledge of the physical world has almost the opposite character. Hume ([1739–40] 2000, 1.4.7, ¶9) famously notes that, at the end of a day of skeptical reflection, he can have a meal in the company of friends, as if to flout his skepticism about the existence of that world of daily pleasure. If there is insincerity, it is about the doubt, not about the content of pragmatic knowledge. It would seem Kafkaesque or, perhaps less elegantly, postmodern to wonder about the *sincerity* of one's own knowledge of the physical world.

The problem here is that of sincerity or of self-doubt, not of doubt of the religious beliefs themselves. One could doubt the latter without any insincerity in one's commitments still to follow them as the best judgment one can make—just as one can doubt any other bit of pragmatic knowledge without any insincerity in one's commitments to act on it as the best judgment one can make. The problem of insincerity arises from the mismatch between *incentives to express* beliefs and the content of one's actual beliefs. There can also, of course, be a mismatch between the dictates of one's religious beliefs and other, perhaps momentary, interests one might have. But there can be such mismatches between different interests that one might have, as in some accounts of the problem of weakness of will, without any implication that one's beliefs about these interests are problematic, should be misrepresented, or could profitably be misrepresented. The peculiar problem of religious beliefs is that they can pervasively be misrepresented with profit. This is the insincerity of the salesperson.

Although the problem of sincerity of beliefs may be pervasive for religious belief, it is not uniquely associated with such belief. It is motivated by the fact that there are rewards for the mere expression of beliefs. Consider two other realms of knowledge in which sincerity is at risk for the same reason: that reward accompanies expression that might differ from belief. First, in politics, rewards are clearly attached to advocacy of positions and to working on behalf of them. Politicians are commonly thought to be masters of insincerity, somehow winning support from

---

[5]For every Augustine with self-doubts there might be a hundred Torquemadas and Savonarolas who appear not to be troubled with the slightest hint of doubt in their beliefs, some of them so firmly that they are willing to kill with impunity in the cause of their beliefs.

people who do not believe them. Politics might be seen as an instance of advocacy. In advocacy of virtually all kinds, the task of the advocate is to represent views that she may not personally hold and, hence, to be insincere.[6] Some advocates, however, work on behalf of the client or other whose views they represent. Politicians sometimes are representatives in this sense. But sometimes they seem to adopt views for the principal purpose of securing their own place in office. Representation and self-serving might be hard to separate, and there is therefore great scope for insincerity. Senator Bill Frist, a Harvard M.D., absurdly claimed that he could see "through medical eyes" from a brief videotape that Terri Schiavo was not in a persistent vegetative state despite her having been apparently brain dead for fifteen years ("Terri Schiavo: The Misery Goes on." *Economist*, 26 March 2005: 29–30). An autopsy showed that she had been brain dead, her brain reduced to about half its normal size ("The Hard Facts Behind a Heartbreaking Case," *New York Times*, 19 June 2005: 4.5).

Second, it is a central supposition of postmodern social science that any academic claims might be motivated by interests rather than by belief in their truth. There is a sense in which this could well be true. I will be rewarded for the work I do, and those who control the rewards may reward some kinds of work far more generously than other kinds. I might therefore do what brings rewards rather than what compels by its seeming truth. In some fields, however, truth might be a far more compelling concern than in others, so that interests might well be strongly associated with truth in those fields. If other physicists cannot replicate the finding of cold fusion, for example, the physicists who purport to have found it suffer loss of respect if they do not concede the issue. In literary criticism there are no such tests, and in the social sciences the tests are commonly less compelling. Hence, the postmodern critique of knowledge might be crucial for literary criticism, less so for the social sciences, and hardly at all for physics or biology. Of course, it might be especially apt in application to the postmodern vision itself, as is suggested by the embarrassment of physicist Alan Sokal's spoof of the enterprise, which was published with seeming enthusiasm by the leading postmodern journal, *Social Text* (Sokal 1996a, 1996b).[7] The greatest difficulty postmodernists face in academic life is the pervasive suspicion from others that they are insincere, that their motivation is more to be audacious and nihilistically critical than to be meaningful or compelling in their claims.

Despite the importance of such instances of insincerity in merely pragmatic contexts, insincerity seems to be a massively more pervasive con-

[6]For discussion of moral problems of advocacy, see Audi 1995.

[7]Stanley Fish, director of the Duke University Press, the publisher of *Social Text* at the time of Sokal's publication, criticizes Sokal's views and defends postmodernists' views (Fish 1996). Also see *New York Times* 26 May 1996: 4.6.

cern in moral and religious contexts. Indeed, in these contexts insincerity seems to threaten at every moment, so pervasively that we may often wonder whether we can judge people to be genuine in their asserted views unless they take extreme actions that entail self-denial. When we praise those who have acted in saintly self-denial, it is plausibly not so much the self-denial as such that motivates us but the apparent proof of their actual sincerity of belief. The mortification of self practiced by such people as Saint Francis of Assisi is surely not in response to any plausible demand of a decent god. Its value, if it has any, is on Earth in giving credible witness to the sincerity of the beliefs of those people.

FUNDAMENTALIST, INFALLIBLE BELIEF

This is an inherently liberal account, and therefore perhaps an inherently subversive account of religious belief. It is about the sources and causes of belief, whereas religious beliefs are commonly defended as simply true by revelation or authority and beyond such explanatory investigation. Liberalism is part of the tradition of the Enlightenment and the investigative spirit of modern science. These come as a package. A liberal account takes for granted that there is a possibility of error, and that open, encompassing investigation must generally be useful for correcting error. Error can be grim. John Locke supposed that credally, just as much as politically, we are required to put our trust in what may prove to betray us (Dunn 1984, 298).

A liberal account is also inherently normative in the following limited sense. Because it is about the grounds for belief, it is about the reasons for belief. To say that one has reasons for a belief that trumps reasons for not holding the belief is to say that one ought to hold the belief. Or, if the explanation of a belief turns out to be socially generated *incentives* for holding it, rather than *reasons* for holding it, one ought to question the content of the belief. In both cases here, the "ought" is the limited one of rational ought. Science shares with liberalism the fundamentally important ethic of accepting the possibility that we are wrong. Fundamentalist religious believers deny the possibility that they could be wrong.

An interesting fact of religious beliefs is that they often come with a meta-level belief about the nature of the belief: that it was acquired in an oddly infallible way. There is a peculiar quality of religious knowledge that one would not claim for ordinary practical knowledge, or that liberals would not claim for any kind of knowledge. In the vocabulary of writings on religious belief, this quality is infallibilism. To be a fallibilist "is essentially to embrace the ideal of self-critical rationality" (Perry 1991, p. 100). A fallibilist holds her beliefs subject to error and correction. Many fundamentalist religious believers evidently believe that *even to suppose error possible* in their beliefs is to fail to live up to those beliefs. Doubt is itself a sin or a wrong. Clearly, a fallibilist cannot give honor to anyone else's claim to have infallible knowledge, and a liberal cannot give credit to any political claims to ground restrictions on supposedly infallible knowledge. Although there might be political difficulties in including religious views in a pluralist polity if those views entail restrictions on the behavior of nonbelievers, there are especially egregious problems in giving recognition to claims of infallibilism. On the economic theory of knowledge, we can make sense even of the view that their belief in infallibility is merely a bit of the knowledge that people come to have.

Moreover, whereas any theory of knowledge acquisition might be able to explain belief in the infallibility of some bit of knowledge, standard theories and sociologies of knowledge are incapable of recognizing any factual knowledge about the world as actually infallible. Indeed, it seems virtually incumbent on a theory of knowledge to be fallibilist. To inquire into the sources of infallible beliefs is therefore inherently to doubt them and, for the believer, to cast aspersions on *her* religiosity by casting doubt on her belief. The meta-level belief in the infallibility of some of one's beliefs is itself just another bit of ordinary knowledge and nothing more. Hence, *it would be incoherent for the ostensibly infallible believer to suppose a nonbeliever could believe the infallibility of her beliefs.* Imagine the oddity of the injunction: "I know you do not believe what I believe, but you must nevertheless believe that what I believe is true." The claim of infallibility simply brings discussion to a close. By definition, there is no point in pursuing dialogue between a liberal and an infallible believer on an issue of infallible belief other than to subvert not merely each other's views but, more profoundly, each other's ways of knowing things.

David Smolin, a law professor and an evangelical Christian who perhaps has infallible beliefs, complains that a requirement of fallibilism in knowledge for participation in political debate would exclude "from dialogue a number of culturally significant religious communities in America, including various Christian groups . . . and theologically conservative representatives of other monotheist[ic] religions" (in a letter quoted in Perry 1991, p. 139). Smolin's central point is to argue against the exclusion of religious claims from political discourse, as many others also argue (e.g., Quinn 1995). But his complaint seems oddly misplaced, at least in its wording. It is the claim of infallibility that closes off dialogue *by denying its relevance.* This is a logical, not a political, point. Those with infallible knowledge on some issue might not be excluded from *participating in politics* on that issue, but they exclude themselves from *dialogue* on it. For the infallibilist, politics is not a matter of dialogue and potential agreement but only of separating into secluded communities or of fighting to prevail and vanquish. The Amish separate; the Ayatollahs vanquish. It is distressing but not surprising that successful leaders with infallible beliefs—religious or secular—have established regimes that are numbered among the grisliest of human political history.

It is not clear on what grounds an infallibilist should tolerate holders of contrary views, except on the pragmatic political ground of incapacity to suppress them. A fallibilist, however, can value even putatively wrong theories as potential routes to better understanding. Fallibilism is the natural economic stance on knowledge, because it holds open the possibility of competition of ideas and the improvement of our knowledge. Freedom of speech is a fallibilist's ideal. Indeed, Mill's defense of free speech is grounded in its public (not its private) value to potential hearers, not its value to speakers. It is through hearing what you have to say that I might come to correct my fallible political knowledge. Hobbes argues that *you* cannot trust *my* claim of revelation ([1651] 1994 chap. 26, ¶40.). Therefore a revelation "obliges only him to whom it is revealed" (chap. 31, ¶3n).

It is common to argue against political toleration—especially by those strongly committed to their own views—that to tolerate is to put up with something bad or wrong. And if it is bad or wrong, we have reason to rid the world of it. It follows that toleration is misguided. But this is not the point of political toleration. Liberals do not simply tolerate something thought to be bad; rather, they tolerate persons whose views or actions are thought to be bad or wrong. They do so in part because they are fallibilists. They might outlaw certain actions, such as ritual sacrifice or suttee, for which the evidence of harm seems clearly to trump the evidence of benefit. But they do not outlaw beliefs or advocacy of beliefs. Openness to alternative beliefs and knowledge claims is, contra the standard defense of intolerance, rational for a fallibilist who, by definition, does not suffer the hubris of certainty.

What once gave many, maybe even most, religious visions their claim as knowledge in popular views was the fact that no competitive source of knowledge existed, other than fairly untutored observation. Since the rise of history and science, both in Greece, religious views no longer stand uncontested, and many of them can increasingly be seen as false. The arguments of the classical Jewish Midrash and of Christian exegetes of the Bible had some claim on the beliefs of people in their time. Today, they can be treated as anthropological oddities. They are products of what anthropologists once unfortunately called the "primitive mind" (Lévy-Bruhl [1910] 1926; [1922] 1923). That mind tends not to distinguish the seen from the unseen, such as spirits that inhabit stones and other seemingly inanimate objects. Lucien Lévy-Bruhl ([1922] 1923, 61–62) says, "The beings of the unseen world are no less directly present than those of the other; they are more active and more formidable. Consequently that world occupies [primitive] minds more entirely than this one, and it diverts their minds from reflecting, even to a slight extent, upon the data which we call objective." The chief difference between his primitives and our neighbors is arguably that there is virtually no distinction at all for the primitive, whereas for our religious neighbors it is primarily religious personages and perhaps devils and the dead who are among us as much as are the living.

If the Bible or the Koran were discovered for the first time in some desert cave today, it would not be taken at all seriously as the ground for belief in any of the principles of the three major religions founded on those texts.[8] For example, discovery of the Mesopotamian *Enuma Elish* in the nineteenth century has presumably led no one to believe its creation story (J. Moore 2002, 41–46). And the discovery in 1945 of the Nag Hammadi library of Gnostic texts in Upper Egypt has presumably led no one to reject the official Christian beliefs of our time and to replace them with Gnostic beliefs, some of which are arguably far more compelling and certainly less vicious than the official views—no one burns in a Gnostic hell (see Pagels 1979; Meyer 2005).

The three middle eastern religions as we know them today are social creations. For example, very little of Catholic practice is based on biblical passages. The church is a much later institutional creation. As a large and intrusive institution, it has massively affected the beliefs of hundreds of millions of people. It did so for more than a thousand years while keeping the biblical text essentially secret from the masses, who could not read any language, let alone the Latin of the Catholic Vulgate Bible, which historically was accessible more to those at universities than even to leaders in the church. Until relatively recently, few popes had read from a Bible (Stark 2003, 73–75).

Moreover, the actual texts of the Bible were determined in hard-fought contests in various conclaves. For example, the Gnostics were suppressed. Bart Ehrman therefore refers to "lost Christianities" and "the faiths we never knew" (Ehrman 2003a; Metzger 1987; for texts that were not adopted, see Ehrman 2003b). A large number of texts, none of which originated in the time from which they supposedly came, and none of which was written in the original languages, were reduced to the 27 books of the New Testament "as a canon of scripture" (Ehrman 2003a, 229). The struggle for exclusions and inclusions was long and was largely settled in the fourth century, but with finality only much later, in 1546, during the Council of Trent. Even then, there were many mistranslations of both the Old and the New Testaments along the way, including the unfortunate translation of the Hebrew word for "young woman" into the

[8]Suppose, contrariwise, that the cave held documents showing that one of the two texts had been a fraud perpetrated by identifiable people for their own benefit. One doubts that there would be a significant reduction in belief in the relevant religion.

Greek for "virgin" (in Isaiah 7.14).[9] Splinter groups adopted different texts in part. Today's literalists have a difficult case to make.

If we were to explain all the beliefs of any religion, we would then have explained them away and we would then no longer take the content of the religion seriously. Even then, however, we should take the believers seriously, and we should commonly even suppose that they have come by their beliefs in a relatively rational way. Hence, without criticizing the believers, one can, in the manner of standard philosophy of science, criticize and even dismiss the content of their beliefs. We might reasonably criticize the believers at the level of political action if they wish to impose their beliefs or practices on others. When individuals view themselves as the center of the world or even the sole concern in the world, we call them solipsists. It would be a case of group-solipsism if any group were to claim that their religion is true while all others (almost entirely uninvestigated) are necessarily false and can therefore be politically opposed. This is as much as to say that by reason of growing up in Alabama or Basra, we happen to know which religion is true.[10]

The parenthetical remark, "almost entirely uninvestigated," suggests a very peculiar fact about religious beliefs when considered alongside many other beliefs. Believers do not often comparison shop for the best religion. Given how much hinges on one's choice of religion, with its possibility of eternal damnation, one should expect that people would take great effort and incur high cost to discover the true religion (Frey 1997, 281). No doubt there are people who do shop around, including many of the younger Americans who attend more than one church each week. Conservative evangelicals and the ministers of some denominations criticize this as a consumerist approach (Neela Banerjee, "Going Church to Church to Find a Faith That Fits," *New York Times*, 30 December 2005: A18). But in general, it might be relatively normal, in all realms, to keep to a truth that one has come to believe until there is imposing evidence against it. The most stable religious communities may be those that are held together by strong norms of exclusion and by deliberate denial of internal debate on their religious views.

It is often asserted that religious beliefs should be given a special status, that they deserve a special degree of respect. We should not criticize them as readily as we criticize apparently poorly grounded or wrong factual beliefs. Religious beliefs are somehow more central or important to a person's identity. Against this view, there are many religious beliefs that should get no respect at all. More generally, the view that religious belief is special and distinctive is itself merely a matter of supposed knowledge,

---

[9]An irreverent Texas spoof recounts the preacher who objects to teaching Spanish in the schools. Why? "If English was good enough for Jesus, it's good enough for our kids."

[10]One recalls a philosopher's joke. If it is only the philosophers at the Australian National University who believe something, is that thing necessarily false?

enhanced in the case of any particular religious group by a group-solipsist distortion.

For example, many Muslims around the world wish to restrict the speech of Danish, French, and other news media that have published political cartoons featuring Muhammad, including one that depicts him as a terrorist suicide bomber. Several groups have threatened to kill randomly selected Danes, French, et al., to show that Islamists are deeply insulted by such cartoons (Jeffrey Stinson, "Protests over Prophet Cartoons Escalate across Muslim World," USA Today, 3 February 2006: 8A). Some Islamic leaders have called for the execution of the editors who allowed the printing of such material, and for cutting off the right hands of the cartoonists. Apparently, the Koran should govern the punishment even of unbelievers. Clearly, Islamists in our time have become the largest and most powerful instance of group-solipsists in world history. They are given some deference by Western leaders and observers only for that reason, therefore, not because the canons of free speech should include deference to religious views per se. The deference is to the hundreds of millions of mobilizable believers, not to their sometimes brutally violent beliefs. Islamists see Islam as special and therefore not eligible for criticism or parody. Fundamentalist Christians also see their own private perspectives this way. The two cannot both be uniquely special, and outsiders need not defer to the internal views of any such groups.

The signal difference between the two in this context is that Muslims can apparently be mobilized by demagogues to act with collective violence. The demagogues among fundamentalist Christians, such as Pat Robertson, come off as little more than silly. Robertson blames the people of New Orleans, thought to be a favorite home for homosexuals, for their bringing the wrath of god, as impersonated by hurricane Katrina, upon themselves. An imam declaring that a political cartoonist should have his or her hand cut off should similarly be dismissed as grandiosely silly, not religiously credible. When self-importance and solipsism are turned into murderous moral views, they deserve ridicule roughly equivalent to that which Robertson frequently receives. When thousands of European aristocrats were killing each other in duels for the sake of "honor," Sir Francis Bacon, England's attorney general, proposed to ridicule them in order to strip their actions of any honor (Hardin 1995, 92–93). We need to follow Bacon's advice today.[11]

[11]Deference has so far carried the day all too often. In 2000 a Dutch theater was to stage an opera, "Aisha and the Women of Medina." The opera was canceled in deference to pressure from Muslim clerics. That opera was based on a novel by a French-Algerian writer who also wrote the libretto, its music was composed by a Moroccan, and it was to be performed by Moroccans (New York Times 10 December 2000, §1, p. 40). It could have been a wonderful cross-cultural event, not a grievous disappointment.

Concluding Remarks

There is a recent strain of argument that religiosity, faith, and religion in general as a phenomenon are somehow genetically evolved in our brains. There is supposedly a biology of belief (Newberg, D'Aquili, and Rause 2001), a god-gene (Hamer 2004), or a god part of the brain (Alper 2001). At best, these authors argue from neurophysiological studies of so-called mystical states. Their books are at least a few decades too early for them to present or argue from compelling data, and they present none—pure speculation is their method. In any case, it is self-evident that, if any of these theses turns out to be true in some sense, nothing much follows for our grasp of what specific beliefs people have. The god part of your brain may tell you to kill the Midianitish woman in our midst, but that cannot be a genetic claim, because others' god parts give no such instruction in what it means to uphold a religion. We still have no explanation of why people believe what they do. Nor would a genetic explanation make any-one's beliefs compelling.

The crucial move in understanding the content of religious beliefs emerges when we recognize that we learn religious things the same way we learn other things—there is no added mystery. This claim is made clearer and more forceful by showing how the ordinary person comes to know (or believe) anything at all, and hence by showing that religious knowledge is not a mysterious separate category but merely part of the general category of knowledge. The economic theory handles religious belief just as it handles ordinary factual, scientific, political, moral, and other knowledge. As with all of these, learning religious beliefs is costly unless it just happens without our making any effort. Perhaps more than any other body of belief or knowledge, it comes to many people in a mas-sive flood, pouring over them from their parents and community, so that it costs virtually nothing for them to learn it. They can put their hands in their pockets and still they will catch lots of religious knowledge. Not even Samuel Johnson could have escaped the communal flood of it.

One who doubts the veracity of religious beliefs because they do not fit anything we actually see in the world must similarly wonder about much of science, which is about things and conceptions of things that are utterly incredible if belief is to turn on what ordinary people observe. The solid table at which I write this is seemingly dense and hard, yet physics for the past century says it is essentially vacuous space barely occupied with scat-tered particles. This mismatch has helped to spur the development of the philosophy of science on the part of major physicists such as Ludwig Boltzmann (see, e.g., Blackmore 1995; Cercignani 1998). Sociologically and psychologically, we should take the fact of religious beliefs seriously, but philosophically or scientifically we should not take the content of such beliefs seriously. Yet most of us should generally take the content of the science that we know only as 'opiniatretry' seriously. It stands behind much of technology, which could only be seen as magical if it were not demonstrably the product of careful, systematic science.

An economic theory of knowledge seemingly makes sense of much of the phenomenon of religious belief as merely a body of knowledge. Such a theory must, of course, be concerned with the *incentives for and costs of coming to discover* some bit of knowledge, which is the common focus of the economics of information. And it must be concerned with the structure or pattern of the happenstance availability of plausibly relevant knowledge in moments of decision. But it must also be concerned with the causing and maintaining of belief through the forceful incentives of norms of exclusion, functional reinforcement, Hobbes's communal teaching, and adaptive belief formation. These mechanisms concern the way *incentives actually bring one to come to believe* some range of knowledge or beliefs, not merely the incentives for coming across the content of that knowledge. This concern might be of interest in virtually all areas of pragmatic, that is, useful knowledge.

Additionally, when a bit of knowledge or belief has normative implications, especially when it is rewarded by the reactions—rewards or sanctions—of others for normative reasons, it can be subject to the problem of insincerity. Insincerity would generally be an odd problem for most of ordinary pragmatic knowledge, but it might be commonplace for moral knowledge, including such knowledge grounded in religious belief.[12] As is the case in Hume's claim that normative and objective visions are inherently, logically separate, so insincerity depends on the predication of normative concerns and not merely on assessments of objective facts.

Religious belief and ordinary knowledge are kin. Forced to abjure his knowledge publicly, Galileo still could not abjure it privately, and he supposedly muttered sotto voce that, despite his abjuration, still the Earth moves about the sun: eppur si muove. Earth is not, as the institutionalized church insisted, the center of the universe. Galileo could not stop knowing this and other facts because he had observed them, some of them through his magnificent telescope, which the church fathers refused to look through. We are like Galileo, in the sense that our faith and knowledge are not subject to compulsion by others. We might, of course, be forced to change our circumstances, and this might lead us to revise our beliefs in time, as Blaise Pascal famously argued, and as any view of the social construction of knowledge suggests is possible (though not certain). But we stand with Galileo in that we cannot literally submit what we know to coerced change.

[12]The problem of sincerity is mentioned in passing by Foley (1994, 53) as a potential problem in our accepting some bit of knowledge from an asserted authority.

CHAPTER 8

Culture

CULTURE is a product of knowledge and the constraints and commitments that follow from that knowledge. These constraints and commitments give culture its bite. Hence, if we are to understand culture and its appeals, we must understand the knowledge from which it is built. The characteristics of cultural knowledge and the characteristic manner in which it is obtained tell the story of cultural commitments, and allow us to assess it normatively. Attempting to assess it cold, without understanding the communal knowledge on which it is built, will fail. In particular, if we want to understand cultural commitments, we must understand ordinary knowledge, as characterized by the theory of knowledge presented here.

In an account of culture from ordinary knowledge, we must first explain the knowledge of the individual, or the content of what a particular person knows. Second, we must explain how individuals come to have a *common body* of knowledge—communal knowledge—and how that communal knowledge spontaneously fits and characterizes the culture. This requirement goes beyond much of the prior discussion of ordinary knowledge here. Religious knowledge is similarly held in common but typically it is hierarchically and not merely spontaneously enforced.[1] Third, and finally, we must explain how this body of knowledge motivates individuals.

The first of these tasks—the explication and explanation of individual knowledge and its constraints—has been addressed in chapter 1 and in application to particular ranges of issues in later chapters. Here I will apply this account to the latter two issues, the common body of knowledge and how it motivates individuals. I will begin with an explanation of two phenomena that define certain limits of spontaneous social order: affinity group formation, such as clique formation, and the generation of norms of exclusion. These two phenomena play together—along with the particularities of local bodies of knowledge—as central parts of the workings of a culture, with its combination of closeness and closedness. Then I will turn to the question of the normative goodness of a culture and how

---

[1]Even it is spontaneously enforced to some extent, as an old verse proclaims: "They thieve and plot and toil and plod and go to church on Sunday. It's true enough that some fear god, but they all fear Mrs. Grundy" (quoted by Lovelock 1998).

culture determines collective identity and identification, which is de facto the motivation to live by the culture and to maintain it.

Finally, I will show that this ordinary-knowledge account of culture fits the paradigm of functional explanation, so that culture is self-replicating across generations. Culture therefore provides us with a spontaneous social order. This conclusion is important, because it makes sense of the spontaneous, self-enforcing maintenance of culture on grounds other than the claim that the culture is sustained simply because people are normatively committed to it. For if culture is built on knowledge, that claim is weak, because we know that our knowledge is often challenged and altered, as suggested by the virtual extinction of Puritan, Quaker, and other fundamentalist religions that led to the creation of the United States as a liberal nation and society, one that undercut the religious beliefs of the very religious groups whose existence forced the adoption of constitutional protection of religious beliefs and religious liberty. Moral knowledge is no different; indeed, for the ordinary knowledge of many people there is not even a clear distinction between moral and pragmatic knowledge. The functional account grounds maintenance in the interests of the members of the society.

GROUP-SPECIFIC IMPLICATIONS OF INDIVIDUAL KNOWLEDGE

To move from individual to group level understandings from the economic theory of ordinary knowledge, let us examine two phenomena—clique formation and norms of exclusion—that turn on knowledge and its high costs. Both of these phenomena work through devices that economize on the knowledge that enables us to have relationships with others. I can invest only so much effort in cultivating knowledge of particular other people, and I therefore concentrate my efforts on a relatively small number of people. But your and my efforts aggregate into a body of knowledge that is partly specific to our group, which coordinates us on particular beliefs and practices. There need be little system in the development of a group's group-specific knowledge. That knowledge is apt to differ in highly idiosyncratic ways from one group to another. These differences in central parts of my group's communal knowledge and your group's communal knowledge help to define us as essentially different groups with at least partially different cultures.

Typically, if we are to organize ourselves communally, in a way that maintains particular cultural values and practices, we will generally have to do so spontaneously, through interpersonal relations that are not backed by powerful institutions of government, or even by religious authorities. For example, northern Italian and Sicilian cultures differed substantially even when both were under Catholic religious hegemony. Religion is typically part of the culture of a society, but we will need endogenous, spontaneously motivated reasons or incentives for adhering to our culture. Spontaneous organization even for what is generally agreed to be a simple collective benefit is likely to be very difficult (Olson 1965; Hardin 1982). To sustain it over generations seems likely to be nearly impossible, even if we assume that the individual members of the cultural group must at least substantially be motivated by personal concern with the collective benefit of the culture. And yet, there are many cultures that seemingly have survived many generations with only modest change over time. For example, Armenians and Jews have maintained strong cultures over many centuries, and often despite brutal external attacks.

The chief obstacle to maintenance of such a strong set of governing beliefs is that they must often run against the immediate short-run interests of many of us within the culture. We could partially overcome this obstacle if we could develop close, trusting relationships with enough people. To do so is virtually impossible in even a moderately complex society. As Adam Smith remarks, in civilized society, the individual "stands at all times in need of the cooperation and assistance of great multitudes, while his whole life is scarce sufficient to gain the friendship of a few persons" (Smith [1776] 1976, bk. 1, chap. 2, p. 26).

The most obviously effective way to counter the incentive to follow contrary individual interests would be to introduce other incentives, including sanctions, that would outweigh the incentives to violate the norms and practices of the culture. We know that this tactic is possible even without external regulation or sanction for long-term dyadic and small number interactions, even when those interactions involve a substantial element of conflict along with an element of coordination, thus affording opportunity for cooperation.[2] What we need is to build up from that dyadic and very small-number level to the societal level. To see the limits of this tactic, let us begin discussion at the very small scale by examining cliques and friendships, which we could expect to persist relatively well in their own right, but which might not be expandable to the very large societal level.

Clique Formation

Consider limits on how many individuals one can know as well as one typically knows friends. If you are my friend, I have most likely known you fairly well over a relatively long period of time. We likely have come

---

[2]As in the structure of the game theorists' prisoner's dilemma, with its superficially perverse set of incentives not to cooperate in many contexts but to cooperate in others.

to know and like each other through many interactions of perhaps varied kinds. To speak of you as my friend evokes associations with many of our activities and interactions together. I am able to predict much of your behavior and your reactions to many things, from having learned them from past behavior. All of this must have taken a lot of time, not necessarily time that was deliberately invested in developing our friendship, but nevertheless a lot of time interacting with each other. If I already have several friends I might not think the cost and even the risk of investing in developing another is worth it. As of now, my current set of friends might give me satisfactory pleasures. Indeed, I might not have as much time as I would like to have to spend with each of them.

This problem of limited time might explain at least part of the phenomenon of clique and friendship-group formation (Hardin 2002, 175–76). It might also be part of the explanation of familism in contexts in which families are relatively large, large enough to exhaust the greater part of the resources of time and energy that any member might have for investing in rich relationships. In the vocabulary of Albert Breton and Ronald Wintrobe (1982), members of cliques might concentrate their investments in exchange relations in a small number of intensive relationships and might shun others, merely to avoid the difficulties of dealing with those with whom they do not have intensive relationships. There are two quite different problems in dealing with such people: lack of a past intensive relationship means that we might have little knowledge of the other; and lack of expectation of a future intensive relationship means that we have little capacity for giving the other the incentive to be reliable in dealings with us, except perhaps through reputational effects.

Similarly, groups might actively develop exclusionary devices to keep their membership comfortably associated only with those they know well enough to trust. Trust typically is an assessment of the trustworthiness of the other. That assessment can be based on belief that the trusted wants to maintain a relationship with the potential truster, that the trusted loves, likes, or otherwise directly has the truster's interests at heart, or that the trusted is committed to some moral principle such as reciprocity or has a strong psychological disposition to be a reliable person in various kinds of relationship (Hardin 2002). All of these make substantial knowledge demands. There are limits to how many people I can know well enough to judge their trustworthiness toward me. There are also limits to how many people I can involve in ongoing relationships that would be rich or frequent enough to establish trust.

Clique formation turns on the limits on developing more than a modest number of close relationships. Perhaps the most important of these is investments of time. For example, the members of a family might wind up in conflict with other families primarily because they simply have no time for them while they are heavily engaged in daily life and toil with one another, as reflected in the conditions in Edward Banfield's (1958) account of life in the fictionally named poor farming village of Montegrano in southern Italy. But this means that, because people are not having fairly rich relationships with others beyond their cliques or their families, they are not even in a position to develop trusting relationships with those others, because they do not have the ongoing exchange relationships in which to embed interests in trustworthiness.

Hence, it is the rational structure of the ongoing relationship in which trust is typically based that blocks trusting more universally. Trust as part of a relationship rules out the possibility or coherence of so-called generalized trust (when one supposedly trusts everyone, including the anonymous unnamed other whom one has never seen before and might never see again) and even of very widespread trust by any individual (Hardin 2002, 60–62). And it blocks the possibility of building a sizable cultural community by grounding it in commitments between individuals all of whom have extensive relationships with each other. Except in very small close and closed communities, there is not enough time in daily life to build up social order out of extensive dyadic and small-number interactions that connect each individual to each other and out of the incentives that such relationships give us.

Norms of Exclusion

In the face of the limits to expansion of a clique or network of friends, how can we organize a society that is substantially larger than such groups? For social contexts in which collective action is required but in which we do not have centralized authorities to give us incentives to overcome our individualistic urges against doing our share in a cooperative venture, there are two devices at work (Hardin 1995, chapters 4 and 5). First, we can develop norms that induce cooperative behavior. Such norms are likely to be fairly weak because, when they are invoked, they generally have to contend with the counter pressure of self interest. Second, we can develop similarity of desires for some collective things and activities, so that we all naturally coordinate on the same desire and, hence, action. In effect, we develop shared values and motivations. We need not actually have those values if we can devise incentive systems to get each other to act in accord with them. When we do this, we de facto create norms of exclusion that make membership in our group or community depend on shared values by excluding those who do not share those values.

There are two striking facts about norms when they are viewed systematically as strategic devices. First, norms that serve collective interests are stronger when they are congruent with and reinforced by individual interests, and they are weaker and less effective when they are opposed to individual interests. Second, norms that are focused on groups are more forceful than those that are universalistic. Groups can mobilize incentives to entice stronger commitments, and can reduce opportunities for gaining wider knowledge that would undercut the groups' norms (Hardin 1995, 140–41). They can, for example, use shunning and even banning to keep individuals in line. If life in the community is valuable to its members once their preferences have been formed and their comforts are well met by the community, these sanctions will be powerful. There might be some who would not think being banned was very costly, because their preference might actually be to move on to a different community or even to the cosmopolitan lack of close community. But for many in a close community, being shunned or banned would be enormously destructive, and the risk of bearing such sanctions would add to the value of contributing to the maintenance of the community's norms and practices.

Again, both of these phenomena—clique formation and norms of exclusion—turn on knowledge and its high costs. I can invest only so much in cultivating knowledge of other people, and I therefore concentrate my efforts on a relatively small number, or on a larger number who have been vetted in a sense by my community through our exclusion of anyone who does not follow our norms. In the second case, if I can count on their all having very much in common (our culture), I can know them more readily and can treat a substantially larger number of people as if I almost know them. Moreover, both cases aggregate into a body of knowledge that is partly specific to our group, knowledge that coordinates us on particular bits of behavior. As discussed later, we could also say that the group coordinates us on a similar or collective identity through the knowledge that is specifically ours and definitive of us.

When it defines a culture, ordinary knowledge can be forcefully and spontaneously imposed on us through norms of exclusion, without need of hierarchical authorities to keep us all in line. Culture is backed by a body of knowledge that, in a sense, has a boundary around it, a boundary that is more or less secure against the easy entry of contrary new knowledge. If it is too permeable, the culture will likely be transformed so much over time that we might no longer think of it as merely a later version of the same culture.

KNOWLEDGE AND CULTURE

We can draw several implications from the economic theory of knowledge. These are not logical entailments, but merely modal empirical inferences, some of which might fail an empirical test, either in a particular culture or more generally. These modal inferences include path dependence, conservatism, lack of distinction between belief and knowledge, lack of a clear distinction between moral and factual knowledge, differences between institutional and individual-level knowledge, and a bias toward one's own interests in the knowledge that we acquire. These are spelled out for individual knowledge in chapter 1. Here we apply them to the group.

These characteristics of a culture's knowledge follow simply from the way in which cultural knowledge works. It is the knowledge that is definitive. Still, the culture replicates the knowledge by conveying it into the next generation, and by reinforcing its content and the ways in which it is learned. Part of this sounds like feedback to reproduce the culture's knowledge and is therefore like a functional explanation. I will show later that this implication rings true. The maintenance of culture, when culture is explained as the result of ordinary communal knowledge, fits a functional explanation. This is an important conclusion, because it means that culture is spontaneously maintained by its society, and that it can override and survive individual transgressions to a substantial degree.

Path Dependence

Ordinary knowledge is likely to be path dependent, much as the common law is path dependent. Bits of it get corrected at the margin, but it is not likely to be subject to revolutionary reconsideration. Marginal corrections can lead to what we could call local optimums, but we could not reasonably expect to reach a general optimum naturally (for elaboration, see Elster 1979: 1–35). Because we are not scientists or philosophical epistemologists concerned with demonstrating the truth of our knowledge, we will tend to satisfice, to accept outcomes that are good enough without pushing further to find the best possible outcome. To say that knowledge is path dependent almost naturally fits the idea of a culture that has descended to us from the past and that is largely intact. Whatever changes have occurred during its career, they have likely been marginal in any given instance, or we would wonder whether the present culture is substantially continuous with that of the past.

A standard example of the effects of path dependence is the internal combustion engine. By now, that engine has benefited from more than a century of innovation from tens of thousands of engineers and others, as well as from petrochemists at work on improving the efficiency of its fuels. It has benefited from the natural experiment of using hundreds of millions of cars equipped with that engine. No alternative engine design can be expected to match such a massive effort at marginal improvements, which have created the standard to beat. The internal combustion engine might have been the easiest, best way to go in the initial years of the development of the automobile, or it might have been a nearly accidental choice. But it might in theory be a very bad way to go, perhaps especially once we have recognized some of its external effects in pollution and in the dreadful politics of the oil-exporting states. For any new technology to compete now, however, it would have to be substantially better already, from the moment of its initial use, because it could not yet benefit from a century of marginal improvements as the internal combustion engine has done. Note, incidentally, that this is an example of collective or communal path dependence, not an individual-level example.

Culture similarly benefits from piecemeal marginal adaptations over time, rather than from radical redesign. It too is a collective construction, and it too can be altered incrementally, often for the better in the sense of serving the members of its society better. Individuals and groups might make discoveries that change our communal practices. As with the internal combustion engine, however, those changes will commonly be marginal and not substantial, although in time they might accumulate into massive changes in our society, in comparison to its predecessor society some generations ago.

Because these changes are marginal and relatively slow in taking root, our culture might long ago have happened into structures or practices that ill-serve us today, but that are hard to change through marginal revisions. For example, we might have marriage and family practices that no one would intentionally choose. We might have elevated certain destructive practices to pervasive dominance of many relationships. Great respect for the culture per se might seem to block criticism of such practices, but even within a strong culture these practices might be criticized. If there are powerful institutions on which we might call to intervene in such practices, we might benefit from calling on them. But typically, if there are such institutions, they are at least partially outside the culture, and their intrusion into our practices might be greeted with great hostility. Strangely, it is possible to explain some perversely destructive practices, such as the duel (Hardin 1995, 91–100), in terms that fit the interests of relevant participants so that, although many might be sorely victimized by the practices, others might see themselves clearly as beneficiaries of them—even though their main vocal defense of the practices might be the simple conservative but vacuous claim that they are morally right.

Conservatism

Such unwavering path dependence typically implies conservatism. This process feeds into the natural tendency toward conservatism that follows from the fact that testing our knowledge is costly, and that trying to find new knowledge is also costly. Moreover, if we do find new knowledge that would recommend changing some practice, that change will itself be costly. It will also be risky, in the sense that the new knowledge will not yet be backed by sufficient experience to justify any claim for its superiority. It is often likely to seem less demanding just to hold fast to what we already have. At least we know what we already have and how it works—and we know, especially, *that* it works.

Similarly, conservatism accords naturally with the idea of a culture that we inherit. Bringing in dramatic new influences from outside is a major irritant to defenders of cultures. The complaint that western and, especially, American culture is overwhelming other cultures is partly just a complaint against importations that a bit of openness might allow, importations that might finally tip the balance against conservative commitments to a particular cultural inheritance. The central motor in so-called cultural imperialism may be nothing more than the appeals of openness to ideas and goods. Such openness challenges the conservatism of maintaining some set of cultural beliefs and practices unchanged. Newness and change may especially appeal to the young, who have not yet made more or less final commitments to central tenets of their society's culture. But a culture's future depends on the eventual commitments of the young, so their openness may be death to much of the culture of their forebears. To call this process imperialism is odd; it is more nearly adoption. Efforts to block the adoption of new ideas can succeed only by constraining the next generation. Not even the Ayatollahs of Iran have been able to do that very effectively.

Authoritarian commitment is often a general desire to transfer sovereignty to some collective and to conform to its norms (Stenner 2005 and 2007). Identification with the group is not the central drive. Rather, it is threats to the normative order of the collective that provoke authoritarian responses. If there is one true people and one right way to be, then politics per se simply makes no sense, just as debate over religious views makes no sense for infallibilist believers. Any threat of political change should therefore provoke authoritarian responses, which therefore should rise dramatically at times of major political change. This reaction is an extreme version of cultural conservatism, in which we individually delegate to some form of enlightened or trustworthy leadership the control over our own beliefs and behavior.

The authoritarian attitude is activated by threats to the community. That attitude can encompass extremist national commitment, racism, and intolerance across many domains, including trivial matters of dress and style. The reaction to any threat to the community makes authoritarians hostile to certain others, and leads them to be mobilized against those others. Manifestations of authoritarianism depend on interaction between individual predispositions and societal conditions or events. The defender of communal culture might tend to focus on the benignly sweet times when the behaviors of intolerance are not provoked, while the critic of communal culture might tend to focus on the extreme moments of threat, when those behaviors might be intense and oppressive and even murderous. Both times are, however, part of the life of community, which must be taken and judged whole and not selectively.

We could ask speculatively in what circumstances the seeming conservatism of knowledge might be overcome. There are two partially separate issues here: overcoming it at the individual level and overcoming it at the societal level. For an individual, it is important that others are also open and also quest for new knowledge, and that there is feedback from revision of knowledge to demonstrate its payoff. The invention of science and the scientific method by Galileo and others set Europe on the road to constant change prompted by the innovations of individuals.

For a society, openness is likely a coordination or tipping phenomenon. If enough are open, it is easy and natural to be open. Big science is organized for discovery and knowledge revision, especially since about 1880. Early successes of big science radically altered the way universities are structured, and de facto made innovation a constant organizational goal. This mission of universities (and increasingly of industrial research departments) virtually guarantees that individual innovators will be rewarded, yielding feedback to personal incentives. But experiences with openness in liberal societies do not readily translate into ways that close and closed communities can alter their cultures to the benefit of their members.

Factual versus Moral Knowledge

As already argued, there is no precise distinction between factual and moral knowledge for ordinary persons. There is no reason of usefulness for us to categorize according to the philosophical canons that might differentiate the two. In our daily lives, they both give reasons for acting in some ways rather than in others. We might actually draw the distinction, but then draw it vaguely, thus failing to categorize everything properly. And on any given occasion of its invocation, we might miscategorize even knowledge that we might, under the pressure of tough discussion, readily recognize as belonging in the other category.

Most of our moral knowledge might be put to use as if it were merely factual knowledge, and much of our factual knowledge might seem to us to have a moral basis. Indeed, given the frequent conservatism of ordinary knowledge, we might tend to see most of our knowledge as inherently right morally and not merely factually. This tendency is apt to be even more typically characteristic of cultural knowledge. We will tend to judge all of our cultural practices and norms as the right way to do things.

I know how to plant my crops because I have learned it from my fore-bears, but I might go further and suppose that this is the only right way to plant them. Such easy judgment of the rightness of our own culture's norms and practices might give us ground for criticizing other cultures, and even for general hostility to them.

Our culture takes on the aspect of a whole system of what is right for us. That system is grounded on what there has been. That is to say, *it is grounded in a derivation of ought from is or, more accurately, a derivation of ought from was*. It is hard to think of a more pervasive way in which facts and values can be run together than in the holistic evaluation of a culture as somehow good. In a culture, even more than in ordinary knowledge generally, I might tend to see most of my knowledge as inherently right morally and not merely factually. I know the customs and practices of my culture, and I know them as right for us. I might think they would be right for you as well, but despite this I might also wish not to share them with you, especially if the way to share them is to bring you into my culture. If you are outside my community, you are not my responsibility.

Belief and Knowledge

For the ordinary person, there is no meaningful distinction between knowledge and belief. In contemporary philosophy of science, we seek criteria for claiming that some putative bit of knowledge is justified, so that, in philosophical jargon, we can call it a justified true belief. This is a somewhat odd notion, because there remains the question who is able to say that the belief is justified. But for the typical individual in ordinary contexts, there is commonly no issue of establishing the "truth" of our beliefs. I believe some claim. What more do I have to do to establish that my belief is true? Or is there some super knower who issues that judgment? Whatever happened to lead me into believing the claim to be just is my justification for the belief. Often we will be able to judge the utility of some belief to some degree, but we would have little interest in investing much effort to meeting the criteria for truth in any philosophical epistemology. The buck stops long before it is all spent on further evidence (this is very nearly Herbert Simon's [1955, 1957] definition of satisficing).

As with ordinary knowledge in general, so in a culture there is commonly no issue of establishing the "truth" of our beliefs, so that belief and knowledge are not meaningfully distinguishable for us in the way that philosophers of scientific epistemology distinguish them. They just are correct or right or true for us. Moreover, we cannot, in any meaningful sense, even judge the utility of some of our core beliefs, because they are justified almost entirely by the fact that they are part of our culture. To violate them would be to violate our culture and to threaten its continuity. For many of us, the utility of that culture is so great that it hardly makes sense to attempt to assess just how valuable it is. That is tantamount to assessing just how valuable existence is.

Bias toward Group Interest

If I seek some bit of knowledge because it might benefit me to know it, then acquiring that knowledge may tend to lead me to a bias toward my own interests, even when I am acting or deciding for others or for some group or community. This process presents a fairly obvious potential bias for individual knowledge. Here, our question is whether it might also work for collective or cultural knowledge, where the bias must be in favor of the cultural group or community. There are, of course, ways in which individual-level bias might be at issue for cultural knowledge if there are effectively hierarchical differences between community members, and if some might benefit at costs to others, as is true of the practice of the duel mentioned above.

There are also many cases in which hierarchical *use* of ordinary knowledge substantially serves the interests of political leaders. Slobodan Milosevich, for example, invoked false history, bigoted characterizations of non-Serbs in Yugoslavia, a general myth of Serbian greatness and uniqueness, claims of violation of Serbian rights, all to gain and hold power over Yugoslavia through its grim ordeal of self-destruction. He, Franjo Tudjman, and Radovan Karadzic were parasites on their own societies. It may be that they did not believe the ridiculous things they claimed. Rather, they may merely have used those claims in their own interest to manipulate their own people. They called on brotherhood and faith and kin because it was in their personal interest to do so (Ajami 1993, 9).

Could, however, the bias toward their own interests that individuals often have with ordinary knowledge have an analog at the aggregate or group level? Is there a group whose members benefit from a belief that they might hold in common, so that their benefit reinforces the belief? Perhaps. Imagine a case in which members of one group hold themselves to be superior to another, and in which that group could benefit from suppression of the other. Some Serbs in the Bosnian and Kosovan conflicts may have seen themselves as superior to the Muslim populations. Many Europeans, and not only Germans, have seen themselves as superior to Jews, and have benefited from legal strictures against Jews that many people may have justified as moral.

In a less malign way, a group could tend to see almost everything in terms of how it fits the group's self-definition, and therefore its own definition of its interests. Perhaps all cultural groups possess a strong element of distorted perceptions of reality that fit their own identification with their culture. Even ordinary nationalists or patriots of the most gentle kind probably see their own status in the world through distorting lenses that make their own nation somehow especially good or honorable in comparison to others. The English belief in the inherent superiority of English culture over French is a standing joke among the French, who are certain that their own culture has a far greater claim on our respect.

Part of the explanation of such a bias might be that counter evidence against what we already believe will tend to be rejected or not even sought, whereas confirming evidence will tend to be sought and will tend to become generalized because this course is mentally cheaper. This is, of course, a very general phenomenon, and therefore has a label: the confirmation bias. In psychological decision theory, the confirmation bias is commonly discussed as a mental trick. It might, however, be more constructively seen as an economic bias in favor of marginal rather than whole-cloth revisions to our beliefs, so that it becomes part of the path dependence of our knowledge. It might often be a relatively benign trick, one that has no particular direction other than the conservative direction of path dependence. But in ordinary knowledge, especially cultural knowledge, it may introduce a malign twist, because ordinary knowledge may be rent through by this bias, often effectively supporting our interests as currently determined by commitment to our culture.

This bias might also help to explain conservatism. The tendency beyond a certain age to become settled in one's commitments and values might merely be an implicit economic move to reduce the costs of making further choices, by de facto considering some of such choices as already made in advance. As we have seen in the explanation of path dependence, it is far less costly and risky to make marginal revisions in our commitments than to reconsider them more substantially. This might even be an ethological fact of our developmental stages. If so, then we might require the creation of institutional devices designed to keep us open to innovation by sometimes overriding our ethologically determined tendencies against openness to new things in our later years.

Cultural versus Institutional Knowledge

In general, we can suppose that institutions and individuals often have different capacities for acquiring knowledge (see, further, chap. 6; and Hardin 1994). Institutions are very good at amassing systematic knowledge, such as census data, life histories, large-scale plans, and so forth. Individuals are very good at acquiring idiosyncratic knowledge of other individuals, such as whether a colleague cheats a friend or employer, or has a secret affair. Institutions might even be barred from using some kinds of individual-level facts, unless they are first subjected to standard criteria for assessing their reliability. Institutions are more likely to meet the canons of the philosophy of science, albeit somewhat loosely. Individuals are likely to test the truth of claims in some contexts, such as when you suspect that I am cheating you in some way, and you want to see proof before acting against me and perhaps foolishly wrecking our friendship. But individuals are not generally systematic, whereas organizations and institutions are almost by definition systematic in their acquisition and use of knowledge.

Differences between individual and institutional knowledge might seem to be irrelevant for understanding culture. Behind our culture there need be no formal institutional devices for collecting or assessing the quality of knowledge. There may be only informal devices, such as norms and spontaneously motivated sanctions from other individuals, to govern collective activities. *Culture is almost entirely built of unintended consequences.* Institutions have at least an element of deliberate design, planning, and application. They too are modified over time in unintentional, undirected ways, but the element of design is nevertheless distinctively different from the fully undirected way a culture comes into being and persists. Indeed, organization theorists often speak of "the culture" of an organization or institution, and what they mean is that there are aspects of the institution that have grown as unintended consequences, but which nonetheless govern much of the life of the institution; they can make the institution function better or worse, in important and pervasive ways that no one might have designed. Moreover, such theorists suppose, surely rightly, that this process is common even in the most carefully designed organizations. Still, it makes compelling sense to say that an institution is largely created, whereas culture simply happens over the generations.

A striking difference between cultural knowledge and the knowledge that a typical institution has is that the former is apt to be fairly restricted in its focus and to be relatively immune to correction, whereas the latter can be very systematic, very general, and readily corrected through institutional interventions. If I think my culture has it wrong, there is no one to whom to turn to try to make it right. An institution can virtually legislate a change from within its own knowledge. A culture cannot do this, although, if it is under the management of a state, that state can legislate changes and those changes may stick—if not instantly, then intergenerationally through the creation of a next generation whose beliefs and interests differ from those of their forebears. If some cultures are to be secured, they might need to have the backing of a state. But then they are at risk of legislated change that could quickly alter their commitments. Our unease at the prospects for liberalism in Iraq stem from the realization that each of two powerful groups wishes to seize control of the government, in order to impose its own culture on all Iraqis, as the Ayatollahs in Iran imposed their culture on all Iranians. A liberal order evidently has no appeal to either group.

A Functional Account of Culture

Given the account here of the elements of the communal-knowledge theory of culture, we can show that culture is functionally maintained by such knowledge. As discussed in chapter 7 on religion, the paradigm of functional explanation is as follows (Merton 1968, 73–138; Elster 1979, 28; Hardin 1980 and 1995, 82–86). *An institution or, in the present case, a behavioral pattern is explained by its function for some group or, in the present case, community* if and only if the function is an effect of the behavioral pattern; the function is beneficial for the community; and the function maintains the behavioral pattern.

The pattern here is (communal) cultural knowledge; its function is to maintain a particular culture for the society, with all of the comforts that the culture provides its members. Culture is an *effect* of communal knowledge, that is, culture is built up from relevant knowledge. Their culture is good for—serves the interests of—the members of the society. Their culture maintains their cultural knowledge by feedback from the (other) members of the society, who have and reinforce the relevant knowledge.

As usual, the seemingly difficult part here is the second step: their culture is good for the members of the society. This conclusion is true only if the members of the society have already formed the preferences and adopted the values that give them the collective identity of the culture. If they have these preferences, then the culture gives them support and gives them comfort. (One might also suppose that it reduces conflicts of certain kinds within the society.) Clearly, the culture is not so likely to be good for a newcomer or immigrant to the society, because such a person will not have developed the relevant preferences, tastes, and beliefs, and may be seen as a Trojan horse.

Also, again, the functional account cannot fit children in a given society, but only adults. To say that a culture is good for children would mean that the culture is good for the effects it has on *forming* preferences and value commitments, but this can be true only if there is a somehow "good" set of preferences and value commitments. Academic proponents of the goodness of cultures specifically wish to deny that there is some universally good set of values for a society—only therefore can they argue that each society's values are justified for that society, not for all societies. Therefore, the argument that shows their culture is good for adults does not work for children. We can say only that the children learn the culture as an important part of their knowledge base, and that they generally learn it from adults. It might be in the interest of the adults to keep their children in their culture, but we might suppose that their teaching of their culture is primarily a by-product of daily life. It might become deliberate only in a context in which there is a potential threat from outside the culture.

An important fact of the functional relationship between knowledge and culture is that the knowledge is in a sense explanatorily prior. Because the knowledge does get recreated and reinforced in the next generation by the current generation, one might want to say that the culture influences the next generation, who then go on to maintain it. But in the functional explanation of culture this just is the third condition: feedback in which the knowledge is reproduced through current members of the society. Hence, the communal-knowledge account explains why a culture is self-sustaining so long as there is no external force to alter it or undercut it. Such exogenous effects could include ecological or other collapse of the context of the culture (Diamond 2005), imposition of some kind from outside the culture, or technological innovation within or from outside the culture, such as has affected societies from before history. This conclusion confirms that our first task in understanding culture is to understand the way knowledge works for ordinary people, and to understand the sometimes distorting effects it has at the group level.

Finally, note that functional explanation in the form above is especially likely to fit contexts in which interests are a major motivator. The fact that we have an interest in mastering our culture's knowledge (in order to prosper in our own society) maintains feedback through us—via our acting on our own interests and our efforts to fulfill them—and it is this feedback that maintains our culture. And it is those interests that make the culture good for us, through its capacity to serve them. The loose element here is that the feedback also goes through our children, thus partially creating them.

The Goodness of a Culture

The ordinary-knowledge account of cultural commitments does not have the normative implications favoring community that are sometimes supposed in communitarian and other writings (Taylor 1990; see also Hardin 1995, 189–98). My community gives me its knowledge, and I might restrict other knowledge that might be available to me by staying comfortably at home in my community rather than venturing outside it (Hardin 1995, 53–55, 89, passim). I enjoy the epistemological comforts of home, and I do not need to work at mastering alternative systems of knowledge. Moreover, part of the knowledge my community gives me is moral knowledge. That my community counts some moral principle as true does not, however, make it true.

Charles Taylor says cultures are irreducibly social goods, which implies that they are goods as well as that (in some sense) they are not individual-level goods. To reach this conclusion, he says of certain virtue-theory conceptions of particular virtues that, "If these things are goods, then other things being equal, so must the culture be which makes them possible" (Taylor 1990, 9). But "these things," virtues, may be goods only in a functional sense, as most of them are for Aristotle, the greatest classical virtue theorist. Aristotle supposes that there are different virtues for different roles. Different sets of virtues conduce to running a state well, to being a good soldier, to being a good citizen, and so forth. They do so in contingent ways. What might be a very important virtue in a hunter-gatherer society might be of little significance in the society of Taylor's university world. Hence, "these things" are not per se goods, they are only contingently goods. Therefore, it does not follow that the culture that produced them is a good at all, either intrinsically or instrumentally. Taylor's argument is simply a mistake.

Taylor also says that a particular language is a good that is irreducibly social. Actual language creation is irreducibly social, in the sense that it is the product of contributions and coordinations by necessarily many people, as culture is. In the case of any specific language, most of those people are now dead. Hence, the sense in which a language or culture is socially produced is not dramatically different from the way in which a national system of roads is irreducibly socially produced. And, just as our system of roads may be poorly designed and might disserve us in many ways, so our language might disserve us, especially if it has few speakers and leaves us out of any great literary or other intellectual tradition. Saying that *our* language is good is a poorly articulated claim. Having language is good, yes. But having *our* language might enable me to do no more than speak with the other hundred or so speakers of it in daily life; it would not enable me to speak with vast numbers of others who could enrich my life. If our language is the only one I have, I might rightly conclude that it is an irreducibly social bad.

Consider an unusual case of a culture that is built up in a particular kind of community: the community of the deaf. In a moving documentary, Josh Aronson's 2000 film *Sound and Fury,* tells the story of deaf parents and relatives in their responses to the new technology of cochlear implants to enable deaf people to hear, and especially to enable their young children to hear. It is the young, who have not passed too many years with deafness who have the best prospects for benefiting from the implants and actually learning to speak. Some of the parents and grandparents of an infant boy and a very young girl are glad for the opportunities implants might offer these children. Others are offended at the idea of implicitly judging deafness as disabling. They fear that their children and grandchildren will leave the deaf community once they can hear. The young girl's father, who bars her getting the implant, says, roughly, that the deaf culture will go extinct. (Uncounted elderly speakers of nearly dead languages react similarly to the loss of their communication with the young of their own families.) The father thinks that such extinction of his deaf culture would be a terrible loss. He frames that objection as an abstract, general complaint. It cannot sensibly be seen that way. The loss is to older deaf people who will become a declining remnant of the deaf culture. It is not a loss to future generations.

In all of Taylor's examples, with the arguable exceptions of language and friendship, a flaw arises at the crucial point of moving from the social origins of language and practices to goods that are *irreducibly social in their consumption*. It is true that I can enjoy and benefit from my culture only if there are others who help to sustain it, but the enjoyments I get from it might be mine and not irreducibly social. Moreover, again, they are goods only contingently. At the point at which, perhaps for ethological reasons, we find it very difficult to switch to languages or cultures that might in many ways have served us better, we can say that the ones we now have are good for us.

In passing, Taylor (1990, 11) says we cannot maintain a footing of frank and equal relations "unless the common understanding englobes the rightness of this footing." This sounds like normative "rightness." If so, it appears that Taylor has achieved a naturalistic derivation of a normative principle (as appears to be his intention). If so, this is worth a lot more discussion. If that is not what is intended here, the terms should be changed or qualified so as not to mislead readers. Noncommunitarians can readily suppose that a liberal legal system can enable individuals to maintain frank and equal relations with each other over certain matters that the law covers. Just how much more than this we can expect or want of an open democratic society is unclear.

Taylor (1990, 16) concludes by saying that welfarism, "as a doctrine about the nature of the good, has to be dispelled before the really interesting argument, between welfarism as a theory of *what things are good* and its opponents, can swim into focus." I think, in a very important sense, that this claim is false on Taylor's own view. No one has made any headway in advancing a theory of "what things are good," and there seems to be little prospect that anyone could do so. Indeed, it seems deeply perverse for Taylor, an advocate of communitarianism (for which values are local and do not generalize), even to think that there could be such a theory.

What welfarists *can* readily say, however, is that, if your community serves your values, as these now exist, then your community is good *for you.* Once you are an adult and have strong commitments to doing things in the ways of your culture, then the maintenance of that culture is good for you. Autonomy theorists could similarly argue that once your values, character, and commitments have been formed, your community supports your autonomy in maintaining these. Neither of these claims goes any distance at all in saying that your culture is good per se. It is merely good for you because it serves your interests or supports your autonomy, as now defined. It is functional for you. At the same time, it might be atrocious for me and almost everyone else, both for welfare and autonomy, even though it can be good for you. The principal part of the welfarist claim is that it could be good for you, because the knowledge you now have gives you resources for using your culture to your advantage, but not for using other cultures for as great an advantage. The principal part of the autonomy claim is that the knowledge you now have tends to be confirmed within the community, which makes the community a resource for sustaining your autonomy.

We have lived through a few decades of contemporary communitarian advocacy that so far has taken the form almost exclusively of an attack on welfarist, egalitarian, and fairness theories, and on the methodological and normative suppositions of these theories. If this is to become an enlightening debate, what we now desperately need are real examples of what communitarianism has to offer. If communitarians cannot provide such examples while they are distracted with their largely negative attack on other theories, discussion will not advance. At its best so far, normative communitarianism is the murky claim that what once was ought still to be. That is an appalling general principle.

COLLECTIVE IDENTITY

The conclusion that your community is a resource for your welfare or your autonomy fits only those who have attained an age at which we can suppose that they are unlikely to develop other cultural values or commitments, and at which autonomy theorists would want to say they are autonomous. It would be pointless for most people at that age to say that they could have become much better if they had developed different values and commitments. My present identity is largely constituted of my prior knowledge. To say we act from identity is merely shorthand for saying we act from personal knowledge, whether gained in the past or in the present—but the great bulk of it necessarily gained in the past. Some of that knowledge gives us strong commitments, with which we identify. Ordinarily, it is misleading or even wrong to say that what motivates people is a common *identity*. What motivates is a common *identification* with something (Hardin 1995, 6–10). When identity is determined by knowledge, however, we can suppose that identity as knowledge very nearly determines identification. To say that we act from a collective identity of some kind is merely shorthand for saying that we all act from very much the same personal knowledge of at least many of the most important things in our lives.

Again, however, the conclusion that community is in some way good for its members, through its service to their welfare or autonomy, does not apply to children. One might argue that close communities sometimes use their children to shore up the culture of the current leaders and all adults, who are now set in their ways. An alternative, less invidious way to characterize what one might call parents' use of their child is to say that the parents merely choose an identity for their child, as all parents de facto do for their children to some extent, more thoroughly in narrowly defined communities than in open and diverse communities. The devoutly religious adult person in a small community of similarly devout people is different from the person who would have come to exist if, say, at age twelve or fourteen her family had left the community and, unlike children in the community, she had continued her education in a cosmopolitan school and even beyond, in a liberal arts college. The life of Ayaan Hirsi Ali (2007) is instructive. She left home in Somalia to go to Europe, and she left her Muslim commitments behind in the course of becoming one of the great cosmopolitans of our time.

To say that it is wrong to create the person whose upbringing was kept in the small devout community, rather than the other person, implies that it would be better to create that other person, perhaps on autonomy grounds. Although this might seem to be a defensible claim in a theory of autonomy if the child were going to live in the larger community in which others are more educated, autonomy theory does not readily yield *any* conclusion about what kind of person to *create*.

On this account, the only issue is how adults are treated in the community, and if they are not de facto coerced or manipulated (for example, by their lack of prior education), we could not say that their autonomy is being violated. If we think there would be two different persons, each formed by their particular circumstances of life history, we cannot make the autonomy argument work for a preference for one over the other. And only if people in the community suffer disappointment or resentment could we make a utilitarian argument work—and maybe not even then, because it is not coherent to say we have harmed persons who would not even exist if we had not allowed them to be manipulated as children to become who they are.

Communitarian argument about the good of individual members of a community is about persons who already are, not about persons in a state of creation, so presumptions about identity are irrelevant for children. Many people, of course, object to the idea that my identity would be different if I had lived a dramatically different life. Against them, however, we can forcefully note that the children of many close, devout communities genuinely *are* different from children in the wider society, and that communitarian and other claims about identity are specifically about such differences. Those children would turn out to be quite different people in radically different circumstances of upbringing. Indeed, the usual defenses of community on behalf of individuals' identity turn on the supposition that their identity is, or at some point must have been, malleable, and that it depends on their community to some large extent.

If our collective identity is constituted by a body of shared knowledge, we might ask what is the usefulness of our ordinary cultural knowledge? If we live in a close culture, a large part of what we need to know (for its usefulness) is our culture's norms and practices. Such knowledge enables us to navigate life in our community with ease. In return, unfortunately, it might reduce the chance of our navigating other cultures, so that it might tend to lock us into our own current culture. This means, of course, that the test of my knowledge is that others in the culture share it with me. Indeed, that is virtually the only test of it, because its primary relevance is to enable me to work that culture for my own life and relationships.

In summary, the most we can claim for the goodness of a community is that, for those who have grown up within it and who remain committed to its values, it is functionally good at providing them with a comfortable context in which to live by their values. This does not say that the community is good per se. Indeed, instead of common arguments in defense of community, we can say that *the community is good only derivatively* for the role it plays in giving that context to those already committed to the community's values and practices. The more common claim is that the community gives its members their conception of the good. But it does this only because it de facto creates the individuals who have such a conception.

CONCLUDING REMARKS

To speak of American culture on the knowledge account given here might be odd, because Americans share no coherent, broadly accepted set of cultural beliefs and practices. The most general things one might invoke to characterize American society are principles of individualism, constitutional protections of rights, and other matters that virtually speak against culture, and do speak against the use of the state to ensure the coercive force of any culture. Openness is virtually anti-culture in this sense of culture. High modernity is anti-culture (Scott 1998).

More generally, there might be no modern national state, no matter how small, that could be characterized as having a coherent culture. It is only relatively small communities that typically have culture, in the sense that would matter to communitarians and to many multiculturalists. Actual states subsume or are defined by cultures only in the odd sense that they have many elements that people differentially take to themselves. Of the quasi-common elements, I have some and you have some, but our two sets are not identical. They might overlap, but they might also have many parts that are different and that do not overlap. Each of us may be taken to be a representative of the general culture, but each of us has only a family resemblance to any of the others.

Culture is probably the most extreme instance of ordinary knowledge. It is not merely an instance of such knowledge but a whole system of it, a system that can govern entire lives. One might therefore think it the apotheosis of such knowledge. Sometimes, no doubt, it is. But sometimes it is a disastrous implication of the limits of that knowledge. Why? Because there is a potentially dark side to this account of culture, which is de facto a dark side of the reality of ordinary knowledge. The dark side is a pragmatic or economic explanation of why destructive, objectively irrational prejudices persist. For example, consider the hostile view of homosexuality that is widespread in contemporary society. That view is a received idea that is consistent with other beliefs. It is not in most individuals' interest to challenge the idea; it might even benefit some straights to pose themselves as superior to gays. And the chosen social group of straights reinforces the hostile view of gays. Indeed, such a group might even invoke a norm of exclusion that could be forcefully used against both gays and any straights who might not be hostile to gays. And it might be reinforced by the confirmation bias noted earlier.

There is a Latin proverb that says that the benefits of any novelty are outweighed by its costs. That proverb is not merely a homily; it is often an inference from the economics of knowledge, already at the individual level. But when it shapes the building stones of culture at the societal level, it can be oppressive. The constraints and tendencies discussed here are not the product of culture but the product of the nature of ordinary knowledge. It is ordinary knowledge that gives culture such characteristic qualities as its commitment to conservatism and stasis, and its confusion of facts and values. It is also the nature of individual knowledge that gives individuals an implicit allegiance to their cultures, because the group's knowledge is the source of most of the individual's cultural knowledge.

Many contemporary writers bemoan the cost of efforts to maintain a particular cultural identity against the pressures of the larger world (Kuran

1996; Kymlicka 1989, 186–87; Tamir 1993, 149).[3] Maintenance of a culture, through creation of relevant institutions and practices, can be handled as a direct effort. But it can also follow from the fact that behavior and beliefs are causally related, for several reasons. First, behavior leads to knowledge, much of it happenstance knowledge, that then affects beliefs.

Second, knowledge clearly affects behavior, directly through preferences, but it also affects it in longer-term ways that might not be so evident at a glance. For example, consider the Catholic woman in a society such as the United States, in which Catholic norms are assailed by the greater license of many, even most people. It is clear from the pattern of many lives around her that people sometimes lose their faith. She fears for the future faith of her family and of herself. In this moment, however, she has her faith and wishes to keep it. She might therefore put herself into positions from which it would be very difficult to slide away from her beliefs, both by isolating her from worse influences and by building her own commitments via the first causal relation noted above. For example, she might become an anti-abortion activist. This would effectively isolate her from many irreligious liberals around her. And it would subject her to frequent interactions with people who would give her support for her beliefs, and information confirming them.

This woman goes beyond Derek Parfit's (1984, p. 327) radical young Russian count, who wants to coerce his future self to contribute to the radical causes he now supports by giving his money and land to those causes now, lest he turn conservative later and renege on these commitments. Our Catholic woman chooses now not merely to restrict her options in the future but, more profoundly, to make her future self be the self she now holds to be right.

In general, culture results from individual choices, and we wish to understand those choices. But the results of these choices are essentially institutions and practices at the level of the society. These results are not strictly intended by the individuals as part of their actions, or even an implication of them. When broadly important unintended consequences of individual actions become patterned, we should consider whether the whole pattern fits a functional account, as argued here for culture. But recall that the functional account is only about the continued maintenance of the pattern of behavior and belief—it says nothing about how the pattern gets started.

Such a functional account typically applies only when the support of the pattern of behavior is felt indirectly, through feedback that reinforces

[3]Kymlicka (1989, 187) notes that cultural minority groups "have to spend more of their resources on securing the cultural membership which makes sense of their lives," an expense that cultural majorities are spared because they largely get their cultural support for free.

the behavior. That feedback is not likely to be consciously understood, although often it must finally be discovered by careful observers. People often infer values from the facts of the matter. In the case of cultural commitments, for example, many people note that they have very intense commitments, and they suppose that this means their cultural beliefs therefore deserve great deference. Unfortunately, intensity of commitments gives no such support to any belief. One can imagine utterly appalling beliefs (for example, about the inferiority of certain other people) that are held with great intensity. That fact does not elevate those beliefs to any special or somehow privileged moral status.

Per se, culture just is. It is neither good nor bad in principle. We can pass judgment on behaviors guided by a culture. But unless an important fraction of those behaviors are conspicuously harmful to people, it is not meaningful to say of the culture that it is bad.

CHAPTER 9

Extremism

JEREMY BENTHAM remarked that religious motivations are among the most constant of all motivations. And, although such a motivation need not be especially powerful, it can be among the most powerful. Because of the constancy of the motivation, Bentham continues, "A pernicious act, therefore, when committed through the motive of religion, is more mischievous than when committed through the motive of ill-will" (Bentham [1789] 1970, 156). He explains this conclusion from fanaticism, which of course need not be religiously motivated, and in the twentieth century was as destructively motivated by ideological and nationalist sentiments as by religious sentiments. This is Bentham's explanation:

> If a man happen to take it into his head to assassinate with his own hands, or with the sword of justice, those whom he calls heretics, that is, people who think, or perhaps only speak, differently upon a subject which neither party understands, he will be as inclined to do this [at] one time as at another. Fanaticism never sleeps: it is never glutted: it is never stopped by philanthropy; for it makes a merit of trampling on philanthropy: it is never stopped by conscience; for it has pressed conscience into service. Avarice, lust, and vengeance, have piety, benevolence, honour; fanaticism has nothing to oppose it. (Bentham [1789] 1970, 156n)

Note especially the apt cruelty of his observation: "which neither party understands."

Bentham's remark is about the individual fanatic. The concern here will be, primarily, with groups of such individuals. Seeing the nature of a group of fanatics may help to understand why the fanatic never sleeps. When the fanatic is in a group of like-minded people, and especially when the group isolates itself from others, either by separating itself or by excluding others, that group reinforces the individual's "conscience," indeed reinforces the individual's beliefs, both factual and normative. A fanatic who must live among others who do not share the fanatic's views may finally at least nod. It is generally the group that produces and sustains fanaticism.

Fanaticism is inherently, therefore, a sociological and not merely a psychological matter. A focus on the individual fanatic might lead one to suppose that the issue is the nature of the belief, how it differs from other beliefs. This might typically be the fanatics' own account: that it is the content of the belief that justifies the fanaticism. Focusing on the group leads us to ask how the belief gets inculcated and maintained. That focus suggests that fanaticism is less likely to be defined by its substantive content than by the way it is socially constructed. The most important part of the economic theory of knowledge for understanding fanatically held knowledge, or group-based beliefs, is the role of authority. After a brief discussion of authority, I will then turn to the nature of normal politics, in particular noting how it sets up the possibilities for fanatical politics. I will bring these discussions together in an account of the knowledge basis of extremism, and I will relate this to certain forms of nationalism. Finally, I will discuss connections between fanatical beliefs and actions, and the relationship between interests and knowledge, and I will suggest how a crippled belief system leads to fanaticism, which may in turn lead to fanatical nationalism.

KNOWLEDGE BY AUTHORITY, AGAIN

As argued in chapter 1, it makes eminently good sense to rely on knowledge by authority. The costs of checking out everything one knows, even by hearsay, would be catastrophic for actually living instead of merely deciding how to live. If we insisted on checking out every bit of putative knowledge, we would be, again, virtually catatonic. Even checking out a single bit of knowledge might make little sense, because the costs of having it wrong would seem to be less than the costs of getting it right. We can commonly rely on others to check some facts, and we can benefit from their judgment of the validity and usefulness of those facts.

As a general proposition, these characteristics of ordinary knowledge are exacerbated in acquiring knowledge of moral and ideological matters, because the latter are not well tested by anyone, and because it would be difficult even to imagine relevant tests of them. Moreover, such facts are not subject to being discovered from experience, or by application of any kind of scientific method; rather, they are almost always socially invented.[1] But the person who relies on authority for acceptance of various facts likely has no particular qualification to judge which facts are more likely to be authoritatively correctly held and which are merely invented, perhaps by some fanatic. Indeed, for the ordinary person, moral, ideological, and religious beliefs might well be indistinguishable in their sources from most objective beliefs. To cite standard examples, the beliefs that the

[1]For many examples, consider the range of beliefs among what are called outsider religions in the United States, such groups as Heaven's Gate, the Shakers, the Oneida Community, and many others surveyed by Stein 2000.

Earth is round or that men have walked on the Moon are no more solidly objective for many people than are their beliefs about god or the rightness of not telling a lie. The latter beliefs might get much stronger support from others in one's society, especially from those whom one knows and respects. And the benefits of believing them might be considerably greater than the benefits of believing that the Earth is round or that men have walked on the Moon.

That our beliefs depend in part on the larger society's assessments and reinforcements means that they can also be manipulated by that society. Or, even more significantly in the case of ideological beliefs, they can be manipulated within small segments of that society so long as the larger society and its views are held at bay. If I am in a small community holding beliefs that others outside that community would think very odd, I may find those beliefs not at all odd because, after all, they are held by everyone I know. They may be merely part of the vast catalog of beliefs that I hold from dependence on authority.

NORMAL POLITICS

Turn now to the context in which extreme politics may be played out. The median voter or Downsian model suggests that most voters must see themselves as relative losers at each election (Downs 1957). Some must always be losers. This follows for all views that display a roughly normal distribution of preferences over political outcomes.[2] Winning candidates or policies must be close to the views of some, but farther from the views of most voters. With multiple dimensions of issues, a typical voter might be close to the winner on one or a few issues but still far from the winner on most issues. A major trick of normal, nonextreme politics is to get people to think they do relatively well politically, even though this superficially dismal implication of the median-voter model is correct. In relatively prosperous times, it might reasonably seem true to most citizens that their interests are relatively well served by politics, or that those interests are not substantially affected by politics. Hence, that their preferences might not be those of the elected governors does not matter fundamentally or grievously.

Those in the tails of the distribution of preferences over major issues, however, cannot generally think they do well in normal politics. At best, they can think they have done better this time than last time, or than

[2]Preferences over many issues, such as those that are essentially yes-no, are not likely to be even roughly normal in their distribution. For example, preferences on abortion in the United States are fundamentally bimodal, with a majority of the populace evidently in favor of a liberal regime on abortion and a majority of legislators prepared to vote great restrictions on abortion.

usually. For example, citizens on the far right in the United States must have thought the election of Ronald Reagan as president in 1980 was a clear improvement over the previous half century, although not so great an improvement as they might have liked.

For those who are always big losers in normal politics, exit from such politics might be a common response. Recall that in Hirschman's (1970) account, they have three options: exit, voice, or loyalty. Loyalty seems incredible and self-denying. Voice has completely failed. Only exit is left. Exit can take at least two quite different forms. First, it might simply involve withdrawal in the form of reduced participation in normal politics, with no other form of activity to replace it for its main functions. More worrisome for normal politics is that the permanent losers might hive off into groups whose intent is to oppose normal politics. Such groups are typically viewed as extremist by those committed to normal politics. As I will argue below, a group that hives off faces its members with constraints that may heighten the intensity of their beliefs in the wrongness of their nation's politics, and may strengthen their motivations to do something outside normal politics.

In the brief passage quoted above, Bentham concluded that, unlike other vices, fanaticism has no opposing virtue. Indeed, it has only normalcy to oppose it. Unfortunately, normalcy is merely a condition for living reasonably and it does not greatly motivate us unless, perhaps, we do not have it. Mere normalcy therefore may not be enough to stop over-wrought fanaticism, especially when the fanatics exit from normal politics and even from normal society.

The Belief System of Extremism

A politically extreme view is likely to involve a self-enforcing, even self-strengthening, norm of exclusion. Norms of exclusion define groups to which those with the right views or with the right characteristics are admitted, and from which others are excluded. Under the force of such norms, the less intensely committed members of a group depart while extremists remain (Hardin 1995, chapter 4). Daniel P. Moynihan (1993, 22) supposes that ethnicity is a new social aggregate, and that the clear point to be made about the so-called melting pot in the United States is that it did not happen. Clearly, he is wrong if he means that there has been no substantial intermarriage across ethnic lines, with consequent loss of identification with such groups. But if some melt, those who are left are likely to be the more intensely committed. Hence, there may be both a lot of melting and a lot of residual ethnicity, as, for example, in the case of Orthodox Jews such as the Lubavitch Jews of Brooklyn. As residual, ethnically defined groups shrink, they may become increasingly extreme in their beliefs and actions.

The logic of incentives here is the opposite of that in the account above, of citizens in normal politics. In normal politics it is the extremists who depart and the less intense who remain behind. In fringe politics, the moderates exit, leaving the most intense behind. The out-migration of the less committed from an exclusionary group leaves the hard core in control (Hardin 1995, 101). But the exclusionary practices of an extreme group do more than this. *They affect the knowledge of the group's members.*

Recall Bentham's cruel remark about the fanaticism that flows from beliefs in heresies, "which neither party understands." He perhaps implicitly supposes there might be a truth of the matter, and that neither of the opponents quarreling over the beliefs knows that truth. One might rather say that those who assert the truth of some particular view have inadequate ground for their own assertions. But this is a claim from standard philosophical epistemology. In their own belief system, they may genuinely suppose that they do have such grounds, or even that they do know the truth of what they assert.

Argument from philosophical epistemology is unlikely to motivate a change in beliefs for anyone, other than, perhaps, a deeply committed philosopher or scientist. Physicists have, for example, been convinced of the truth of quantum mechanics, biologists of the truth of the system of DNA structuring of life, and some philosophers of the relevance and correctness of Kantian ethics. All of these beliefs must sound incongruous and incredible to ordinary people, for whom the beliefs are dreamlike nonsense. Most of us do not have the time or incentive to be deeply committed philosophers or scientists, and we need not even suspect that there is anything questionable about our own beliefs.

It might seem astonishing that one could, on the one hand, know that most others generally believe differently and, on the other hand, nevertheless insist strongly on the truth of one's own particular beliefs. But this capacity seems less astonishing if one's particular beliefs are those of the group or society in which one spends one's life, and if those who believe otherwise are outside that group or society. In these conditions, my beliefs may get reinforced constantly by those around me, even though those beliefs might be shared by at most a minute fraction of the world's population. Of course, it is we who choose (or at least act) to isolate ourselves from other views.

If we hold beliefs that are contrary to widespread beliefs in our own society, we can protect our beliefs, to some extent, whether intentionally or unintentionally, by keeping ourselves in the company only of others who share our beliefs. When asked about his relations with traditional Protestants, such as Episcopalians, a professor of theology at one of the conservative seminaries in Los Angeles said he had not talked to an Episcopalian priest in more than twenty-five years (Crapanzano 2000, xxiii). That is extreme intellectual isolation within one of the world's most cosmopolitan cities.

In our isolation, we may even begin to think those outside our group are hostile to us. We may therefore come to have openly hostile relations with people outside our group, and we may harden our judgment of other groups over time. As an example of this self-reinforcing trend, consider the so-called ethnic hatred that was blamed by many for the recent collapse of Yugoslavia. Such group hatred seems more likely to have followed than to have preceded the grisly violence in Yugoslavia. The hostility led to the destruction of long-standing friendships and to the break-up of marriages across ethnic lines. The fact of such friendships and marriages does not fit the brutal assertion of many observers that the hatred was prior and therefore was the fundamental cause of the civil strife (see, for example, Kaplan 1993). The supposed hatred followed the politics of hostility (Hardin 1995, 147–50).

Isolation of people in a group with relatively limited contact with the larger society generates paranoid cognition, in which individuals begin to suppose the worst from those they do not know, or even from those with whom they are not immediately in communication. As Roderick Kramer (1994) describes this psychological phenomenon, when people feel that they are under scrutiny they tend to exaggerate the extent to which they are the target of attention. They therefore attribute unduly personalistic motivations to others and become increasingly distrustful of those others. This is an instance of the sinister attribution error. Although Kramer's studies are of intra-organizational contexts, one might suppose this phenomenon would color relations between relatively separatist, isolated groups and the larger society. If so, it would clearly affect the beliefs of the isolated group members; it would tend to exacerbate their fear and dislike of the larger society.

Although psychologists might suppose that such phenomena as paranoid cognition and the sinister attribution error are the result of complex psychological motors, they may primarily be simple matters of the skewed beliefs that arise from lack of contact with and, hence, lack of accurate knowledge of, relevant others. Separation in order to sustain a group's own beliefs might go much further and actually reinforce or even partially determine those beliefs. The hostility of an isolated extremist group may flow more from this skewing of its members' beliefs than from genuine opposition to the larger society or some other group.

In a study of the ultra-orthodox Jews of Israel, Eli Berman notes that politically driven demands by the group to restrict the activities of others, for example by prohibiting commerce and motor traffic on the Sabbath, may cause antagonism from the others. He notes that such "secular antagonism toward the ultra-orthodox could be desirable and efficient from the point of view of the latter community if it discourages secular activity by [the ultra-orthodox]" (E. Berman 1998). It may be beneficial to those strongly committed to the Ultra position in other ways as well. In particular, it might strengthen the norm of exclusion, thus to keep Ultras in line, and it might strengthen commitments by Ultras in reaction to the heightened hostility of the outside community. Hence, indirectly, the politics of imposing their views on others' actions may contribute to the crippling of the understanding of the Ultras, although their intent might merely be to cripple the understanding of secular Israelis in the hope of leading them to orthodox views.

Part of the crippling of the group's understanding of their place in the world is to lead them to think of themselves as the sole reservoir of truth and the sole object of concern. Groups such as the Ultras are *group-solipsists*. They self-righteously seek laws that constrain others to live by the Ultras' morals, just as the school board members in Dover and many other places self-righteously constrain the education of all children in order to constrain the education of their own. The others are of no concern to them. Group-solipsism is commonly politicized in these and other ways, and when it is, it can be a grimly destructive force. Group-solipsists often do not merely exclude, they deny others. Individual solipsism, which says that my concerns are the only thing that matters (not merely to me but at all) is an odious position. But it is perverse to suppose that elevating it to the group level makes group-solipsism less odious than individual-level solipsism (Hardin 1995, chap. 7).

NATIONALISM

Consider now the views of nationalists, views that are sometimes but not always or even typically fanatic. As many observers of nationalism note, the nationalist vision is perplexing for the vacuity of its belief system, even when it is far from fanatical. Anderson ([1983] 1991, 5) notes three general oddities of the vision. First, while historians and social scientists recognize the modernity and even very recent rise of nationalism as a phenomenon, nationalists insist on the antiquity of their nations, even supposing their origins to be primordial, before history. Second, while historians and social scientists commonly think that nationality as a sociocultural concept is relatively universal, nationalists suffer from a blinkered particularity of its concrete manifestation in their case. Finally, while nationalist claims often have great political power, they suffer from philosophical poverty and incoherence.

Anderson concludes that a nation is an imagined political community. Hobsbawm (1992, 46) asks how a concept so remote from the real experience of most humans as "national patriotism" could become such a powerful political force so quickly. On the account of the belief system of nationalism, one must suppose that it requires either an illogical imagination or an imagination grounded in woeful ignorance. Illogic is not impossible, but the more likely account must be woeful ignorance.

As an example of the philosophical poverty of the nationalist vision, consider the frequent assertion by nationalists of a common national will (Anderson [1983] 1991, 108). Historically, the idea of a common will or sovereignty of a people may simply be a transformation of the idea of the sovereignty of the single willed monarch. Yet, the very fact of a nationalist movement that is not universally supported overtly betrays the lack of a common will. Moreover, in virtually every context that matters in practice, there can be no common will of a people numerous enough to constitute a nation. It is a fallacy of composition to suppose that there is a common will.

Hence, nationalist views share with fanatical views their grounding in an ignorance that is evidently promoted by groups. Unless it is accompanied by a creed, however, nationalism is not typically fanatical. The ignorance that underlies commonplace nationalist views is a relatively general kind of ignorance that can seemingly survive open discussion in a broad society. As Hobsbawm (1992, 169) notes, vagueness and the lack of programmatic content gives nationalism potentially universal support within its own community. For example, ethnic and linguistic nationalism provide no general guidance for the future (168). Such vagueness often underlies negative programs, such as the nationalism that is opposed to a colonial regime, or the movement to overthrow the Shah in Iran. Indeed, because these views fit a quasi-utilitarian assessment of what would benefit the relevant national group, they can be supported by a relatively open society.

But when the views turn fanatic, the ignorance that underlies them must be protected from the intrusions of the broader society. For example, ideological or religious fundamentalism typically provides a real and detailed program for both the individual and the society. Such fundamentalism draws strength from the claim to universal truth, applicable to all (Hobsbawm 1992, 168). Just because it does, however, it can be questioned in detail and with specificity. Such questioning could be the death of fanatical beliefs. Fanaticism is not a kind of belief; rather, it is a characteristic of the way beliefs can be held, including obstinate ignorance of alternative views. Fanaticism requires exclusionary group practices for its maintenance, because it is that isolation that allows spurious beliefs to escape challenge.

Yet it is often directed at the promulgation of a universalist program, which, again, would be inclusive rather than exclusive. This peculiar divergence between the inclusive substance and the exclusionary maintenance of many fanatical views is merely a result of the economics of holding views that are contrary to those of a larger society. The views require protection against corrosive contrary knowledge. This is true to some extent even of milder nationalist views. Nationalism, however powerful the emotion of being in an imagined community, is nothing without the creation of nation-states (Hobsbawm 1992, 177). That is, with neither the plausible, but vague, goal of creating a national state nor the maintenance by an organized state to keep the progam alive, nationalism as a very general urge falters. For example, when a population is diverse and intermingled, we have no choice but to reconcile ourselves to living together (Tamir 1993, 140).

Michael Walzer argues that ethnic pluralism is evidently compatible with the idea of a unified republic (Walzer 1980, 785). But, as he notes, a modern liberal pluralist state is a very different kind of republic from that envisioned by Montesquieu and Rousseau. It lacks the intense political fellowship and pervasive commitment to public affairs that they praised and advocated. Rousseau supposed that the better the constitution of the state, the more do public affairs encroach on private affairs in the minds of citizens. Rousseau's claim might fit a small city state, such as the Geneva of his time, but it is entirely wrong for large, complex states. It is Nazi, Soviet, and Maoist states that most push public affairs to encroach on private affairs. Large states with good constitutions typically leave citizens almost entirely alone to lead their own lives. In good times, there should be little political participation in a well-organized liberal state. Such states might offer assistance to some, and must generally offer coordination of many activities to enable citizens to live with each other despite their varied purposes (Hardin 1999, chap. 1). It is states such as those led by extremists that attempt to go much further in forcing public affairs onto citizens, largely by enforcing values that many citizens might not share. This is one of the reasons that Rousseau, no doubt unfairly, is sometimes seen as an early source of totalitarian thought.

As Tamir (1993, 79) notes, the idea of nationalism tends to be associated with its most fanatical versions, which assume, in a variant of the Rousseauean vision, that the identity of individuals is wholly constituted by their national membership, and that personal will is only free when submerged in the national one. The liberal nationalism for which she argues is, rather, the descendant of the cultural pluralism of Johann Gottfried Herder ([1774] 2004) and J. G. Mazzini. Their German and Italian nationalisms of the eighteenth and nineteenth centuries aimed at creating supranations out of multitudes of diverse communities. The popular idea of nationalism is, however, commonly associated with such problem cases as the later, twentieth-century German and Italian nationalisms, which were radically illiberal.

One might ask of cases of fanatical nationalism, which comes first? The fanaticism or the nationalism? Below I will suggest that fanaticism often seems to require nationalism for its fulfillment or security. Fanaticism is therefore not inherent in nationalism, although nationalism may often be born out of fanaticism, in which case it is likely to be fanatical nationalism. Yet the fanaticism might actually be diverted by the demands of a nationalism that cannot readily be exclusive and that might soon become, if not quite liberal, at least more inclusive. Hence, in principle at least, nationalism might be a counter or even an antidote to fanatical movements, not least because it might offer greater rewards to leaders of any factional group. There is, for example, a strand of Israeli nationalism that has this strong, liberal bent, but it may in time lose to the fanatical bent of the more prolific, rigidly exclusionary, ultra-orthodox Israelis with their fanatically crippled belief system.

On the issue of ethnic and other pluralisms in a large society, recall Moynihan's (1993, 22) overstatement on the failure of the melting pot in the United States. Edward Said supposes that minority immigrant groups no longer need to assimilate because "the simple accessibility of the entire world makes . . . forgetfulness all but unattainable" (quoted in Tamir 1993, 86). But assimilation is primarily a generational effect; hence, this supposition seems unlikely to be true. Members of later generations will commonly succumb to the blandishments of the society in which they grow up and live, and they will find life both easier and generally more rewarding if they adopt the local language and manners. Many will therefore attain "forgetfulness." But those who sustain memories and identifications might come to constitute an extreme group. Against the prospects of their doing so, however, is Said's "simple accessibility of the entire world," which undercuts the possibility of sustaining the crippled understanding behind extremism. Sustaining such understanding requires exclusion of knowledge of, and therefore traffic with, most of the rest of the entire world.

Writers on nationalism commonly ask why individuals are willing to die (or at least to put themselves at great risk of dying) for mere nations. Anderson ([1983] 1991, 7 and 141) asks the question twice and, symptomatically, fails to answer it. He says only that "It is as a community that nations lead so many to die for them despite the relative recency of nationalism (scarcely more than two centuries)." All the other major writers on nationalism, many of whom frame Anderson's question more or less explicitly, also fail to answer it, although some of them seem to think it easy to understand that people can become so radically committed to a nationalist cause. The answer must turn on the fact that nationalist views do not entail fanaticism, but that fanaticism can be directed at nationalist goals. To explain fanatical nationalism, therefore, requires more than merely the explanation of nationalism. For example, most Europeans and Americans might well be nationalist, but few of them are fanatically nationalist.

Fanatical Action without Fanatical Belief

Members of isolated extremist groups can do things that seem extraordinary to others, as if they were audacious beyond measure. But the individuals in an isolated group are not so clearly audacious in their actual context. They merely do what people in their groups do. Such action, if undertaken by an ordinary person whose life is wholly within the larger community, would be audacious.

Although the beliefs that would lead an individual to be profoundly committed to a nation or ethnic group are surely socially instilled and defined, action is finally taken at the individual level of the person and not at the aggregate level. Knowledge can depend on a group's impact on an individual, and in part the effect of the group is through its authority as a source of knowledge. A group's effect might also turn on the incentives it has to influence members' actions in ways that lead them to particular beliefs. Indeed, rewarding or sanctioning members for their apparently right or wrong knowledge might directly affect what the members know, by making their knowledge fit more nearly with their interests.

You might come to hold some important belief or claim of your group in a more complex causal way, as a result of your interest in being in the group. As a result of your participation in the life of the group, you hear many things that actually support the claim. After some time, you may begin to have difficulty separating various things you seemingly know from the beliefs of the group, which begin to be reinforced by this growing body of related knowledge. Eventually, you might even find that the best way to make sense of a lot of related things is actually to suppose the odd claim to be true, and you might therefore come to believe it as an almost necessary or deductively entailed part of this coherent larger body of beliefs. It follows, then, that you are led to your belief in the claim by the incentive for having it, or at least for credibly expressing it. You do not directly believe merely because it is in your interest to do so, but you do other things that are in your interest, and in doing these things you come to believe the claim. The belief may be an unintended consequence of various activities and other beliefs.

As a member of a group, one might recognize the force of the group's impositions without finally believing what seems to define and unite the group. Because one's interests in membership are at stake, however, one might act in ways that fit the group's beliefs. In a sense, then, we might say that actions may be fanatical even when beliefs are not. For example, one of the so-called killers of Mostar during the Bosnian war explained his actions not as a result of beliefs about the evil nature of the Serbian people he was murdering, many of whom were, after all, formerly his friends. Rather, he explained it as a result of his interest in remaining a part of his Croatian community. If he wished to remain, he had to join actively in its horrors (Block 1993; see further Hardin 1995, 148–49).

At the extreme, one might suppose that some group has no genuine believers in its fanatical views, but that all members are coordinated on acting fanatically by the false sense that everyone else or most others do believe. A near-cousin of this possibility is the claim, mentioned earlier, by John Howard Griffin (1976, 153; see further, Hardin 1995, 90) that by about 1960 many, perhaps a majority of, southern whites favored the end of Jim Crow segregation policies, but thought themselves a tiny minority and therefore never acted against white hegemony. Instead, they acquiesced in the prevalent racism.

INTERESTS AND KNOWLEDGE

In general, note that the focus here is almost entirely on knowledge, and not on interests. James Coleman's (1987) account of zealotry is based on interests in the individual's costs and benefits of acting for collective benefit. One must generally suppose that, if action is to be explained, we must finally deal not only with knowledge but also with motivations. Hence, to complete the story of fanatical political commitments, we need not only an explanation of such fanatical beliefs but also a motivational account of why such beliefs produce the extraordinary actions we often see.

Sometimes, as in the case of the killers of Mostar, the motivation for relevant actions is to be structurally explained as part of an imposed system of incentives, such that fanatical beliefs and fanatical actions need not be joined. We might in some contexts be able to argue convincingly that some beliefs virtually entail actions, so that believing is tantamount to acting. For various reasons, including usual concerns with akrasia, or weakness of will, this easy step is not prima facie compelling in general, although it might be in some cases. In particular, it might fit the behavior of very young terrorists who have been indoctrinated in secluded terrorist camps, so that their understanding is particularly constrained and crippled, enough so to convince them that their interests are served by undertaking suicidal actions.

Albert Hirschman (1977) argues that the rise of capitalism helped to displace religious zealotry, because passions were trumped by interests.

At least part of the story, even of this change, is merely that people began to learn the costs of zealotry, costs that rose as the economy was depressed by turmoil, as in seventeenth-century England. Hobbes and Locke essentially wished to push religious conflict out of politics, in order to allow greater material prosperity, and greater personal safety. Hobbes supposed this could be done by imposing some—any—particular variant of Protestant Christianity. Locke supposed it could be done by merely keeping religious issues out of politics and consigning them to the realm of personal conscience (a very Protestant view).

People commonly do not know their own interests, or do not know how to effect their interests. The constrained understanding behind extremism can exacerbate both of these failings. Part of the impact of economic progress is to make clearer to people what their interests are, or how their interests can be served. Fanaticism seems to decline with general prosperity—a generalization of the Marxist worry about the eventual embourgeoisement of increasingly prosperous workers. Those with a large stake in the present state of affairs are less likely to attack it.

Religious zealotry in our time has seen the destruction of the economic prospects of many Islamic nations, which have generally performed far less well than comparable non-Islamic nations (Lewis 2002). The complaint of Islamic fundamentalists is an analog of that of Marxists: materialism saps religious commitment. They therefore wish to gain control of governments and laws in order to suppress material concerns and to impose their religious values. As is true of many extremist groups, therefore, their goal is inherently illiberal. It is a claim for the unquestioned rightness of particular ideas. But they seem fairly clearly to understand that their ideas can prevail only by keeping their people ignorant of alternatives and of material possibilities. Hence, they seem to have a relatively clear sense of the knowledge bases of liberalism and illiberalism. That is to say, they recognize that their problem is not merely one of motivation but, more urgently, of the polluting effects of knowledge.

It is instructive that most of the Islamic states also fail to become democratic. John Mueller argues that this is a matter of deliberate choice on the part of the autocratic national leaders (Mueller 1999, chap. 3), although that explanation leaves open the question why those nations so typically have leadership that is resolutely determined to remain autocratic. Because many of these leaders are not themselves religious fundamentalists, it is perhaps an unintended consequence of their antidemocratic stance that they block the open discussion that would undercut religious extremism by undercutting its belief system. Had they allowed democratic choice, they might well have lost power fairly early. But the cost of maintaining their rigidly antidemocratic stance is the creation of an opposition that could not have flourished as well in an open society, an opposition that tends toward fanatical Islam, much as the Polish opposition to Communism for several decades tended toward adamant Catholicism.

Recall the development of fundamentalist religion in Chapter 7, especially as in the exit model of Montgomery. Thus, Islamic immigrants who become prosperous in the West may become religiously liberal,[3] or even apostate. The Canadian Irshad Manji (2003) seeks reform. Ayaan Hirsi Ali, a Somali-born feminist once in the Dutch legislature (Caldwell 2005), and Wafa Sultan, a Syrian-born doctor in Los Angeles (Broder 2006),[4] are apostates and liberals, as is presumably the novelist Salman Rushdie. But many of the Islamic immigrants might exit in the opposite direction—from liberal mosques into fundamentalist mosques. Muhammad Atta, who led the attacks of September 11, 2001, was evidently from a relatively liberal and well-educated background in Egypt, but in Hamburg he became a suicidal, murderous radical.

This bifurcated pattern of change might augur ill, both for immigrant Islamic groups in western nations and for their western hosts. Many politicians and commentators seem to suppose that these groups must eventually liberalize and become less fractious in their new homes. But the simultaneous movement of some of these immigrants into fundamentalist, extremist sects may lead to far worse fractious behavior, including jihadism. Radical imams are a clear threat to the peaceful assimilation of some immigrants into liberal, democratic society. It is generally a mistake to suppose that all the individuals in such a group, or in any other kind of religion, must follow the average trend. Some will follow Montgomery's path of exit into extremism. If even one in a thousand Islamic immigrants in the West have followed that path, there must already be roughly more than a thousand Islamic extremists in the United States, and about twenty thousand in Europe.[5]

---

[3]It is said of the once radical Quakers that they came to do good and they did well.

[4]Sultan was in a debate on Al Jazeera television in July 2005. "Why does a young Muslim man, in the prime of life, go and blow himself up?" Sultan asked. "In our countries, religion is the sole source of education and is the only spring from which that terrorist drank until his thirst was quenched." She was then in a follow-up debate in February 2006. "The clash we are witnessing around the world is not a clash of religions or a clash of civilizations," she said. It is a clash between two opposites, between two eras. It is a clash between a mentality that belongs to the Middle Ages and another mentality that belongs to the twenty-first century. It is a clash between civilization and backwardness, between the civilized and the primitive, between barbarity and rationality." Her answering machine and email have been flooded with death threats from people who apparently believe and wish to prove thereby that they are not backward, primitive, and barbaric.

[5]One in a thousand is well within the error term in any substantial survey research. Radicalized Islamic immigrants will therefore be very difficult to enumerate, and still more difficult to identify, with standard social science devices. It is unlikely that any extant estimates

Part of the reason for developing such fanaticism may be a motor for group polarization that shows up in small discussion groups, such as juries (Sunstein 2000). This may be an especially harsh fact for political groups in illiberal societies, such as many in the Middle East, or in illiberal subsocieties such as radicalized Islamic immigrants in the West. In common cases, the opposition group has to keep its meetings closed and secret if it is to escape suppression by the state, suppression that is apt to be brutal and violent. Among the most brutally extreme cases of such suppression was Hafez al-Assad's destruction of thousands, maybe tens of thousands, out of perhaps 350,000 inhabitants of the town of Hama in Syria in order to be certain of killing rebellious followers of the Muslim Brotherhood. Hama had been the fourth largest city in Syria before its destruction. American bombing of Afghanistan was less destructive than Assad's action, but still severe. Over the years of his dictatorship, however, Saddam Hussein might have killed far more of his own Iraqi citizens, also to suppress political opposition, especially from Kurds and Shiites (P. Berman 2003).

The need for secrecy and isolation means that the group's discussions become increasingly sharpened on a narrow interpretation of their world, and they become political or religious fanatics or, more likely, political *and* religious fanatics. They begin to support programs such as those proposed by Sayyid Qutb, an intellectual leader of the Muslim Brotherhood in Egypt and author of *Milestones* and other politico-religious tracts, before he was executed by Nasser's regime in 1966. Members of an offshoot of that Brotherhood later assassinated Anwar Sadat for making peace with Israel. Sadat wanted to control leftist secular groups, and in so doing he allowed a great deal of room for their opponents, such as the Brotherhood. While limiting and controlling the left, Sadat gave religious extremists of the right room to expand (Farhad Kazemi, personal communication, 21 February 2006). He paid a heavy price. Incidentally, Qutb is said to have been a mentor to Ayman Zawahiri, who became a mentor to and partner of Osama bin Laden.

Note that in the case of many of the Middle Eastern states, the availability of massive oil reserves may be a resource curse, enabling regimes to ignore their populace because they can fully fund all programs by pumping and selling oil (see, e.g., Ross 1999; Wantchekon 2002; Weinthal and Luong 2006, 36–38; Humphreys, Sachs, and Stiglitz 2007). Moreover, they can invest heavily in military and police forces to control their own populations. The populations might benefit little if at all from the

---

of the number of radical Islamists are of any value. A brutal Nazi or Stalinist regime might ferret out many of them, even most of them. Democratic regimes are unlikely to be able to find even a small fraction of them before they identify themselves by their violent actions.

national resources, which can be managed with foreign workers who have no stake or interest in the governments for which they work. As a result, the regimes become autocratic and have no interest in democracy, even as a sham exercise. A colonel or general can ensconce himself in power and thereafter ignore virtually all potential opposition. One might say that the autocrat is a parasite on the society, but in fact the autocrat lives from the oil reserves, not from extracting taxes from the populace, and is therefore a parasite only in an indirect sense. Occasionally, such an autocrat might even provide beneficial programs to poor citizens, as Muammar Qaddafi does in Libya.

Knowledge, Fanaticism, and Nationalism

In the end, it is arguably the nexus between knowledge and interests that explains fanatical nationalism. This causal connection is important negatively, in the sense that many fanatical nationalists could not sustain their fanatical commitments if their knowledge were not so radically crippled. But the nexus may also be important positively. Perhaps it is not so much that nationalists become fanatics, although this path is evidently often followed. Rather, it may be fanatics and psychologically potential fanatics who become nationalists if that path is available to them. The causal story is that a crippled understanding leads to fanaticism, which then leads to the urge for governmental control, so as to narrow popular focus on nationalism.

In the modern era, it is only through gaining control of a state that a fanatical group can expect to exclude contrary views and thereby maintain the crippled belief system of their followers. With the power of a state behind them, they can coerce, as the Taliban have done. If knowledge then tends to follow interests, coercion will work to convert some to the fanatical beliefs. We can probably safely suppose, for example, that religious belief in Iran a decade after the Ayatollahs came to power was firmer than it was before they had begun to coerce those who dared to show insufficiently strong belief.

It would be false to suppose that people believe simply what is in their interest, especially when merely *acting* as if they believed might serve their interest just as well. The Croatian killer of Mostar did not need to do even this much. He could act as one might have acted if one had the fanatical belief in Croatian righteousness, and that was sufficient to maintain his status in his Croatian society. But belief is not a matter of choice or decision. Commonly, it happens to us because the facts compel us, although many beliefs, religious and perhaps otherwise, are not grounded in demonstrable facts at all. Still, there can be a causal connection between our interests and what we perceive to be the facts. Moreover, among the facts that compel us are the testimony of others around us. At some level, fanatics seem to understand this, and they therefore often want to couple their fanatical beliefs with the power to coerce and influence others whose beliefs are weaker. In the twentieth century, this commonly meant to connect their beliefs with the power of national control.

There may have been instances of pure nationalism that were fanatical as well. Hitler's Nazi program was at least partly a matter of pure nationalism. But most nationalisms that are fanatical seem to be connected with a program that is not specifically nationalist, but merely opportunistic in seeking control of the nation. Because national independence has seemed to be a worthy goal to many who were not fanatics on any cause, fanatics may sometimes have gained from the support of at least their nationalism. Moreover, as noted previously, fanatical movements have benefited from the enforced ignorance that authoritarian governments have imposed for reasons of their own interest, rather than as part of any program of fanaticism. Hampering open discussion cripples the belief system of a populace and makes it more readily susceptible to the blandishments of fanatics. Counter to the slogan 'knowledge is power,' very nearly the opposite is true for fanatics. Suppressing knowledge is the route to power, strangely enough even to the power of a crippled and crippling idea.

COERCED IGNORANCE

The U.S. Supreme Court ruled, in *Wisconsin v. Yoder,* that the Old Order Amish in Wisconsin could end the education of their children at age 14 (contrary to Wisconsin law that mandates education for all until age 16). One of the arguments of *Yoder* is that Amish children have no need of the education that would let them fit successfully into the larger U.S. society, because they will live in the extraordinarily restrictive Amish society, in which a low level of education is sufficient for a normal level of success in occupational life.

The Court noted the view of the Amish that secondary school education (beyond eighth grade or age 14) was "an impermissible exposure of their children to a 'worldly' influence in conflict with their beliefs" (*Wisconsin v. Yoder,* 211). The Court decided that it is permissible to cripple their children's belief system and their capacity for eventually choosing their own lives. Its decision is as merciless to these children as the church leaders are: "It is one thing to say that compulsory education for a year or two beyond the eighth grade may be necessary when its goal is the preparation of the child for *life in modern society* as the majority live, but it is quite another if the goal of education be viewed as the *preparation of the child for life in the separated agrarian community that is the keystone of the Amish faith*" (222, emphases added). The sad fact of an education that is merely adequate for the latter life is that it is likely crippling for any alternative life these woefully undereducated people might choose later.[6] In fact, much of the education of Amish children in earlier years is provided in private community schools with Amish teachers. The decision, then, is about enforced ignorance and not about protecting Amish children from worldly influences through schooling.

Justice William O. Douglas, the sole dissenter (in part) in the *Yoder* decision correctly notes that "despite the Court's claim, the parents are seeking to vindicate not only their own free exercise claims, but also those of their high-school-age children." He thinks the interests of the children are ignored, and only the interests of the state and of the parents are taken into account in the *Yoder* decision. An Amish child of 16 or 18 who wishes to try a different life will have great difficulty, because in the larger community of the United States, education through high school is required for many jobs from which the Amish teenager in Wisconsin will be excluded. Recall the data on the apparent growth of evangelical church membership in recent decades (Hout, Greeley, and Wilde 2001). Of that seeming growth, 30 percent comes from the evangelicals' greater success in holding on to their own members. They discourage higher education, but they have not been legally empowered to block their children's high school education as the Amish have been. The Amish success rate in holding onto their members is now secured more firmly by *Yoder* than it had been.[7]

---

[6]The *Yoder* decision is not as sweeping as it might seem to be. Other religious groups, such as evangelical groups and deeply conservative Jewish groups in urban settings, cannot make the claim that ending education at age fourteen while continuing a kind of apprenticeship in farming serves future farmers in the narrow group's world very well. The Amish claim that this organization of their lives is a crucial part of their faith. Few of the evangelicals are in such geographically restrictive, close communities that geographically exclude others and are genuinely dedicated economically to farming. Leaders of the Amish community have an interest in maintaining a simple way of life, which they see as threatened by further education. *Yoder* ruled that this interest is a genuinely religious concern, and that it outweighed the state's interest in schooling through the tenth grade. The Supreme Court had not previously exempted religious groups from such laws, and its decision stresses that the 300–year Amish tradition was crucial to its decision.

[7]It is a saving grace of the badly argued decision in *Yoder* that it is very narrowly construed, so that it cannot be readily generalized to other religious issues. Subsequent decisions on religious exercise have largely repudiated that decision, buttressed by Justice Antonin Scalia's declaration that applying the standards of *Yoder* to further cases would be "courting anarchy." Chief Justice Warren Burger, the inconsistent author of *Yoder*, essentially reversed himself in *United States v. Lee* (1982), a case concerning Amish neglect of payment of social security taxes for their employees. *Yoder* ends rather than begins the move to partition public policy into religiously grounded segments (see Peters 2003, 175–78). Oddly, the Amish community in New Glarus, Wisconsin, which sparked the Yoder appeal, was virtually torn apart by the conflicts and the notoriety that it generated; most of its members soon moved away to various places (166–71). It is an ostensibly religious principle that the Amish do not go to law.

The Amish practice of "rumspringa" (roughly: jumping around) is some-times offered as a defense of the liberalism of the *Yoder* decision (Mazie 2005). At age 16, young Amish adults are licensed to roam into the larger world and to indulge in its offerings, which typically today include beer, music, drugs, movies, television, and things that other teenagers enjoy. Whenever they wish, the young Amish may return to the community and be baptized as adult believers who have themselves voluntarily accepted Amish life. Ostensibly, this means that they act with autonomy, but the real burden of *Yoder* cannot be overcome by allowing this odd lark. The deep burden is that Amish youth are so poorly educated that they are not qualified even to take on some of the pleasures of the larger world. They are disqualified from all but the most mundane jobs in the larger econ-omy. Even worse, they are disqualified from continuing with education, unless someone takes a special interest in them to get them into school or university. Most of them will therefore never be qualified for most jobs. *Yoder* poses a very high barrier between the Amish community and the rest of the world. It does not entirely bar individual choice in life, but it severely restricts the range of plausibly attractive choices.

CONCLUDING REMARKS

Explanations of individual and group fanaticism pose different problems, but they are both matters of constrained belief systems. For the most part, individuals become fanatics through the backing of groups, although some individuals might manage to become fanatics essentially on their own (as appears to have happened for the Unabomber). In the course of living more or less within a fanatical group, the individual's knowledge becomes massively distorted. This is a peculiar result in some ways, be-cause we all live to some large extent within groups, but most of us are not monomaniacally fanatic. Moreover, virtually all of our knowledge comes from our larger society, not from our own discovery. Hence, it is fundamentally group based in large part, but the groups from which most of our knowledge comes are open and inclusive, whereas the knowledge of the fanatic comes from an essentially exclusive group. Often, however, such groups choose to include others, but only by converting those oth-ers rather than merely being open to them with whatever differences they might have.

Hence, again, the fundamental problem is to explain the fanaticism of certain groups. Fanatical groups may arise in many ways, through any way that cripples the knowledge of the groups' members. A single fanat-ical and charismatic individual might preach to others and all the while sequester them from the influences of the larger society. Or the belief system of a group that has become isolated, perhaps by exclusion from other groups in the society, might eventually become constrained and might therefore acquire increasingly extremist views. But group formation cannot, in general, have a single explanatory story. Rather, it must be essentially a phenomenon of coordination on a limited set of views. Coordinations develop in many and varied ways, and in any particular group it might be virtually impossible even to tell the story of how the coordination got underway, because the vast number of facts constituting that story may be unrecorded and not coherently remembered.

Coordination of a group of people brings power, often to a small leadership within the group (Hardin 1995, chap. 2). Such a leadership may then recognize that its interest is tied to the cohesion of the group that constitutes their power. It is the coordinated group, focused on some issue, that constitutes their power. The leadership need not even hold the beliefs of the group members to covet such power. Leaders often see the benefits to the group, and hence to themselves, of keeping members ignorant, and they might attempt to impose substantial ignorance on their members, as the Old Order Amish in Wisconsin impose ignorance on their children.

Once such a group is underway, its fanaticism may be intensified through the exit of its more moderate members. They might exit of their own accord because, say, the group's mindset has become stultifying, or because they have better opportunities outside it. Or they might exit because they are de facto shunned and excluded by others in the group, which is more guided by its strengthened norm of exclusion. A group's fanaticism might also be intensified intergenerationally, through blinkered education, as is the case of the Amish children of Wisconsin, or of the children governed by the Taliban in Afghanistan, the Ayatollahs in Iran, the ultra-orthodox rabbis of Israel, and many others.

Winston Churchill reputedly quipped that fanatics are people who cannot change their minds and will not change the subject. He got their belief system just right with his first point. But perhaps he got them wrong with his second point. It is not so much that they will not change the subject. Rather, they cannot change it, because they have no other subject. That is the nature of their crippled belief system, without which they would not be fanatics. This is a good place to end, lest I become fanatical in defense of the theory of knowledge of the ordinary person. I will change the subject.

References

The typography but not the wording of some classical texts has been modernized for ease of reading. Additional works of my own are listed at the end of the preface. Cases cited in the text are listed at the conclusion of the references.

Adler, Jonathan E. 2002. *Belief's Own Ethics.* Cambridge, Mass.: MIT Press.

Ajami, Fouad. 1993. "The Summoning." *Foreign Affairs* 72 (September-October): 2–9.

Albritton, Rogers. 1985. "Freedom of Will and Freedom of Action." *Proceedings and Addresses of the American Philosophical Association* 59 (No. 2): 239–51.

Alper, Matthew. 2001. *The "God" Part of the Brain: A Scientific Interpretation of Human Spirituality and God.* Brooklyn, N.Y.: Rogue Press.

Anderson, Benedict. [1983] 1991. *Imagined Communities.* London: Verso, revised edition.

Anscombe, G.E.M. [1974] 1981. "On Transubstantiation." In Anscombe, *Ethics, Religion and Politics.* Minneapolis: University of Minnesota Press: 107–12.

Aronson, Josh. 2000. *Sound and Fury* (film). Aronson Film Associates, Inc., and Public Policy Productions.

Arrow, Kenneth J. [1951] 1963. *Social Choice and Individual Values.* New Haven, Conn.: Yale University Press, second edit.

Audi, Robert. 1995. "The Ethics of Advocacy." *Legal Theory* 1: 251–81.

———. 1997. "The Place of Testimony in the Fabric of Knowledge and Justification." *American Philosophical Quarterly* 34 (no. 4): 404–42.

Banfield, Edward C. 1958. *The Moral Basis of a Backward Society.* New York: Free Press.

Baron, Jonathan. [1988] 2000. *Thinking and Deciding.* Cambridge: Cambridge University Press.

Barry, Brian. 1980. "Is It Better to Be Powerful or Lucky?" *Political Studies* (June and September 1980) 28: 183–94, 338–52.

Bartels, Larry M. 1996. "Uninformed Votes: Information Effects in Presidential Elections." *American Journal of Political Science* 40 (no. 1, February): 194–230.

Becker, Gary S. 1996. *Accounting for Tastes.* Cambridge, Mass.: Harvard University Press.

Beckwith, Francis J. 2003. *Law, Darwinism, and Public Education: The Establishment Clause and the Challenge of Intelligent Design.* Lanham, Md.: Rowman & Littlefield.

Behe, Michael J. 1996. *Darwin's Black Box: The Biochemical Challenge to Evolution.* New York: Free Press.

Bennett, Stephen Earl. 2003. "Is the Public's Ignorance of Politics Trivial?" *Critical Review* (fall): 307–37.

Bentham, Jeremy. [1789] 1970. *An Introduction to the Principles of Morals and Legislation,* ed. J. H. Burns and H.L.A. Hart. London: Methuen.

Berle, Adolph A., and Gardner C. Means. 1932. *The Modern Corporation and Private Property.* New York: Macmillan.

Berman, Eli. 1998. "Sect, Subsidy, and Sacrifice: An Economist's View of Ultra-Orthodox Jews." *Quarterly Journal of Economics* 115 (no. 3, August): 905–53.

Berman, Paul. 2003. *Terror and Liberalism.* New York: Norton.

Biagioli, Mario. 1993. *Galileo, Courtier: The Practice of Science in the Culture of Absolutism.* Chicago: University of Chicago Press.

Blackmore, John, ed. 1995. *Ludwig Boltzmann, His Later Life and Philosophy, 1900–1906.* Kluwer.

Block, Robert. 1993. "Killers," *New York Review of Books* (18 November): 9–10.

Bloom, Allan. 1987. *The Closing of the American Mind.* New York: Simon and Schuster.

Bodin, Jean. [1576] 1606. *The Six Books of the Republic.* Cambridge, Mass.: Harvard University Press, reprint of 1606 transl. of Richard Knolles.

Bonnefoy, Yves, and Wendy Doniger, eds. 1991. *Mythologies,* 2 vols. Chicago: University of Chicago Press.

Boswell, James. [1791] 1976. *Boswell's Life of Johnson.* London: Oxford University Press.

Boyer, Pascal. 2001. *Religion Explained: The Evolutionary Origins of Religious Thought.* New York: Basic.

Brandt, Richard B. 1979. *A Theory of the Good and the Right.* Oxford: Oxford University Press.

Bretherton, Inga. 1992. "The Origins of Attachment Theory: John Bowlby and Mary Ainsworth." *Developmental Psychology* 28: 759–75.

Breton, Albert, and Ronald Wintrobe. 1982. *The Logic of Bureaucratic Conduct.* Cambridge: Cambridge University Press.

Brink, David O. 1988. "Sidgwick's Dualism of Practical Reason." *Australasian Journal of Philosophy* 66: 291–307.

———. 1989. *Moral Realism and the Foundations of Ethics.* Cambridge: Cambridge University Press.

Broder, John M. 2006. "For Muslim Who Says Violence Destroys Islam, Violent Threats." *New York Times* (11 March): A1, 6.

Buchan, James. 2003. *Crowded with Genius.* New York: HarperCollins.

Caldwell, Christopher. 2005. "Daughter of the Enlightenment." *New York Times Magazine* (3 April): 26–31.

Campbell, Jeremy. 2001. *The Liar's Tale: A History of Falsehood.* New York: Norton.

Cercignani, Carlo. 1998. *Ludwig Boltzmann: The Man Who Trusted Atoms.* Oxford: Oxford University Press.

Chace, James. 2004. *1912: Wilson, Roosevelt, Taft, and Debs—The Election That Changed the Country.* New York: Simon & Schuster.

Coady, Tony. 1992. *Testimony: A Philosophical Study.* Princeton: Princeton University Press.

———. 1994. "Speaking of Ghosts," in Frederick Schmitt, ed., *Socializing Epistemology: The Social Dimensions of Knowledge.* Lanham, Md.: Rowman and Littlefield: 75–92.

Cohen, Jon. 1994. "The Duesberg Phenomenon" and related stories. *Science* (9 December): 1642–49.

Coleman, James S. 1987. "Free Riders and Zealots." In Karen S. Cook, ed., *Social Exchange Theory.* Newbury Park, Calif.: Sage, pp. 59–82.

Converse, Philip. 1964. "The Nature of Belief Systems in Mass Publics." In David E. Apter, ed., *Ideology and Discontent.* New York: Free Press.

———. 1975. "Public Opinion and Voting Behavior." In Fred I. Greenstein and Nelson W. Polsby, eds. *Handbook of Political Science.* Reading Mass.: Addison-Wesley, vol. 4.

———. 1990. "Popular Representation and the Distribution of Information." In John A. Ferejohn and James Kuklinski, eds., *Information and Democratic Processes.* Urbana, Ill.: University of Illinois Press: 369–88.

———. 2000. "Assessing the Capacity of Mass Electorates." *Annual Review of Political Science* 3:331–53.

Converse, Philip, and Roy Pierce. 1986. *Political Representation in France.* Cambridge, Mass.: Harvard University Press.

Couzin, Jennifer. 2005. "Plan B: A Collision of Science and Politics." *Science* 310 (7 October): 38–39.

Coyne, George. 2005. "Infinite Wonder of the Divine." *The Tablet* (10 December). (URL: http://www.thetablet.co.uk/cgi-bin/register.cgi/tablet-01118)

Craig, Edward. 1990. *Knowledge and the State of Nature.* Oxford: Oxford University Press.

Crapanzano, Vincent. 2000. *Serving the Word: Literalism in America from the Pulpit to the Bench.* New York: The New Press.

Dahl, Robert A. 1961. *Who Governs?* New Haven, Conn.: Yale University Press.

Dalrymple, William. 2005. "Inside the Madrasas." *New York Review of Books* (1 December): 16–20.

Danson, Edwin. 2006. *Weighing the World: The Quest to Measure the Earth.* Oxford: Oxford University Press.

Darwin, Charles. [1859] 1964. *On the Origin of Species by Means of Natural Selection, or the Preservation of Favoured Species in the Struggle for Life.* Cambridge, Mass.: Harvard University Press.

Davidson, Donald. [1970] 1980. "Mental Events." In Davidson. *Actions and Events.* Oxford: Oxford University Press.

Davis, Percival, and Dean H. Kenyon. [1993] 2004. *Of Pandas and People: The Central Question of Biological Origins.* Foundation for Thought & Ethics; 2nd edition.

Dawkins, Richard. [1986] 1996. *The Blind Watchmaker: Why the Evidence of Evolution Reveals a Universe Without Design.* New York: Norton.

Delli Carpini, Michael X., and Scott Keeter. 1996. *What Americans Know about Politics and Why It Matters.* New Haven, Conn.: Yale University Press.

Dembski, William A. 2004. *The Design Revolution: Answering the Toughest Questions about Intelligent Design.* Downers Grove, Ill.: InterVarsity Press.

Dewey, John. [1920] 1948. *Reconstruction in Philosophy.* Boston: Beacon Press.

———. [1927] 1954. *The Public and Its Problems.* Chicago: Swallow.

———. [1929] 1984. *The Quest for Certainty: A Study of the Relation of Knowl-*

edge and Action. The Later Works, vol. 4, ed. by Jo Ann Boydson. Carbondale, Ill.: Southern Illinois University Press.

Diamond, Jared. 2005. *Collapse: How Societies Choose to Fail or Succeed.* New York: Viking.

Downs, Anthony. 1957. *An Economic Theory of Democracy.* New York: Harper.

Doyle, Arthur Conan. [1887] 1993. *A Study in Scarlet.* New York : Oxford University Press, ed. Owen Dudley Edwards.

Duesberg, Peter. 1988. "HIV Is Not the Cause of AIDS." *Science* 241(29 July): 514.

———. 1996. *Inventing the AIDS Virus.* Washington, D.C.: Regnery.

Dunn, John. 1984. "The Concept of 'Trust' in the Politics of John Locke." In Richard Rorty, J. B. Schneewind, and Quentin Skinner, eds., *Philosophy in History.* Cambridge: Cambridge University Press: 279–301.

Ehrman, Bart. 2003a. *Lost Christianities: The Battle for Scripture and the Faiths We Never Knew.* Oxford: Oxford University Press.

———. 2003b. *Lost Scriptures: Books That Did Not Make It into the New Testament.* Oxford: Oxford University Press.

Elster, Jon. 1979. *Ulysses and the Sirens: Studies in Rationality and Irrationality.* Cambridge: Cambridge University Press.

Enserink, Martin. 2005. "Is Holland Becoming the Kansas of Europe?" *Science* 308 (3 June): 1394.

Estrich, Susan. 1998. *Getting Away with Murder: How Politics Is Destroying the Criminal Justice System.* Cambridge, Mass.: Harvard University Press.

Evans-Pritchard, E. E. 1937. *Witchcraft, Oracles, and Magic among the Azande.* Oxford: Oxford University Press.

Everett, Daniel L. 2005. "Cultural Constraints on Grammar and Cognition in Pirahã: Another Look at the Design Features of Human Language." *Current Anthropology* 46 (no. 4, August–October): 621–46.

Fenno, Richard F., Jr. 1978. *Home Style: House Members in Their Districts.* Boston: Little, Brown.

Ferguson, Adam. [1767] 1980. *An Essay on the History of Civil Society.* New Brunswick, N.J.: Transaction.

Figes, Orlando. 2007. *The Whisperers: Private Life in Stalin's Russia.* New York: Henry Holt.

Finocchiaro, Maurice. 2005. *Retrying Galileo, 1633–1992.* Berkeley, Calif.: University of California Press.

Fish, Stanley. 1996. "Professor Sokal's Bad Joke." *New York Times,* 21 May: op-ed page.

Fitzgerald, F. Scott. 1945. *The Crack-up.* New York: New Directions.

Foley, Richard. 1994. "Egoism in Epistemology," in Frederick Schmitt, ed., *Socializing Epistemology: The Social Dimensions of Knowledge.* Lanham, Md.: Rowman and Littlefield: 53–73.

Forrest, Barbara, and Paul R. Gross. 2004. *Creationism's Trojan Horse: The Wedge of Intelligent Design.* Oxford: Oxford University Press.

France, Anatole. 1892. *Le livre de mon ami.* Paris: Calmann Levy.

Franklin, James. 2001. *The Science of Conjecture: Evidence and Probability before Pascal.* Baltimore, Md.: Johns Hopkins University Press.

Frey, Bruno S. 1997. "Rational Choice in Religion—and Beyond." *Journal of Institutional and Theoretical Economics* 153 (no. 1, March): 279–84.

Friedman, Jeffrey. 1998. "Public Ignorance and Democratic Theory." *Critical Review* (nos. 3 and 4, summer-fall): 397–411.

Gass, William. 1966. *Omensetter's Luck.* New York: New American Library.

Gauthier, David. 1986. *Morals by Agreement.* Oxford: Oxford University Press.

Gellner, Ernest. 1983. *Nations and Nationalism.* Ithaca, N.Y.: Cornell University Press.

Gelman, Rochel, and C. R. Gallistel. 2004. "Language and the Origin of Numerical Concepts." *Science* 306 (15 October): 441–43.

Gilkey, Langdon. 1985. *Creationism on Trial.* Minneapolis: Winston Press.

———. 1988. "Reply from the Author." *Biology and Philosophy* 3: 485–95.

Gilovich, Thomas, Dale Griffin, and Daniel Kahnemann, eds. 2002. *Heuristics and Biases: The Psychology of Intuitive Judgment.* Cambridge: Cambridge University Press.

Goldman, Alvin I. [1992] 1993. "Epistemic Folkways and Scientific Epistemology." In Goldman, ed., *Readings in Philosophy and Cognitive Science.* Cambridge, Mass.: MIT Press, pp. 95–116.

Gompers, Samuel. 1905. "Discussion at Rochester, N.Y., on the Open Shop—'The Union Shop Is Right'—It Naturally Follows Organization." *American Federationist* 12 (April, no. 4): 221–23.

Goodstein, Laurie. 2005. "Intelligent Design Might Be Meeting Its Maker." *New York Times* (4 December): 4.1 and 4. 4.

Gould, Stephen J. 1993. *Eight Little Piggies: Reflections in Natural History.* New York: Norton.

Govier, Trudy. 1997. *Social Trust and Human Communities.* Montreal: McGill-Queens University Press.

Griffin, John Howard. [1961] 1976. *Black Like Me.* New York: New American Library.

Grofman, Bernard, and Julie Withers. 1993. "Information-Pooling Models of Electoral Politics." In Grofman, ed., *Information, Participation, and Choice.* Ann Arbor, Mich.: University of Michigan Press: 55–64.

Hall, Richard J., and Charles R. Johnson. 1998. "The Epistemic Duty to Seek More Evidence." *American Philosophical Quarterly* 35 (no. 2, April): 129–39.

Hamer, Dean. 2004. *The God Gene: How Faith Is Hardwired into Our Genes.* New York: Doubleday.

Hanson, R. Brooks, and Floyd E. Bloom. 1999. "Fending off Furtive Strategists." *Science* 285 (17 September): 1847.

Hardin, Russell. 1980. "Rationality, Irrationality, and Functionalist Explanation." *Social Science Information* 19 (September): 755–72.

———. 1982. *Collective Action.* Baltimore, Md.: Johns Hopkins University Press, for Resources for the Future.

———. 1988a. "Constitutional Political Economy: Agreement on Rules." *British Journal of Political Science* 18 (October): 513–30.

———. 1988b. *Morality Within the Limits of Reason.* Chicago: University of Chicago Press.

———. 1989. "Ethics and Stochastic Processes." *Social Philosophy and Policy* 7 (Autumn): 69–80.

———. 1991. "Hobbesian Political Order." *Political Theory* 19 (May): 156–80.

———. 1994. "My University's Yacht: Morality and the Rule of Law." In NOMOS 36, *The Rule of Law*, edited by Ian Shapiro. New York: New York University Press: 205–27.

———. 1995. *One for All: The Logic of Group Conflict.* Princeton, N.J.: Princeton University Press.

———. 1996. "Magic on the Frontier: The Norm of Efficiency." *University of Pennsylvania Law Review* 144 (May): 1987–2020.

———. 1999. *Liberalism, Constitutionalism, and Democracy.* Oxford: Oxford University Press.

———. 2000. "Democratic Epistemology and Accountability." *Social Philosophy and Policy* 17: 110–26.

———. 2002. *Trust and Trustworthiness.* New York: Russell Sage Foundation.

———. 2003. *Indeterminacy and Society.* Princeton, N.J.: Princeton University Press.

———. 2004a. "Representing Ignorance." *Social Philosophy and Policy* 21 (no. 1, Winter): 76–99.

———. 2004b. "Transition to Corporate Democracy?" In *Building a Trustworthy State in Post-Socialist Transition*, edited by Janos Kornai and Susan Rose-Ackerman. New York: Palgrave Macmillan: 175–97.

———. 2006a. "Rational Choice Political Philosophy." In Irwin L. Morris, Joe Oppenheimer, and Karol Soltan, eds., *From Anarchy to Democracy*, Stanford: Stanford University Press: 95–109.

———. 2006b. *Trust.* London: Polity.

———. 2006c. "The Genetics of Cooperation." *Analyse & Kritik* 28 (July): 57–65.

———. Forthcoming. *The Mystery of Nationalism.*

Harris, Sam. 2004. *The End of Faith: Religion, Terror, and the Future of Reason.* New York: Norton.

Hayek, F. A. 1944. *The Road to Serfdom.* Chicago: University of Chicago Press.

———. 1960. *The Constitution of Liberty.* Chicago: University of Chicago Press.

———. 1980. *Individualism and Economic Order.* Chicago: University of Chicago Press.

Herder, Johann Gottfried. [1774] 2004. *Another Philosophy of History and Selected Political Writings.* Indianapolis, Ind.: Hackett, transl. by Ioannis D. Evrigenis and Daniel Pellerin.

Hirschman, Albert O. 1970. *Exit, Voice, and Loyalty: Responses to Decline in Firms, Organizations, and States.* Cambridge, Mass.: Harvard University Press.

———. 1977. *The Passions and the Interests: Political Arguments for Capitalism Before Its Triumph.* Princeton, N.J.: Princeton University Press.

Hobbes, Thomas. [1651] 1994. *Leviathan*, edited by Edwin Curley. Indianapolis, Ind.: Hackett.

Hobsbawm, E. J. 1992. *Nations and Nationalism since 1870.* Cambridge: Cambridge University Press, 2nd edition.

Holmes, Stephen. 1990. "The Secret History of Self-Interest." In Jane J. Mansbridge. *Beyond Self-Interest.* Chicago: University of Chicago Press: 267–86.

Holston, James. 1989. *The Modernist City: An Anthropological Critique of Brasília*. Chicago: University of Chicago Press.

Holton, Gerald. 1986. *The Advancement of Science, and Its Burdens: The Jefferson Lectures and Other Essays*. Cambridge: Cambridge University Press.

———. 1996. *Einstein, History, and Other Passions*. Reading, Mass.: Addison-Wesley.

Horton, Richard. 1996. "Truth and Heresy about AIDS" (review of Duesberg books). *New York Review of Books* (23 May): 14–20.

Hout, Michael, Andrew Greeley, and Melissa Wilde. 2001. "The Demographic Imperative in Religious Change." *American Journal of Sociology* 107 (September): 468–500.

Hull, David L. 1988. *Science As a Process: An Evolutionary Account of the Social and Conceptual Development of Science*. Chicago: University of Chicago Press.

Hume, David. [1739–40] 2000. *A Treatise of Human Nature*. Oxford: Oxford University Press, ed. David Fate Norton and Mary J. Norton.

———. [1748] 2000. *An Enquiry Concerning Human Understanding*. Oxford: Oxford University Press, ed. Tom L. Beauchamp.

———. [1779] 1976. *Dialogues Concerning Natural Religion*. In *David Hume on Religion*. Oxford: Oxford University Press, ed. by John Valdimir Price.

Humphreys, Macartan, Jeffrey D. Sachs, and Joseph E. Stiglitz, eds. 2007. *Escaping the Resource Curse*. New York: Columbia University Press.

Iyengar, Shanto. 1990. "Shortcuts to Political Knowledge: The Role of Selective Attention and Accessibility." In John A. Ferejohn and James Kuklinski, eds., *Information and Democratic Processes*. Urbana, Ill.: University of Illinois Press: 160–85.

Jacobs, Jane. 1961. *The Death and Life of Great American Cities*. New York: Random House.

James, Clive. 1996. "Sex and Reason" (a review of Ray Monk, *Bertrand Russell: The Spirit of Solitude*, New York: Free Press, 1996). *New Yorker* (9 December): 104–17.

Johns, Adrian. 2001. "The Birth of Scientific Reading." *Nature* 409 (18 January): 287.

Kahnemann, Daniel, and Amos Tversky. 2000. *Choices, Values, and Frames*. Cambridge: Cambridge University Press; and New York: Russell Sage Foundation.

Kaiser, Jocelyn. 2002. "Software Glitch Threw off Mortality Estimates." *Science* 296 (14 June) 1945–47.

Kaplan, Robert D. 1993. "A Reader's Guide to the Balkans." *New York Times Book Review* (18 April): 1, 30–33.

Kelly, Paul J. 2004. *Liberalism*. London: Polity.

Kinsley, Michael. 1995. "The Intellectual Free Lunch." *New Yorker* (6 February): 4–5.

Kitcher, Philip. 1994. "Contrasting Conceptions of Social Epistemology," in Frederick Schmitt, ed., *Socializing Epistemology: The Social Dimensions of Knowledge*. Lanham, Md.: Rowman and Littlefield: 111–34.

Koertge, Noretta, ed. 1998. *A House Built on Sand: Exposing Postmodernist Myths about Science*. Oxford: Oxford University Press.

Kolata, Gina. 2004. "A Glimmer of Hope for Fading Minds." *New York Times* (13 April): F1 and 6.

Krakauer, Jon. 1990. *Eiger Dreams: Ventures among Men and Mountains.* New York: Knopf.

Kramer, Roderick M. 1994. "The Sinister Attribution Error: Paranoid Cognition and Collective Distrust in Organizations." *Motivation and Emotion* 18: 199–230.

Kuhn, Thomas. [1962] 1996. *The Structure of Scientifc Revolutions.* Chicago: University of Chicago Press, 3rd edition.

Kull, Steven, and I. M. Destler. 1999. *Misreading the Public: The Myth of a New Isolationism.* Washington, D.C.: Brookings Institution Press.

Kuran, Timur. 1996. "The Discontents of Islamic Economic Morality." *American Economic Review* 86 (no. 2, May): 438–42.

Kymlicka, Will. 1989. *Liberalism, Community, and Culture.* Oxford University Press.

Lahiri, Jhumpa. 1999. "The Treatment of Bibi Haldar." In Lahiri, *Interpreter of Maladies.* New York: Houghton Mifflin: 158–72.

Lane, Harlan. 1976. *The Wild Boy of Aveyron.* Cambridge, Mass.: Harvard University Press; reprinted New York: Bantam, 1977.

Larson, Edward J. 1997. *Summer for the Gods: The Scopes Trial and America's Continuing Debate over Science and Religion.* Cambridge, Mass.: Harvard University Press.

Larson, Edward J., and Larry Witham. 1998. "Leading Scientists Still Reject God." *Nature* 394 (23 July): 313.

———. 1999. "Scientists and Religion in America." *Scientific American* (September): 88–93.

Lehrer, Keith. 1990. *Theory of Knowledge.* Boulder, Colo.: Westview.

———. 1995. "Knowledge and the Trustworthiness of Instruments." *Monist* 78 (no. 2): 156–70.

Lenin, V. I. [1917] 1954. *The Agrarian Programme of Social-Democracy in the First Russian Revolution, 1905–1907.* Moscow: Progress Publishers, 2nd revised edition.

Lévy-Bruhl, Lucien. [1910] 1926. *How Natives Think.* London: Unwin Brothers.

———. [1922] 1923. *Primitive Mentality.* London: George Allen & Unwin.

Lewis, Bernard. 2002. *What Went Wrong? Western Impact and Middle Eastern Response.* Oxford: Oxford University Press.

Lewontin, R.C. 1991. *Biology as Ideology: The Doctrine of DNA.* Ontario, Calif.: Stoddart.

Lingua Franca. 2000. The editors. *The Sokal Hoax.* Lincoln, Nebr.: University of Nebraska Press.

Locke, John. [1689] 1975. *An Essay Concerning Human Understanding.* Oxford: Oxford University Press, ed. by Peter H. Nidditch. (Quotations from this text are slightly modernized.)

Louis, Pierre-Charles-Alexandre. [1835] 1836. *Researches on the Effects of Bloodletting in Some Inflammatory Diseases.* Boston: Hilliard, Gray, and Co.

Lovelock, James. 1998. "A Book for All Seasons." *Science* (8 May) 280: 832–33.

Luther, Martin. [1523] 1991.

Lyell, Charles. [1830–33] 1990. *Principles of Geology.* Chicago: University of Chicago Press, vol. 1.

Lyons, David. 1965. *Forms and Limits of Utilitarianism.* Oxford: Oxford University Press.

Machamer, Peter. 2005. "The Many Trials of Galileo Galilei." Review of Finocchiaro 2005. *Science* 309 (1 July): 58.

MacIntyre, Alasdair. 1984. "Is Patriotism a Virtue?" Lindley Lecture. Lawrence, Kans.: University of Kansas.

Mackie, J. L. 1995. "Evil and Omnipotence." *Mind,* New Series, 64 (no. 254, April): 200–212.

Maclean, Charles. 1980. *Island on the Edge of the World: The Story of St. Kilda.* New York: Taplinger.

Mandeville, Bernard. [1705, 1714] 1988. *The Fable of the Bees,* 2 vols. Indianapolis, Ind.: Liberty Press.

Manji, Irshad. 2003. *The Trouble with Islam Today: A Muslim's Call for Reform in Her Faith.* Toronto: Random House.

Mann, Charles C. 2002. "Has GM Corn 'Invaded' Mexico?" *Science* 295 (1 March): 1617–19.

Margolis, Howard. 1987. *Patterns, Thinking, and Cognition.* Chicago: University of Chicago Press.

———. 2002. *It Started with Copernicus: How Turning the World Inside out Led to the Scientific Revolution.* New York: McGraw-Hill.

Marty, Martin E. 2005. *When Faiths Collide.* Malden, Mass.: Blackwell.

Mayr, Ernst. 1997. *This Is Biology: The Science of the Living World.* Cambridge, Mass.: Harvard University Press.

Mazie, Steven V. 2005. "Consenting Adults? Amish *Rumspringa* and the Quandary of Exit in Liberalism," 3 *Perspectives on Politics* (December, no. 4): 745–59.

Merton, Robert K. 1968. *Social Theory and Social Structure.* New York: Macmillan, enlarged edition.

Metzger, Bruce. 1987. *The Canon of the New Testament: Its Origin, Development, and Significance.* Oxford: Oxford University Press.

Meyer, Marvin. 2005. *The Gnostic Discoveries: The Impact of the Nag Hammadi Library.* San Francisco: HarperSanFrancisco.

Michaels, David. 2005. "Doubt Is Their Product." *Scientific American* (June): 96–101.

Mill, John Stuart. [1848] 1965. *Principles of Political Economy.* In J. M. Robson, ed., *Collected Works of John Stuart Mill.* Toronto: University of Toronto Press, 7th edition, vols. 2 and 3.

———. [1859] 1977. *On Liberty.* In J. M. Robson (ed.), *Collected Works of John Stuart Mill.* Toronto: University of Toronto Press, vol. 18, pp. 213–310.

———. [1861] 1977. *Considerations on Representative Government,* in Mill, *Essays on Politics and Society,* vol. 19 of *Collected Works of John Stuart Mill.* Toronto: University of Toronto Press, ed. J. M. Robson: 371–613.

Miller, Arthur I. 2005. *Empire of the Stars: Obsession, Friendship, and Betrayal in the Quest for Black Holes.* New York: Houghton Mifflin.

Miller, Jon D. 1983. *The American People and Science Policy: The Role of Public Attitudes in the Policy Process*. New York: Pergamon.

Miller, Laura. 2004. "How Many Books Are Too Many?" *New York Times Book Review* (18 July): 23.

Mises, Ludwig von. [1922] 1981. *Socialism*. Indianapolis, Ind.: Liberty Fund.

Mitgang, Herbert. 1999. "Death of a President: A 200-Year-Old Malpractice Debate." *New York Times* (14 December): D7.

Montgomery, James D. 1996a. "Dynamics of the Religious Economy: Exit, Voice and Denominational Secularization." *Rationality and Society* 8: 81–110.

———. 1996b. "Contemplations on the Economic Approach to Religious Behavior." *American Economic Review* 86 (no. 2, May): 443–47.

Montmarquet, James A. 1993. *Epistemic Virtue and Doxastic Responsibility*. Lanham, Md.: Rowman & Littlefield.

Mooney, Chris. 2005. *The Republican War on Science*. New York: Basic Books.

Moore, G. E. 1903. *Principia Ethica*. Cambridge: Cambridge University Press.

Moore, John A. 2002. *From Genesis to Genetics: The Case of Evolution and Creationism*. Berkeley: University of California Press.

Morabia, Alfredo. 2004. "Pierre-Charles-Alexandre Louis and the Evaluation of Bloodletting." James Lind Library (www.jameslindlibrary.org).

Morgan, Edmund S. 2005. "Back to Basics" (a review of Vincent Crapanzano, *Serving the Word: Literalism in America from the Pulpit to the Bench*). *New York Review of Books* (20 July): 47–49.

Morris, Henry M., and John C. Whitcomb. 1961. *The Genesis Flood*. Philadelphia: Presbyterian & Reformed Publishing.

Moynihan, Daniel Patrick. 1993. *Pandaemonium: Ethnicity in International Politics*. Oxford: Oxford University Press.

Mueller, John. 1999. *Democracy, Capitalism, and Ralph's Pretty Good Grocery*. Princeton, N.J.: Princeton University Press.

Nagel, Thomas. 1998. "Concealment and Exposure," *Philosophy and Public Affairs* 27: 3–30.

Narveson, Jan. 2002. "Fixing Democracy." In Narveson, *Respecting Persons in Theory and Practice: Essays on Moral and Political Philosophy*. Lanham, Md.: Rowman & Littlefield: 163–84.

Newberg, Andrew, Eugene D'Aqili, and Vince Rause. 2001. *Why God Won't Go Away: Brain Science and the Biology of Belief*. New York: Ballantine.

Niebuhr, Reinhold. 1932. *Moral Man and Immoral Society: A Study in Ethics and Politics*. New York: Scribner's.

Nyberg, David. 1993. *The Varnished Truth: Truth Telling and Deceiving in Ordinary Life*. Chicago: University of Chicago Press.

Olson, Mancur, Jr. 1965. *The Logic of Collective Action*. Cambridge, Mass.: Harvard University Press.

Orr, H. Allen. 2005. "Devolution: Why Intelligent Design Isn't." *New Yorker* (20 May): 40–52.

Overbye, Dennis. 2004. "A Wrinkle in Space-Time." *New York Times* (13 April): F1 and 4.

Page, Benjamin I., and Robert Y. Shapiro. 1992. *The Rational Public*. Chicago: University of Chicago Press.

Pagel, Mark, ed. 2002. *Encyclopedia of Evolution.* Oxford: Oxford University Press, 2 vols.

Pagels, Elaine. 1979. *The Gnostic Gospels.* New York: Random House.

Pareto, Vilfredo. [1927] 1971. *Manual of Political Economy.* New York: Kelley, trans. from French edition by Ann S. Schwier.

Parfit, Derek. 1984. *Reasons and Persons.* Oxford: Oxford University Press.

Park, Robert. 2000. *Voodoo Science.* Oxford: Oxford University Press.

———. 2006. "Scorched Earth: Why Did NASA Kill a Climate Change Project?" *New York Times* (15 January): 4.13 op-ed.

Pennock, Robert T. 2001. *Intelligent Design Creationism and Its Critics: Philosophical, Theological, and Scientific Perspectives.* Cambridge, Mass.: MIT.

Perkins, Sid. 2006. "Evolution in Action: The Trials and Tribulations of Intelligent Design." 169 *Science News* (25 February): 120–21.

Perry, Michael J. 1991. *Love and Power: The Role of Religion and Morality in American Politics.* New York: Oxford University Press.

Peters, Shawn Francis. 2003. *The* Yoder *Case: Religious Freedom, Education, and Parental Rights.* Lawrence, Kans.: University Press of Kansas.

Piller, Charles. 1991. *The Fail-Safe Society: Community Defiance and the End of American Technological Optimism.* New York: Basic Books.

Plous, Scott. 1993. *The Psychology of Judgment and Decision Making.* Philadelphia: Temple University Press.

Popkin, Samuel L. [1991] 1994. *The Reasoning Voter: Communication and Persuasion in Presidential Campaigns.* Chicago: University of Chicago Press, 2nd edition.

Portney, Kent E. 1991. *Siting Hazardous Waste Treatment Facilities: The NIMBY Syndrome.* New York: Auburn House.

Posner, Richard A. 1999. *The Problematics of Moral and Legal Theory.* Cambridge, Mass.: Harvard University Press.

Prichard. H. A. [1912] 1968. "Does Moral Philosophy Rest on a Mistake?" In Prichard, *Moral Obligation and Duty and Interest.* London: Oxford University Press: 1–17.

Puccini, Giacomo. [1904] 1992. *Madama Butterfly.* New York: Metropolitan Opera Guild (libretto by Giuseppe Giacosa and Luigi Illica).

Quinn, Philip L. 1995. "Political Liberalisms and Their Exclusion of the Religious." *Proceedings and Addresses of the American Philosophical Association* 69 (November): 35–56.

Rawls, John. [1971] 1999. *A Theory of Justice.* Cambridge, Mass.: Harvard University Press.

Reid, Thomas. [1764] 1970. *An Inquiry into the Human Mind.* Chicago: University of Chicago Press, ed. by Timothy J. Duggan.

———. [1788] 1969. *Essays on the Active Powers of the Human Mind.* Cambridge, Mass.: MIT Press.

Rieger, Mary A., Michael Lamond, Christopher Preston, Stephen B. Powles, and Richard T. Roush. 2002. "Pollen-Mediated Movement of Herbicide Resistance between Commercial Canola Fields." *Science* 296 (28 June): 2386–88.

Rorty, Richard. [1985] 1991. "Postmodernist Bourgeois Liberalism," in Rorty, *Objectivity, Relativism, and Truth: Philosophical Papers.* Cambridge: Cambridge University Press, vol. 1: 197–202.

———. 1998. *Achieving Our Country*. Cambridge, Mass.: Harvard University Press.

Rosenblum, Nancy L. 1989. "Introduction." In Rosenblum, ed., *Liberalism and the Moral Life*. Cambridge, Mass.: Harvard University Press: 1–17.

Ross, Michael. 1999. "The Political Economy of the Resource Curse." *World Politics* 51 (January 1999): 297–322.

Ryle, Gilbert. [1946] 1971. "Knowing How and Knowing That." In Ryle, *Collected Essays*, vol. 2 of *Collected Papers*. New York: Barnes and Noble: 212–25.

Sanders, Lisa. 2006. "On Her Last Legs: A nearly Obsolete Disease Makes a House Call." *New York Times Magazine* (26 February): 19–20.

Schmitt, Frederick F. 1987. "Justification, Sociality, and Autonomy." *Synthese* 73: 43–85.

———, ed. 1994. *Socializing Epistemology: The Social Dimensions of Knowledge*. Lanham, Md.: Rowman and Littlefield.

Schönborn, Cardinal Christoph. 2005. "Finding Design in Nature." *New York Times* (7 July): A23 (op-ed page).

Schumpeter, Joseph A. [1942] 1950. *Capitalism, Socialism and Democracy*. New York: Harper, 3rd edition.

Schwartz, Barry. 1986. *The Battle for Human Nature*. New York: Norton.

Schwartz, James. 2000. "Death of an Altruist: Was the Man Who Found the Selfless Gene Too Good for This World?" *Linqua Franca* (July–August): 51–61.

Schwartz, Robert S. 2005. "Faith Healers and Physicians—Teaching Pseudoscience by Mandate." *New England Journal of Medicine* 353 (6 October): 1437–39.

Scott, James C. 1998. *Seeing Like a State: How Certain Schemes to Improve the Human Condition Have Failed*. New Haven, Conn.: Yale University Press.

Scott , John Finley. 1971. *Internalization of Norms: A Sociological Theory of Moral Commitment*. Englewood Cliffs, N.J.: Prentice-Hall.

Shapin, Steven. 1996. *The Scientific Revolution*. Chicago: University of Chicago Press.

Shermer, Michael. 2000. *How We Believe: The Search for God in an Age of Science*. New York: W. H. Freeman.

Sidgwick, Henry. 1876a. "Professor Calderwood on Intuitionism in Morals," *Mind* 1: 563–66.

———. 1876b. "The Theory of Evolution in Its Application to Practice," *Mind* 1: 52–67.

———. 1895 [1905]. "The Philosophy of Common Sense." *Mind* 4 (April): 145–58.

———. 1907. *The Methods of Ethics*. London: Macmillan, seventh edition.

Simon, Herbert A. 1955. "A Behavioral Model of Rational Choice," *Quarterly Journal of Economics* 69: 99–118.

———. 1957. *Models of Man: Social and Rational*. New York, John Wiley and Sons.

———. 1984. "Scientific Literacy as a Goal in a High-Technology Society." Sterling M. McMurrin, ed., *The Tanner Lectures on Human Values*, vol. 5. Salt Lake City, Ut.: University of Utah Press: 121–53.

Singer, Marcus George. 1961. *Generalization in Ethics*. New York: Knopf.

Smith, Adam. [1776] 1976. *An Inquiry into the Nature and Causes of the Wealth of Nations.* Oxford: Oxford University Press; Indianapolis, Ind.: Liberty Classics, 1981, reprint.

Sokal, Alan D. 1996a."Transgressing the Boundaries: Toward a Transformative Hermeneutics of Quantum Gravity." *Social Text* 14: 217–43.

———. 1996b. "A Physicist Experiments with Cultural Studies." *Lingua Franca* (May/June): 62–64.

Somin, Ilya. 1998. "Voter Ignorance and the Democratic Ideal." *Critical Review* (fall): 413–58.

Specter, Michael. 2004. "Miracle in a Bottle." *New Yorker* (2 February): 64–75.

Stark, Rodney. 2003. *For the Glory of God: How Monotheism Led to Reformations, Science, Witch-Hunts, and the End of Slavery.* Princeton, N.J.: Princeton University Press.

Stark, Rodney, and William Sims Bainbridge. 1985. *The Future of Religion: Secularization, Revival, and Cult Formation.* Berkeley: University of California Press.

Stark, Rodney, Laurence R. Iannacone, and Roger Finke. 1996. "Religion, Science, and Rationality." *American Economic Review* 86 (no. 2, May): 433–37.

Stein, Stephen J. 2000. *Alternative American Religions.* New York: Oxford University Press.

Stendahl [Marie Henri Beyle]. [1831] 1953. *Scarlet and Black.* Baltimore: Penguin.

Stenner, Karen. 2005. *The Authoritarian Dynamic.* Cambridge: Cambridge University Press.

———. 2007. "The Authoritarian Dynamic: Racial, Political and Moral Intolerance under Conditions of Societal Threat." In *Toleration and Conflict,* ed. by Ingrid Creppell, Russell Hardin, and Stephen Macedo. Lanham, N.J.: Rowman & Littlefield: 225–256.

Stigler, George J. 1961. "The Economics of Information." 69 *Journal of Political Economy* (No. 3, June): 213–25.

Stimson, James. 1990. "A Macro Theory of Information Flow." In John A. Ferejohn and James Kuklinski, eds., *Information and Democratic Processes.* Urbana, Ill.: University of Illinois Press: 345–68.

———. 2004. *Tides of Consent: How Public Opinion Shapes American Politics.* Cambridge: Cambridge University Press.

Stokstad, Erik. 2002. "A Little Pollen Goes a Long Way." *Science* 296 (28 June): 2314.

Sunstein, Cass R. 2000. "Deliberative Trouble? Why Groups Go to Extremes." *Yale Law Journal* 110 (no. 1, October): 71–119.

Swets, John A., Robyn M. Dawes, and John Monahan. 2000. "Better Decisions through Science." *Scientific American* (October): 82–87.

Talbot, Margaret. 2005. "Darwin in the Dock: Intelligent Design Has Its Day in Court." *New Yorker* (5 December): 66–77.

Tamir, Yael. 1993. *Liberal Nationalism.* Princeton, N.J.: Princeton University Press.

Taylor, Charles. 1990. "Irreducibly Social Goods." In *Rationality, Individualism, and Public Policy,* edited by Geoffrey Brennan and Cliff Walsh. Canberra, Australia: Centre for Research on Federal Financial Relations: 45–63.

Thomson, Keith. 2005. *Before Darwin: Reconciling God and Nature.* New Haven, Conn.: Yale University Press.

Trilling, Lionel. [1972] 2000. "Mind in the Modern World: The 1972 Jefferson Lecture in the Humanities." In Trilling, *The Moral Obligation To Be Intelligent: Selected Essays*, ed. by Leon Wieseltier. New York: Farrar, Straus and Giroux: 477–500.

Vyse, Stuart. 1997. *Believing in Magic: The Psychology of Superstition*. Oxford: Oxford University Press.

Wallace, Anthony F. C. 1966. *Religion: An Anthropological View*. New York: Random House.

Walzer, Michael. 1980. "Pluralism: A Political Perspective." In Stephen A. Thernstrom, ed., *Harvard Encyclopedia of American Ethnic Groups*. Cambridge, Mass.: Harvard University Press: pp. 781–87.

Wantchekon, Leonard. 2002. "Why Do Resource Dependent Countries Have Authoritarian Governments?" *Journal of African Finance and Economic Development* 5 (no. 2): 57–77.

Weinthal, Erika, and Pauline Jones Luong. 2006. "Combating the Resource Curse: An Alternative Solution to Managing Mineral Wealth." *Perspectives on Politics* 4 (March): 35–53.

Wells, Jonathan. 2000. *Icons of Evolution: Science or Myth?* Washington, D.C.: Regnery.

Williams, D. C. 1947. *The Ground of Induction*. Cambridge, Mass.: Harvard University Press.

Wills, Garry. 2000. *Papal Sin: Structures of Deceit*. New York: Doubleday.

Wilson, David Gordon. [1974] 2004. *Bicycling Science*. Cambridge, Mass.: MIT Press, 3rd edition.

Wittgenstein, Ludwig. 1969. *On Certainty*. New York: Harper, ed. by G.E.M. Anscombe and G. H. von Wright.

Wittman, Donald. 1996. *The Myth of Democratic Failure*. Chicago: University of Chicago Press.

Wood, E. Thomas, and Stanislaw M. Jankowski. 1994. *Karski: How One Man Tried to Stop the Holocaust*. New York: Wiley.

Wright, Lawrence. 2002. "Lives of the Saints." *New Yorker* (21 January): 40–57.

Wuthnow, Robert. 1985. "Science and the Sacred." In Phillip E. Hammond, ed., *The Sacred in a Secular Age*. Berkeley: University of California Press: 187–203.

CASES CITED

California Democratic Party v. Jones, 530 U.S. 567 (2000).

Edwards v. Aguillard, 482 U.S. 578 (1987).

Kitzmiller et al. v. Dover Area School District et al. Memorandum Opinion, December 20, 2005.

Modrovich v. Allegheny County, 385 F.3d 397 (3d Cir. 2004).

United States v. Lee, 455 U.S. 252 (1982).

Wisconsin v. Yoder et al., 406 U.S., pp. 205–49 (1972).

Index

220 · Index

Converse, Philip, 77
Costa, Lucio, 86
Council of Trent, 156
courts of equity, 133–34
Coyne, George, 48–49
Craig, Edward, 31–32
cultural knowledge: bias toward group
interest and, 172–73; conservatism and,
168–70; institutional knowledge and,
173–75; path dependence and, 167–68
culture: America and, 181–82; communal
knowledge and, 161–62, 166–67, 175–76;
community of the deaf and, 177–78;
conservatism and, 168–70; functionality
and, 162, 167, 175–76; goodness of,
176–79; individual interests and, 163;
modern states and, 182; norms of exclusion and, 165–66; as ordinary knowledge,
182; path dependence and, 167–68;
shared values and motivations and, 165;
unintended consequences and, 174

Dahl, Robert, 65–66
Darwin, Charles, *Origin of Species*, 49
Davis, Percival, 52
democracy: economic theory of knowledge
and, 63–69, 79; left and right parties
and, 80–81; median-voter model and,
64; multidimensional issues and, 78–80
Descartes, René, 33
Dewey, John, 5, 54; pragmatic-rule of, 26,
31; on science, 55
distributed knowledge, policy and, 91–93
division of labor: errors and, 15; Hume
and Smith on, 10; individual knowledge
and, 14–15; reliance on authority or
testimony and, 14
Dodgson, C. L., 78
Douglas, William O., 204
*Dover Area School District, et al.,
Kitzmiller et al. v.*, 50, 52–55, 137
Downs, Anthony, 62–65, 66, 71, 187
Driggs, Ken, 147–48
Duesberg, Peter, 22
Durkin, John, 71

echinacea, 37–38
economic theory of knowledge, 4–9; acquisition costs and, 2–3; beliefs versus
knowledge and, 6; coherence and, 109;
costs versus benefits and, 4–5, 111–14;

culture and, 166; definition of, 2;
democracy and, 63–69, 79; economic
theory and, 6–7; government and, 99;
happenstance and, 3; institutional versus
individual capacities and, 9; moral
versus factual knowledge and, 6, 9; path
dependency and, 8–9; pragmatism and,
5–6, 34; rationality and, 112; religious
belief and, 135, 159–60; time and, 6;
value of knowledge and, 2; voting and,
66–67. *See also specific knowledge types*
Edwards v. Aguillard, 53, 57, 137
Ehrman, Bart, 156
Einstein, Albert, 59
Encyclopedia of Evolution, 56
Enormous Theorem, 122, 123
Enuma Elish, 156
epistemology: coherentist, 20–21; com-
munalist, 23; externalist, 21–22; fundamentalist, 20; justification and, 26;
knowledge versus belief and, 26; ordinary knowledge and, 24–27; proceduralist, 22–23
evolution, 33, 49–58, 136–37. *See also*
intelligent design (ID)
externalism. *See* epistemology, externalist

fallibilism: Bible and, 156–57; religious
belief and, 153–58
fanaticism/extremism, 185–86; actions
versus beliefs and, 195–96; Amish and,
201–3; constrained belief systems and,
203; discussion groups and, 199; Islam
and, 197–98; leadership and, 203–4;
nationalism and, 193–94, 200–201;
normal politics and, 187–88; norms of
exclusion and, 188–90; prosperity and,
197
Fenno, Richard, 68
Ferguson, Adam, 124
Fitzgerald, F. Scott, 4
Fleischmann, Martin, 54
foreign aid, 60–62
France, Anatole, *Le livre du mon ami*,
146–47
Frankfurter, Felix, 40
Frist, Bill, 57, 152
fundamentalism, 20, 192

Galileo, 46–49, 58, 160
Gass, William, *Omensetter's Luck*, 150

St. Kilda, 115
Sultan, Wafa, 198
superstition, academics and, 140n

Taft, William Howard, 100
Tamir, Yael, 192
Taylor, Charles, 177–78
Templeton Foundation, 55–56
three-strikes sentencing law, 68–69
Tintoretto, Jacopo, "Creation of the
    Animals," 53
tobacco, lung cancer and, 56
Trilling, Lionel, 41–42
Tudjman, Franjo, 172
Tzotil language, 12

Ullmann-Margalit, Edna, 31
Ultras, 190–91
unintended consequences, 114; beliefs
    as, 145, 195; culture as, 174, 184; func-
    tional explanation and, 183–84; institu-
    tions as, 114; religious fundamentalism
    and, 197; synoptic design and, 92
Ussher, James, 49–50
utilitarianism, 79–80, 116, 199–200; Aus-
    trian social theory and, 96; knowledge
    requirements of, 124–25; Sidgwick on,
    101, 108

voting: costs and benefits of, 75–76, 81;
    knowledge and, 66–69; logic of collec-
    tive action and, 70–77; low information
    rationality and, 67; making a difference
    and, 71, 93; median-voter model and,
    64, 69–70; ordinary knowledge and,
    65–66; psychological foibles and, 65–66;
    status and, 65–66; voter ignorance and,
    65–69, 81
Vyse, Stuart, 42

Wallace, Anthony F. C., 139, 141
Walzer, Michael, 192
welfarism, 96–99, 131–33, 178–79
Whitcomb, John C., 50
White, Andrew Dickson, 55
Williams, D. C., 92–93, 100
Wilson, Woodrow, 100, 117
Wintrobe, Ronald, 164
Wisconsin v. Yoder et al., 88, 201–3
Wittgenstein, Ludwig, 5, 26; *On Certainty*, 8
Wyman, Louis, 71

Yoder et al., Wisconsin v., 88, 201–3
Yugoslavia, 190. *See also* Bosnian/Kosovan
    conflicts

Zawahiri, Ayman, 199

CPSIA information can be obtained at www.ICGtesting.com
Printed in the USA
BVOW03s0907070314

346820BV00009B/19/P